Summary of Contents

D0515136

THE CSS ANTHOLOGY

101 ESSENTIAL TIPS, TRICKS & HACKS

BY **RACHEL ANDREW**
2ND EDITION

The CSS Anthology: 101 Essential Tips, Tricks & Hacks

by Rachel Andrew

Editor: Georgina Laidlaw

Managing Editor: Simon Mackie

Technical Editor: Matthew Magain

Expert Reviewer: Simon Willison

Printing History:

   First Edition: November 2004

   Second Edition: May 2007

Index Editor: Bill Johncocks

Technical Director: Kevin Yank

Cover Design: Alex Walker

Latest Update: September 2007

Notice of Rights

Notice of Liability

Trademark Notice

Published by SitePoint Pty Ltd

424 Smith Street Collingwood
VIC Australia 3066
Web: www.sitepoint.com
Email: business@sitepoint.com

ISBN 978-0-9758419-8-3
Printed and bound in Canada

About the Author

Rachel Andrew is a web developer and the director of web solutions provider edgeofmyseat.com. When not writing code, she writes *about* writing code and is the coauthor of several books promoting the practical usage of web standards alongside other everyday tools and technologies. Rachel takes a common sense, real world approach to web standards, with her writing and teaching being based on the experiences she has in her own company every day.

Rachel lives in the UK with her partner Drew and daughter Bethany. When not working, they can often be found wandering around the English countryside hunting for geocaches and nice pubs that serve Sunday lunch and a good beer.

About the Technical Editor

Before joining the SitePoint team as a technical editor, Matthew Magain worked as a software developer for IBM and also spent several years teaching English in Japan. He is the organizer for Melbourne's Web Standards Group,[1] and enjoys swimming, listening to classical jazz, and drinking Coopers Pale Ale, though not all at the same time. Matthew lives with his wife Kimberley and their daughter Sophia.

About the Technical Director

As Technical Director for SitePoint, Kevin Yank oversees all of its technical publications—books, articles, newsletters and blogs. He has written over 50 articles for SitePoint on technologies including PHP, XML, ASP.NET, Java, JavaScript and CSS, but is perhaps best known for his book, *Build Your Own Database Driven Website Using PHP & MySQL*, also from SitePoint. Kevin now lives in Melbourne, Australia. In his spare time he enjoys flying light aircraft and learning the fine art of improvised acting.

About SitePoint

SitePoint specializes in publishing fun, practical, and easy-to-understand content for web professionals. Visit http://www.sitepoint.com/ to access our books, newsletters, articles and community forums.

---

[1] http://webstandardsgroup.org/

For Bethany

Table of Contents

Chapter 6   Forms and User Interfaces 175

Chapter 7   Cross-browser Techniques 215

Preface

When I'm not writing books like this one, I'm writing code. I make my living by building web sites and applications as, I'm sure, will many readers of this book. I use CSS to get jobs done every day, and I know what it's like to struggle to get something to work when the project needs to be finished the next morning.

When I talk to designers and developers who don't use CSS, or use CSS only for simple text styling, one thing that I hear over and over again is that they just don't have time to learn this whole new way of working. After all, tables and spacer GIFs function, they get the job done, and they pay the bills.

I was lucky. I picked up CSS very early in the piece, and started to play with it because it interested me. As a result of that early interest, my knowledge grew as the CSS techniques themselves were developed, and I can now draw on six years' experience building CSS layouts every time I tackle a project.

In this book, I've tried to pass on the tricks and techniques that allow me to quickly and easily develop web sites and applications using CSS.

You won't find pages and pages of theory in this book. What you will find are solutions that will enable you to do the cool stuff today, but which should also act as starting points for your own creativity. In my experience, it's far easier to learn by doing than by reading, so while you can use this book to find solutions that will help you get that client web site up and running by the deadline, please do experiment with these examples and use them as a means to learn new techniques.

The book was designed to let you quickly find the answer to the particular CSS problem with which you're struggling at any given point in time. You don't need to read it from cover to cover—just grab the technique that you need, or that interests you, and you're set to go. Along with each solution, I've provided an explanation to help you to understand why the technique works. This knowledge will allow you to expand on, and experiment with, the technique in your own time.

I hope you enjoy this book! It has been great fun to write, and my hope is that it will be useful as a day-to-day reference, as well as a tool that helps give you the confidence to explore new CSS techniques.

Who Should Read this Book?

This book is aimed at people who need to work with CSS—web designers and developers who have seen the cool CSS designs out there, but don't have the time to wade through masses of theory and debate in order to create a site. Each problem is solved with a working solution that can be implemented as-is or used as a springboard to creativity.

This book isn't a tutorial; while Chapter 1 covers the very basics of CSS, and the early chapters cover simpler techniques than those that follow, you will find the examples easier to grasp if you have a basic grounding in CSS.

What's Covered in this Book?

Chapter 1: *Getting Started with CSS*

This chapter does not follow the same format as the rest of the book—it's simply a quick CSS tutorial for anyone who needs to brush up on the basics of CSS. If you've been using CSS in your own projects, you might want to skip this chapter and refer to it on a needs basis if you find you want to look into basic concepts in more detail.

Chapter 2: *Text Styling and Other Basics*

This chapter covers techniques for styling and formatting text in your documents; font sizing, colors, and the removal of annoying extra whitespace around page elements are explained as the chapter progresses. Even if you're already using CSS for text styling, you'll find some useful tips here.

Chapter 3: *CSS and Images*

Combining CSS and images can create powerful visual effects. This chapter looks at the ways in which you can do this, covering background images (not just on the body), and positioning text with images, among other topics.

Chapter 4: *Navigation*

We all need navigation, and this chapter explains how to create it, CSS-style. The topics of CSS replacements for image-based navigation, CSS "tab" navigation, combining background images with CSS text to create attractive and accessible menus, and using lists to structure navigation in an accessible way are addressed in this chapter.

Chapter 5: *Tabular Data*

While the use of tables for layout should be avoided wherever possible, tables should be used for their real purpose: the display of tabular data, such as that contained in a spreadsheet. This chapter will demonstrate techniques for the application of tables to create attractive and usable tabular data displays.

Chapter 6: *Forms and User Interfaces*

Whether you're a designer or a developer, it's likely that you'll spend a fair amount of time creating forms for data entry. CSS can help you to create forms that are attractive and usable; this chapter shows how we can do that while bearing the key accessibility principles in mind.

Chapter 7: *Cross-browser Techniques*

How can we deal with older browsers, browsers with CSS bugs, and alternative devices? These questions form the main theme of this chapter. We'll also see how to troubleshoot CSS bugs—and where to go for help—as well as discussing the ways you can test your site in as many browsers as possible.

Chapter 8: *Accessibility and Alternative Devices*

It's all very well that our pages look pretty to the majority of our site's visitors—but what about that group of people who rely upon assistive technology such as screen magnifiers and screen readers? Or those users who prefer to navigate the Web using the keyboard rather than a mouse, for whatever reason? In this chapter we'll see how we can make our site as welcoming and accessible as possible for *all* users, not just able-bodied visitors with perfect vision.

Chapter 9: *CSS Positioning and Layout*

In this chapter, we explore the use of CSS to create beautiful and accessible pages. We cover a range of different CSS layouts, and a variety of techniques, which can be combined and extended upon to create numerous interesting page layouts.

The Book's Web Site

Located at http://www.sitepoint.com/books/cssant2/, the web site that supports this book will give you access to the following facilities.

The Code Archive

As you progress through this book, you'll note file names above many of the code listings. These refer to files in the code archive, a downloadable ZIP file that contains all of the finished examples presented in this book. Simply click the **Code Archive** link on the book's web site to download it.

Updates and Errata

No book is error-free, and attentive readers will no doubt spot at least one or two mistakes in this one. The Corrections and Typos page on the book's web site will provide the latest information about known typographical and code errors, and will offer necessary updates for new releases of browsers and related standards.[1]

The SitePoint Forums

If you'd like to communicate with other designers about this book, you should join SitePoint's online community.[2] The CSS forum, in particular, offers an abundance of information above and beyond the solutions in this book, and a lot of fun and experienced web designers and developers hang out there.[3] It's a good way to learn new tricks, get questions answered in a hurry, and just have a good time.

The SitePoint Newsletters

In addition to books like this one, SitePoint publishes free email newsletters including *The SitePoint Tribune*, *The SitePoint Tech Times*, and *The SitePoint Design View*. Reading them will keep you up to date on the latest news, product releases, trends, tips, and techniques for all aspects of web development. If nothing else, you'll get useful CSS articles and tips, but if you're interested in learning other

---

[1] http://www.sitepoint.com/books/cssant2/errata.php

[2] http://www.sitepoint.com/forums/

[3] http://www.sitepoint.com/launch/cssforum/

technologies, you'll find them especially valuable. Sign up to one or more SitePoint newsletters at http://www.sitepoint.com/newsletter/.

Your Feedback

If you can't find an answer through the forums, or if you wish to contact us for any other reason, the best place to write is books@sitepoint.com. We have an email support system set up to track your inquiries, and friendly support staff members who can answer your questions. Suggestions for improvements as well as notices of any mistakes you may find are especially welcome.

Acknowledgments

Firstly, I'd like to thank the SitePoint team for making this book a reality, and for being easy to communicate with despite the fact that our respective time zones saw me going to bed as they started work each day. Particular thanks must go to Simon Mackie, whose encouragement throughout the writing process was a great support.

Thanks also to both Simon Willison, who reviewed the first edition of this book, and to Matthew Magain, who edited this second edition, not only for picking up technical errors and inconsistencies, but for reminding me of different ideas and approaches to the solutions.

To those people who are really breaking new ground in the world of CSS, those whose ideas are discussed throughout this book, and those who share their ideas and creativity with the wider community, thank you.

Thanks to Drew for his support and encouragement, for being willing to discuss CSS concepts as I worked out my examples for the book, for making me laugh when I was growing annoyed, and for putting up with our entire lack of a social life. Finally, thanks must go to my daughter Bethany, who is very understanding of the fact that her mother is constantly at a computer, and who reminds me of what is important every day. You both make so many things possible, thank you.

Conventions Used in this Book

You'll notice that we've used certain typographic and layout styles throughout this book to signify different types of information. Look out for the following items.

Markup Samples

Any markup—be that HTML or CSS—will be displayed using a fixed-width font like so:

```
<h1>A perfect summer's day</h1>
<p>It was a lovely day for a walk in the park. The birds
were singing and the kids were all back at school.</p>
```

If the markup forms part of the book's code archive, the name of the file will appear at the top of the program listing, like this:

```
                                                      example.css
.footer {
  background-color: #CCC;
  border-top: 1px solid #333;
}
```

If only part of the file is displayed, this is indicated by the word *excerpt*:

```
                                                 example.css (excerpt)
  border-top: 1px solid #333;
```

Tips, Notes, and Warnings

Hey, you!

Tips will give you helpful little pointers.

Ahem, Excuse Me ...

Notes are useful asides that are related—but not critical—to the topic at hand. Think of them as extra tidbits of information.

Make Sure You Always ...

... pay attention to these important points.

Watch Out!

Warnings will highlight any gotchas that are likely to trip you up along the way.

Getting Started with CSS

Cascading Style Sheets sound intimidating. The name alone conjures up images of cryptic code and syntax too difficult for the layperson to grasp. In reality, however, CSS is one of the simplest and most convenient tools available to web developers. In this first chapter, which takes a different format than the rest of the book, I'll guide you through the basics of CSS and show you how it can be used to simplify the task of managing a consistently formatted web site. If you've already used CSS to format text on your sites, you may want to skip this chapter and jump straight to the solutions that begin in Chapter 2.

Defining Styles with CSS

The basic purpose of CSS is to allow the designer to define **style declarations** (formatting details such as fonts, element sizes, and colors), and to apply those styles to selected portions of HTML pages using **selectors**—references to an element or group of elements to which the style is applied. Let's look at a basic example to see how this is done.

Consider the following HTML document outline:

```
<!DOCTYPE html PUBLIC "-//W3C//DTD XHTML 1.0 Strict//EN"
    "http://www.w3.org/TR/xhtml1/DTD/xhtml1-strict.dtd">
<html xmlns="http://www.w3.org/1999/xhtml" lang="en-US">
<head>
<title>A Simple Page</title>
<meta http-equiv="content-type"
    content="text/html; charset=utf-8" />
</head>
<body>
<h1>First Title</h1>
<p>…</p>

<h2>Second Title</h2>
<p>…</p>

<h2>Third title</h2>
<p>…</p>
</body>
</html>
```

This document contains three headings, which have been created using <h1> and
<h2> tags. Without CSS styling, the headings will be rendered using the browser's
internal style sheet—the h1 heading will be displayed in a large font size, and the
h2 headings will be smaller than the h1, but larger than paragraph text. The document
that uses these default styles will be *readable*, but it probably won't be as attractive
as you might like. We can use some simple CSS to change the look of these elements:

```
<!DOCTYPE html PUBLIC "-//W3C//DTD XHTML 1.0 Strict//EN"
    "http://www.w3.org/TR/xhtml1/DTD/xhtml1-strict.dtd">
<html xmlns="http://www.w3.org/1999/xhtml" lang="en-US">
<head>
<title>A Simple Page</title>
<meta http-equiv="content-type"
    content="text/html; charset=utf-8" />
<style type="text/css">
h1, h2 {
 font-family: sans-serif;
 color: #3366CC;
}
</style>
</head>
<body>
```

```
<h1>First Title</h1>
<p>…</p>

<h2>Second Title</h2>
<p>…</p>

<h2>Third Title</h2>
<p>…</p>
</body>
</html>
```

All the magic lies between the `<style>` tags in the `head` of the document, where we define our light blue, sans serif font and apply it to all `h1` and `h2` elements in the document. Don't worry about the syntax—I'll explain it in detail in a moment. We don't need to add anything to the markup itself—changes to the style definition at the top of the page will affect all three headings, as well as any other headings that might be added to the page at a later date.

Now that you have an idea of what CSS does, let me explain the different ways in which you can use CSS styles in your HTML documents.

Inline Styles

The simplest method of adding CSS styles to your web pages is to use **inline styles**. An inline style is applied via the `style` attribute, like this:

```
<p style="font-family: sans-serif; color: #3366CC;">
  Amazingly few discotheques provide jukeboxes.
</p>
```

As you can see, no selectors are required when we use an inline style—all we need is a style declaration. The `style` attribute clearly identifies the element to which the style is to be applied.

Inline styles have one major disadvantage: they can't be reused. For example, if we wanted to apply the style above to another `p` element, we would have to type it out again in that element's `style` attribute. Additionally, inline styles are located alongside the page's markup, making the code difficult to read and maintain.

Embedded Styles

Another approach you can take to applying CSS styles to your web pages is to use the `style` element, as I did in the first example we looked at. Using this approach, you can declare any number of CSS styles by placing them between the opening and closing `<style>` tags, as follows:

```
<style type="text/css">
  CSS Styles here
</style>
```

The `type` attribute specifies the language that you're using to define your styles. CSS is the only language in wide use at the time of writing, and is indicated with the value `text/css`.

While it's nice and simple, the `<style>` tag has one major disadvantage: if you want to use a particular set of styles throughout your site, you'll have to repeat those style definitions within the `style` element at the top of every one of your site's pages.

A more sensible alternative is to place those definitions into a plain text file, then link your documents to that file. This external file is referred to as an external style sheet.

External Style Sheets

An **external style sheet** is a file (usually given a **.css** filename) that contains a web site's CSS styles, keeping them separate from any one web page. Multiple pages can link to the same **.css** file, and any changes you make to the style definitions in that file will affect all the pages that link to it. This achieves the objective of creating site-wide style definitions that I mentioned above.

To link a document to an external style sheet (say, **styles.css**), we simply place a `link` element in the document's header:

```
<link rel="stylesheet" type="text/css" href="styles.css" />
```

Remember our original example in which three headings shared a single style rule? Let's save that rule to an external style sheet, and link it to the web page like so:

```
<!DOCTYPE html PUBLIC "-//W3C//DTD XHTML 1.0 Strict//EN"
    "http://www.w3.org/TR/xhtml1/DTD/xhtml1-strict.dtd">
<html xmlns="http://www.w3.org/1999/xhtml" lang="en-US">
<head>
<title>A Simple Page</title>
<meta http-equiv="content-type"
    content="text/html; charset=utf-8" />
<link rel="stylesheet" type="text/css" href="styles.css" />
</head>
<body>
<h1>First Title</h1>
<p>...</p>

<h2>Second Title</h2>
<p>...</p>

<h2>Third Title</h2>
<p>...</p>
</body>
</html>
```

The linked **styles.css** file contains the style definition:

```
h1, h2 {
  font-family: sans-serif;
  color: #3366CC;
}
```

As with an image file, you can reuse this **styles.css** file in any pages in which it's needed. Not only will it save you from re-typing the styles, it also ensures that your headings display consistently across the entire site.

CSS Selectors

Every CSS style definition has two components:

- A list of one or more **selectors**, separated by commas, define the element or elements to which the style will be applied.
- The **declaration block** specifies what the style actually does.

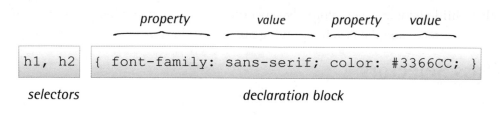

Figure 1.1. The components of a CSS rule: a list of selectors and a declaration block

In Figure 1.1, the selectors are h1 and h2, which means that the style should apply to all h1 and h2 elements. The remainder of the style definition—the declaration block—comprises the properties (fonts, colors, and other settings that should be applied by the style), and the values these properties should take. In this section, I'll describe the basic CSS selector types and give you some examples of each; the solutions in the rest of the book focus mainly on the different properties and the values they can take.

Type Selectors

The most basic form of selector is a **type selector**, which we've already seen. By naming a particular HTML element, you can apply a style rule to every occurrence of that element in the document. Type selectors are often used to set the basic styles that will appear throughout a web site. For example, the following style rule might be used to set the default font for a web site:

```
body, p, td, th, div, blockquote, dl, ul, ol {
  font-family: Tahoma, Verdana, Arial, Helvetica, sans-serif;
  font-size: 1em;
  color: #000000;
}
```

This rather long selector comprises a list of elements for which the font, size, and color will be styled according to the declaration block.

In theory, applying these styles to a page's body element should be all we need to do to have the styles appear across the site—all the other page elements appear between the <body> tags, and should thus inherit the styles applied to the body. But in reality, many browsers don't properly apply style properties into tables and other child elements. Therefore, I've specified those other elements to ensure that browsers make no mistakes in applying my new style rule.

Class Selectors

Assigning styles to elements is all well and good, but what happens if you want to assign different styles to identical elements that occur in different places within your document? This is where CSS **classes** come in.

Consider the following style, which turns all the paragraph text on a page blue.

```
p { color: #0000FF; }
```

Great! But what would happen if you had a sidebar on your page with a blue background? You wouldn't want the text in the sidebar to display in blue as well—then it would be invisible. What you need to do is define a class for your sidebar text, then assign a CSS style to that class.

To create a paragraph of the `sidebar` class, first add a `class` attribute to the opening tag:

```
<p class="sidebar">This text will be white, as specified by the
   CSS style definition below.</p>
```

Now we can write the style for this class:

```
p { color: #0000FF; }
.sidebar { color: #FFFFFF; }
```

This second rule uses a class selector to indicate that the style should be applied to any element of the `sidebar` class. The period indicates that we're naming a class—not an HTML element.

Now, what would happen if there were links in your sidebar? By default, they'd be rendered just like any other links in your page; however, add a `class="sidebar"` attribute to the link element, and they'll turn white, too:

```
<p class="sidebar">This text will be white, <a class="sidebar"
      href="link.html">and so will this link</a>.</p>
```

That's fairly neat, but what if you wanted to make the links stand out a bit more? Perhaps you want to display them in bold text? Adding the `bold` text attribute to the `sidebar` class will turn your whole sidebar bold, which would be no good. You need a CSS selector that selects links of the `sidebar` class only, and, by combining a type selector with a class selector, you can do exactly that:

```
p { color: #0000FF; }
.sidebar { color: #FFFFFF; }
a.sidebar:link, a.sidebar:visited { font-weight: bold; }
```

Note that we've also used the `:link` and `:visited` pseudo-classes here—we'll look at pseudo-classes in more detail later in this chapter.

If you were to add these style rules to your style sheet and reload the page in your browser, you'd see that your sidebar links display in a font that's white *and* bold—both of the styles that we defined above for the `sidebar` class are applied to our sidebar links. If we were to specify a different color in the third style, however, links would adopt that new color, because the third selector is more specific, and CSS style rules are applied in order of increasing selector specificity.

Incidentally, the process of applying multiple styles to a single page element is called **cascading**, and is where Cascading Style Sheets got their name.

ID Selectors

In contrast with class selectors, **ID selectors** are used to select one particular element, rather than a group of elements. To use an ID selector, first add an `id` attribute to the element you wish to style. It's important that the ID is unique within the document:

```
<p id="tagline">This paragraph is uniquely identified by the ID
   "tagline".</p>
```

To reference this element by its ID selector, we precede the `id` with a hash (#). For example, the following rule will make the above paragraph white:

```
#tagline { color: #FFFFFF; }
```

ID selectors can be used in combination with the other selector types. The following style, for example, applies to elements with a class of new appearing within the paragraph that has an id of tagline:

```
#tagline .new {
  font-weight: bold;
  color: #FFFFFF;
}
```

Descendant Selectors

If your sidebar consisted of more than just one paragraph of text, you *could* add the class to every opening p tag in the sidebar. However, it would be much neater to apply an id of sidebar to a container element, and set the color of every p element within that container to white, with a single CSS style rule. This is what **descendant selectors** are for.

Here's the new CSS:

```
p { color: #0000FF; }
.sidebar p { color: #FFFFFF; }
```

And here's the updated HTML:

```
<div class="sidebar">
  <p>This paragraph will be displayed in white.</p>
  <p>So will this one.</p>
</div>
```

As you can see, a descendant selector comprises a list of selectors (separated by spaces) that matches a page element (or group of elements) "from the outside in." In this case, because our page contains a div element that has a class of sidebar, the descendant selector .sidebar p refers to all p elements inside that div.

Child Selectors

The descendant selector matches all elements that are descendants of the parent element, including elements that are *not direct descendants*.

Consider the following markup:

```
<div class="sidebar">
  <p>This paragraph will be displayed in white.</p>
  <p>So will this one.</p>
  <div class="tagline">
    <p>If we use a descendant selector, this will be white too.
       But if we use a child selector, it will be blue.</p>
  </div>
</div>
```

In this example, the descendant selector we saw in the previous section would match the paragraphs that are nested directly within div.sidebar *as well as* those inside div.tagline. If you didn't want this behavior, and you only wanted to style those paragraphs that were *direct* descendants of div.sidebar, you'd use a **child selector**. A child selector uses the > character to specify a direct descendant.

Here's the new CSS, which turns only those paragraphs directly inside .sidebar (but not those within .tagline) white:

```
p { color: #0000FF; }
.sidebar>p { color: #FFFFFF; }
```

 Internet Explorer 6 Doesn't Support the Child Selector

Unfortunately, Internet Explorer 6 doesn't support the child selector, so until usage of that browser decreases significantly, you should only use the child selector to specify non-essential styles. If, as a result of using a child selector, the information on your page becomes unreadable (or the layout suffers unacceptably), try to use a different method (such as an ID selector) to apply the style.

Pseudo-class Selectors

The formatting options available for the a element in HTML are more extensive than those on offer for most other elements. By specifying link, vlink, and alink attributes in the <body> tag, you can set the colors for the various states of the links in your page (unvisited, visited, and being clicked on, respectively).

CSS provides its own way of setting these styles, and adds a fourth state that's applied when the cursor hovers over the link. Consider the following example:

```
a:link { color: #0000FF; }
a:visited { color: #FF00FF; }
a:hover { color: #00CCFF; }
a:active { color: #FF0000; }
```

This code contains four CSS style definitions. Each of the selectors uses what is termed a **pseudo-class** of the a element.

- The first, `link`, applies to unvisited links only, and specifies that they should be blue.
- The second, `visited`, applies to visited links, and makes them magenta.
- The third style definition, `hover`, overrides the first two by making links light blue when the cursor is moved over them, whether they've been visited or not.
- The final style definition makes links red when they're clicked on.

The order in which you specify these pseudo-class selectors in your style sheet is important; because `active` appears last, it overrides the first three, so it will take effect whether the links have been visited or not, and whether the cursor is over them or not.

The `hover` and `active` states are officially known as **dynamic pseudo-class selectors**, as they only occur when the user interacts in some way with the element, by clicking on the link or holding the cursor over it.

Summary

This chapter has given you a taste of CSS and its usage at the most basic level. If you haven't used CSS before, but have an understanding of the concepts discussed in this chapter, you should be able to start using the examples in this book.

The examples in the early chapters are somewhat simpler than those found near the end, so, if you haven't worked with this technology before, you might want to begin with the earlier chapters. These will build on the knowledge you gained in this chapter to get you using and, I hope, enjoying CSS.

Chapter

Text Styling and Other Basics

This chapter explores the applications of CSS for styling text, and covers a lot of CSS basics as well as answering some of the more frequently asked questions about these techniques. If you're new to CSS, these examples will introduce you to a variety of properties and their usages, and will give you a solid foundation from which to start your own experiments. For those who are already familiar with CSS, this chapter will serve as a quick refresher in those moments when you can't quite remember how to achieve a certain effect.

The examples I've provided here are well supported across a variety of browsers and versions, though, as always, testing your code in different browsers is important. While there may be small inconsistencies or a lack of support for these techniques in older browsers, none of the solutions presented here should cause you any serious problems.

How do I replace `<font>` tags with CSS?

Once upon a time, before CSS was widely supported, web developers styled the text on their pages using the `<font>` tag. However, now that the use of CSS to style text is supported by version 4 browsers and above, there's no longer a compelling reason to continue to use <font> tags.

Here's an example: if you used <font> tags, you'd need to set the style for each paragraph on your page, like so:

```
<p><font color="#800080" face="Verdana, Geneva, Arial, Helvetica,
   sans-serif">These stuffed peppers are lovely as a starter, or as
   a side dish for a Chinese meal. They also go down well as part
   of a buffet and even children seem to like them.</font></p>
```

Solution

Using CSS, you can specify in the style sheet the color and font you want to apply to the paragraph. To replace the <font> tags in the example above, we'd set the p element's color property to #800080, and set its font-family to Verdana, Geneva, Arial, Helvetica, sans-serif:

basicfont.css (excerpt)

```
p {
  color: #800080;
  font-family: Verdana, Geneva, Arial, Helvetica, sans-serif;
}
```

Now, every time you add to your document text enclosed by <p> tags, it will take on this style—no extra markup is required. It also makes life a lot easier if your client suddenly wants to change the font from Verdana to Times on 100 pages of the site!

Should I use pixels, points, ems, or something else to set font sizes?

You can size text in CSS using the font-size property, like so:

```
font-size: 12px;
```

We've used pixel sizing here, but the `font-size` property can take a variety of other values. Before you can decide which to use, you'll need to know something of the relative merits of each option.

Solution

Sizing Fonts Using Units of Measurement

Table 2.1 identifies the units that you can use to size fonts.

Table 2.1. Units available for setting font size

Unit Identifier	Corresponding Units
pt	points
pc	picas
px	pixels
em	ems
ex	exes
%	percentages

Let's look at each of these units in turn.

Points and Picas

```
p {
   font-size: 10pt;
}
```

You should avoid using **points** and **picas** to style text for display on screen. This unit is an excellent way to set font sizes for print design, as the point measurement was created for that purpose. A point has a fixed size of 1/72 of an inch, while a pica is one-sixth of an inch. A printed document whose fonts are specified using these units will appear exactly as you intended—after all, one-sixth of an inch is the same physical measurement whether you're printing on an A4 page or a billboard. However, computers cannot accurately predict the physical size at which elements will appear on the monitor, so they guess—and guess badly—at the size of a point or pica, with results that vary between platforms.

If you're creating a print style sheet, or a document that's intended for print—not on-screen—viewing, points and picas are the units to use. However, a general rule of thumb indicates that we should avoid them when designing for the Web.

Pixels

```
p {
  font-size: 12px;
}
```

Many designers like to set font sizes in **pixel measurements**, as this unit makes it easy to achieve consistent text displays across various browsers and platforms. However, pixel measurements ignore any preferences users may have set in their own browsers and, in many browsers, font sizes that the designer has dictated in pixels cannot be resized by users. This limitation presents a serious accessibility problem for users who need to make text larger in order to read it clearly.

While pixels may seem like the easiest option for setting font sizes, pixel measurements should be avoided if another method can be used, particularly for large blocks of content. If you're creating a document for print, or creating a print style sheet, you should avoid pixels entirely. Pixels have no meaning in the world of print and, like the application of points to the on-screen environment, when print applications are provided with a pixel measurement, they will simply try to guess the size at which the font should appear on paper—with erratic results.

Ems

The **em** is a relative font measurement: one em is equal to the height of the capital letter M in the default font size. Where CSS is concerned, 1em is seen to be equal to the user's default font size, or the font size of the parent element when it is set to something other than the default.

If you use ems (or any other relative unit) to set all your font sizes, users will be able to resize the text, which will comply with the text size preferences they have set in their browsers. As an example, let's create a declaration that sets the text within a p element to display at a size of 1em:

```
p {
  font-size: 1em;
}
```

A visitor who uses Internet Explorer 6, in which the text size is set to **Medium**, will see the paragraph shown in Figure 2.1 when he or she views the page.

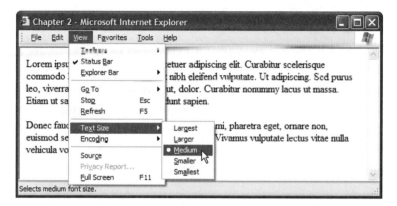

Figure 2.1. Viewing the display when the `font-size` is set to `1em` and text size is **Medium**

If the users have set the text size to **Largest**, the `1em` text will display as shown in Figure 2.2.

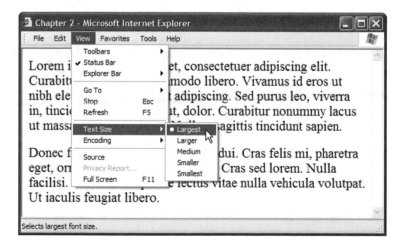

Figure 2.2. Viewing the display when the `font-size` is set to `1em` and text size is set to **Largest**

It's true that using ems to size text gives you less control over the way users view the document. However, this approach means that users who need a very large font size, for instance, can read your content—which, presumably, is the reason why you're publishing the text to the page.

Em values can be set using decimal numbers. For example, to display text at a size 10% smaller than the user's default (or the font size of its parent element), you could use this rule:

```
p {
  font-size: 0.9em;
}
```

To display the text 10% larger than the default or inherited size, you'd use this rule:

```
p {
  font-size: 1.1em;
}
```

Exes

The **ex** is a relative unit measurement that corresponds to the height of the lowercase letter x in the default font size. In theory, if you set the `font-size` of a paragraph to `1ex`, the uppercase letters in the text will display at the height at which the lowercase letter x would have appeared if the font size had not been specified (and the lowercase letters will be sized relative to those uppercase letters).

Unfortunately, modern browsers don't yet support the typographical features needed to determine the size of an ex precisely—they usually make a rough guess for this measurement. For this reason, exes are rarely used at the time of writing.

Percentages

```
p {
  font-size: 100%;
}
```

As with ems and exes, font sizes that are set in **percentages** will honor users' text size settings, and can be resized by the user. Setting the size of a p element to `100%` will display your text at users' default font size settings (as will setting the font size to `1em`). Decreasing the percentage will make the text smaller:

```
p {
  font-size: 90%;
}
```

Increasing the percentage will make the text larger:

```
p {
  font-size: 150%;
}
```

Sizing Fonts Using Keywords

As an alternative to using numerical values to set text sizes, you can use absolute and relative keywords.

Absolute Keywords

We can use any of seven absolute keywords to set text size in CSS:

- `xx-small`
- `x-small`
- `small`
- `medium`
- `large`
- `x-large`
- `xx-large`

These keywords are defined relative to each other, and browsers implement them in different ways. Most browsers display `medium` at the same size as unstyled text, with the other keywords resizing text accordingly, to varying degrees. Internet Explorer 5 (and version 6, depending on the document type), however, treats `small` as being the same size as unstyled text.

These keyword measurements are considered absolute in that they don't inherit from any parent element. Yet, unlike the absolute values provided for height, such as pixels and points, they do allow the text to be resized in the browser, and will honor the user's browser settings. The main problem with using these keywords is the fact that, for example, `x-small`-sized text may be perfectly readable in one browser, and minuscule in another.

Relative Keywords

Text sized using relative keywords—`larger` and `smaller`—takes its size from the parent element in the same way that text sized with `em` and `%` does. Therefore, if you set the size of your p element to `small` using absolute keywords, and decide that you want emphasized text to display comparatively larger, you could add the following to the style sheet:

relative.css

```
p {
  font-size: small;
}
em {
  font-size: larger;
}
```

The following markup would display as shown in Figure 2.3, because the text between the `<em>` and `</em>` tags will display larger than its parent, the p element:

relative.html *(excerpt)*

```
<p>These <em>stuffed peppers</em> are lovely as a starter, or as a
   side dish for a Chinese meal. They also go down well as part of
   a buffet and even children seem to like them.</p>
```

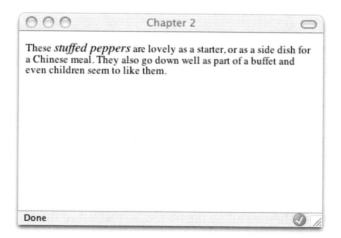

Figure 2.3. The emphasized text displaying larger than its containing paragraph

Relative Sizing and Inheritance

When you use any kind of relative sizing, remember that the element you're considering will inherit its starting size from its parent element, then adjust its size accordingly. This is fairly easy to understand in layouts in which elements are nested in a simple manner; however, this inheritance pattern can become problematic in nested-table layouts in which the parent element is not always obvious—things can seem to inherit very strangely indeed! The following example demonstrates this point.

My style sheet contains the following style rule, which sets text in a `td` element to display at 80%. This is slightly smaller than users' default font sizes, but they will be able to resize the text:

nesting.css

```
td {
  font-size: 80%;
}
```

On a page in which there are no nested table cells, the text will display consistently at that slightly smaller size. However, in a nested-table layout like that defined in the markup below, the text within each nested table will display at 80% of the font size of its containing table:

nesting.html *(excerpt)*

```
<table>
  <tr>
    <td>This is a table
      <table>
        <tr>
          <td>This is the second table
            <table>
              <tr>
                <td>This is the third table</td>
              </tr>
            </table>
          </td>
        </tr>
      </table>
    </td>
  </tr>
</table>
```

```
      </td>
    </tr>
  </table>
```

This markup will display as in Figure 2.4. As you can see, the text becomes progressively smaller in each nested table.

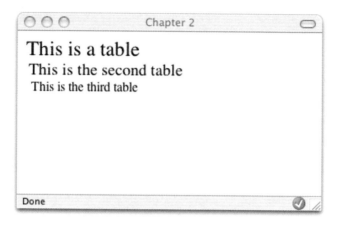

Figure 2.4. Using relative font sizing within nested tables

Discussion

When you're deciding which method of text sizing to use, it's best to select one that allows all users to resize the text, and that ensures that the text complies with the settings users have chosen within their browsers. Relative font sizing tends to work well with CSS layouts and simple table-based layouts, but it can be tricky to implement in a complex nested-table layout because of the way the elements inherit sizing. However, in order to achieve even a basic level of accessibility, enabling users to set fonts to a comfortable level is necessary.

Designing your layout with resizable text in mind also allows you to avoid an issue that's often seen in browsers that do allow the resizing of pixels, on pages where designers have assumed that setting font sizes in pixels will allow them to fix the heights of containers, or place text on top of a fixed-height image. This approach will work in Internet Explorer, which doesn't resize text whose size is set in pixels, but may result in a complete mess of overflowing text in Firefox, where the heights of boxes containing text cannot ever be known.

How do I set my text to display in a certain font?

Solution

Specify the typeface that your text will adopt using the `font-family` property, like so:

```
p {
  font-family: Verdana;
}
```

Discussion

As well as specific fonts, such as Verdana or Times, CSS allows the specification of some more generic font families:

- `serif`
- `sans-serif`
- `monospace`
- `cursive`
- `fantasy`

When you specify fonts, it's important to remember that users probably don't have the fonts you have on your computer. If you define a font that they don't have, your text will display in their browsers' default fonts, regardless of what you'd have preferred.

To avoid this eventuality, you can simply specify generic font names and let users' systems decide which font to apply. For instance, if you want your document to appear in a sans-serif font such as Arial, you could use the following style rule:

```
p {
  font-family: sans-serif;
}
```

Now, you'll probably want to have more control than this over the way your site displays—and you can. It's possible to specify both font names and generic fonts in the same declaration block. Take, for example, the following style rule for the p element:

```
p {
  font-family: Verdana, Geneva, Arial, Helvetica, sans-serif;
}
```

Here, we've specified that if Verdana is installed on the system, it should be used; if it's not installed, the browser is instructed to see if Geneva is installed; failing that, the computer will look for Arial, then Helvetica. If none of these fonts are available, the browser will use that system's default sans-serif font.

Fonts that you can feel fairly confident to use are:

Windows   Arial, Lucida, Impact, Times New Roman, Courier New, Tahoma, Comic Sans, Verdana, Georgia, Garamond

Mac   Helvetica, Futura, Bodoni, Times, Palatino, Courier, Gill Sans, Geneva, Baskerville, Andale Mono

This list reveals the reason why we chose the fonts we specified in our style rule: we begin by specifying our first preference, a common Windows font (Verdana), then list a similar Mac font (Geneva). We then follow up with other fonts that would be usable if neither of these fonts was available.

How do I remove underlines from my links?

The widely accepted default visual indication that text on a web page links to another document is that it's underlined and displays in a different color from the rest of the text. However, there may be instances in which you want to remove that underline.

Solution

We use the `text-decoration` property to remove the underlines from link text. By default, the browser will set the `text-decoration` of an `a` element to `underline`.

To remove the underline, simply set the `text-decoration` property for the link to none:

```
text-decoration: none;
```

The CSS used to create the effect shown in Figure 2.5 is as follows:

textdecoration.css

```
a:link, a:visited {
    text-decoration: none;
}
```

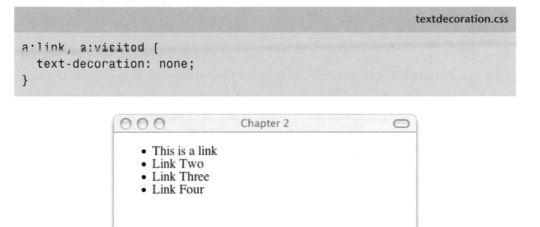

Figure 2.5. Using `text-decoration` to create links that aren't underlined

Discussion

In addition to `underline` and `none`, there are other values for `text-decoration` that you can try out:

- `overline`
- `line-through`
- `blink`

You can combine these values. For instance, should you wish to have an underline and overline on a particular link, as illustrated in Figure 2.6, you'd use the following style rule:

textdecoration2.css

```
a:link, a:visited {
  text-decoration: underline overline;
}
```

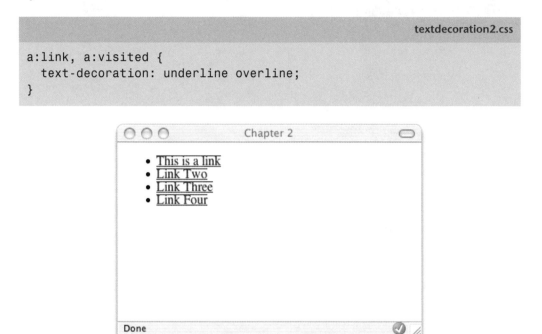

Figure 2.6. Combining text-decoration values to create links with underlines and overlines

Avoid Applying Misleading Lines

You can use the text-decoration property to apply underlines to text that's not a link, but be wary of doing this. The underlining of links is such a widely-accepted convention that users tend to think that *any* underlined text is a link to another document.

When is Removing Underlines a Bad Idea?

Underlining links is a standard convention followed by all web browsers and, consequently, users expect to see links underlined. Removing the underline from links that appear within text can make it very difficult for people to realize that these words are in fact links, and not just highlighted text. I'd advise against removing the underlines from links within text. There are other ways in which you can style links so they look attractive, and removing the underline is rarely, if ever, necessary.

Links that are used as part of a menu, or appear in some other situation in which the text is quite obviously a link—for instance, where the text is styled with CSS to resemble a graphical button—are a different story. If you wish, you can remove the underline from these kinds of links, because it should be obvious from their context that they're links.

How do I create a link that changes color when the cursor moves over it?

One attractive link effect changes the color or otherwise alters the appearance of a link when the cursor is moved across it. This effect can be applied to great advantage on navigation menus created with CSS, but it can also be used on links within regular paragraph text.

Solution

To create this effect, we need to style the :hover and :active dynamic pseudo-classes of the anchor element differently from its other pseudo-classes.

Let's look at an example. Here's a typical style rule that applies the same declarations to all of an anchor element's pseudo-classes:

textdecoration3.css

```
a:link, a:visited, a:hover, a:active {
  text-decoration: underline;
  color: #6A5ACD;
  background-color: transparent;
}
```

When this style sheet is applied, our links will display in the blue color #6A5ACD with an underline, as shown in Figure 2.7.

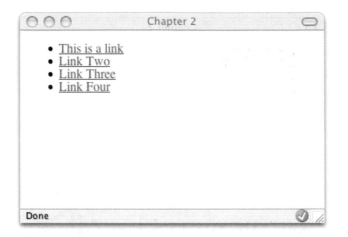

Figure 2.7. Using the same declaration for all of the links' pseudo-classes

To style our `:hover` and `:active` pseudo-classes differently, we need to remove them from the declaration with the other pseudo-classes and give them their own separate declaration. In the CSS below, I decided to apply an overline in addition to the underline. I've also set a background color and made the link's text a darker color; Figure 2.8 shows how these styles display in a browser:

```
                                            textdecoration4.css
a:link, a:visited {
  text-decoration: underline;
  color: #6A5ACD;
  background-color: transparent;
}
a:hover, a:active {
  text-decoration: underline overline;
  color: #191970;
  background-color: #C9C3ED;
}
```

As you've probably realized, you can style the anchor's other pseudo-classes separately, too. In particular, you might like to apply a different style to links that users have visited. To do so, you'd simply style the `:visited` pseudo-class separately.

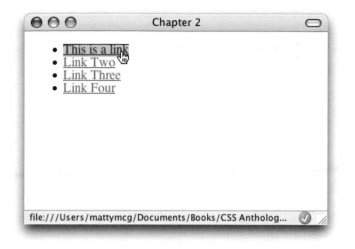

Figure 2.8. Moving the cursor over a link to which a hover style is applied

When styling pseudo-classes, take care that you don't change either the size or weight (or boldness) of the text. If you do, you'll find that your page appears to jiggle, as the surrounding content has to move to make way for the larger text to display when your cursor hovers over the link.

> ### Ordering Pseudo-class Declarations
>
> The anchor pseudo-classes should be declared in the following order: `link`, `visited`, `hover`, `active`. If they aren't, you may find that they don't work as you intended. One way to remember this order is the mnemonic: LoVeHAte.

How do I display two different styles of link on one page?

The previous solution explained how to style the different selectors of the anchor element, but what if you want to use different link styles within the same document? Perhaps you want to display links without underlines in your navigation menu, yet make sure that links within the body content are easily identifiable. Or maybe part of your document has a dark background color, so you need to use a light-colored link style there.

Solution

To demonstrate how to create multiple styles for links displayed on one page, let's take an example in which we've already styled the regular links:

linktypes.css *(excerpt)*

```css
a:link, a:visited {
  text-decoration: underline;
  color: #6A5ACD;
  background-color: transparent;
}

a:hover, a:active {
  text-decoration: underline overline;
  color: #191970;
  background-color: #C9C3ED;
}
```

These should be taken as the default link styles—they reflect the way links will normally be styled within your documents. The first rule makes the link blue, so if an area of our page has a blue background, the links that appear in that space will be unreadable. We need to create a second set of styles for links in that area.

First, let's create a `class` or an `id` for the element that will contain the differently colored links. If the container is already styled with CSS, it may already have a `class` or `id` that we can use. Suppose that our document contains the following markup:

linktypes.html *(excerpt)*

```html
<div class="boxout">
  <p>Visit our <a href="store.html">online store</a>, for all your
    widget needs.</p>
</div>
```

We need to create a style rule that affects any link appearing within an element of class `boxout`:

linktypes.css *(excerpt)*

```
.boxout {
  color: #FFFFFF;
  background-color: #6A5ACD;
}
.boxout a:link, .boxout a:visited {
  text-decoration: underline;
  color: #E4E2F6;
  background-color: transparent;
}
.boxout a:hover, .boxout a:active {
  background-color: #C9C3ED;
  color: #191970;
}
```

As you can see in Figure 2.9, this rule will display all links in the document as per the first style *except* those that appear within the boxout—these links will be displayed in the lighter color.

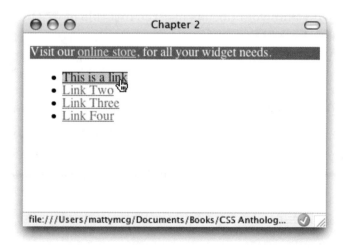

Figure 2.9. Using two different link styles in one document

How do I style the first item in a list differently from the others?

Frequently, designers find that we need to style the first of a set of items—be they list items or a number of paragraphs within a container—differently from the rest of the set. One way to achieve this would be to assign a class to the first item, and style that class differently from the other items. There is, however, a more elegant way to create this effect in modern browsers: using the pseudo-class selector first-child.

Solution

Here's a simple list of items marked up as an unordered list:

firstchild.html *(excerpt)*

```
<ul>
  <li>Brie</li>
  <li>Cheddar</li>
  <li>Red Leicester</li>
  <li>Shropshire Blue</li>
</ul>
```

Using `first-child`

To change the color of the first item in the list without affecting its neighbors, we can use the first-child selector. This allows us to target the first element within the ul element, as shown overleaf; the result is shown in Figure 2.10:

firstchild.css *(excerpt)*

```
li:first-child {
  color: red;
}
```

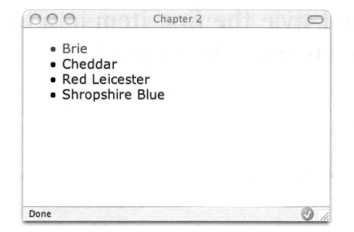

Figure 2.10. Displaying the first list item in red text

Unfortunately `first-child` is not supported by Internet Explorer 6, so until the number of visitors using this browser to view your site becomes negligible, you'll need to find another method to create this effect. One such method is to use a class selector.

Using a Class Selector

To create this effect in Internet Explorer 6, we add a `class` or `id` attribute to the element that we wish to style differently. For this example, let's use a `class`:

firstchildwithclass.html *(excerpt)*

```
<ul>
  <li class="unusual">Brie</li>
  <li>Cheddar</li>
  <li>Red Leicester</li>
  <li>Shropshire Blue</li>
</ul>
```

Once this in place, we create a style rule to implement the desired effect:

firstchildwithclass.css *(excerpt)*

```
li.unusual {
  color: red;
}
```

How do I add a background color to a heading?

CSS allows us to add a background color to any element, including a heading.

Solution

Below, I've created a CSS rule for all the level-one headings in a document. The result is shown in Figure 2.11.

headingcolor.css (excerpt)

```
h1 {
  background-color: #ADD8E6;
  color: #256579;
  font: 1.6em Verdana, Geneva, Arial, Helvetica, sans-serif;
  padding: 0.2em;
}
```

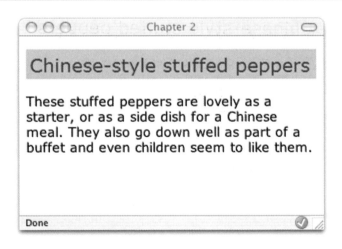

Figure 2.11. Displaying a heading with a background color

Make Way for Color!

When you add a background to a heading, you may also want to adjust the padding so that there's space between the heading text and the edge of the colored area, as I've done in this example.

How do I style headings with underlines?

Solution

There are two ways in which you can add an underline to your text. The simplest is to use the `text-decoration` property that we encountered earlier in this chapter in "How do I remove underlines from my links?". This method will allow you to apply to text an underline that's the same color as the text itself, as this code, and Figure 2.12, show:

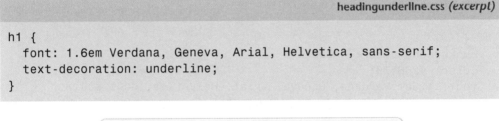

```
                                          headingunderline.css (excerpt)

h1 {
    font: 1.6em Verdana, Geneva, Arial, Helvetica, sans-serif;
    text-decoration: underline;
}
```

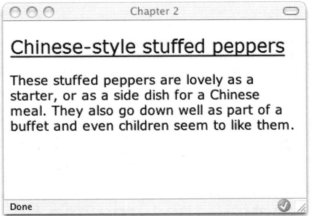

Figure 2.12. Adding an underline to a heading using `text-decoration`

You can also create an underline effect by adding a bottom border to the heading. This solution, which produces the result shown in Figure 2.13, is more flexible in that it allows you to separate the underline from the heading with the use of padding, and you can change the color of the underline so that it's different than that of the text.

A heading to which this effect is applied is also less likely to be confused with underlined link text than is a heading whose underline is created using the `text-decoration` property. However, this effect may display with slight inconsistencies in different browsers, so you'll need to test it to make sure the effect looks reasonable on the browsers your visitors may use. Here's the style rule you'll need:

headingunderline2.css

```
h1 {
  font: 1.6em Verdana, Geneva, Arial, Helvetica, sans-serif;
  padding: 0.2em;
  border-bottom: 1px solid #aaaaaa;
}
```

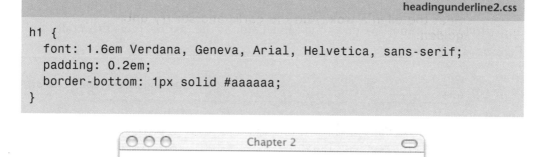

Figure 2.13. Creating an underline effect using a bottom border

How do I remove the large gap between an h1 element and the following paragraph?

By default, browsers render a gap between all heading and paragraph elements. The gap is produced by default top and bottom margins that browsers apply to these elements. The margin on the heading shown in Figure 2.14 reflects the default value. This gap can be removed using CSS.

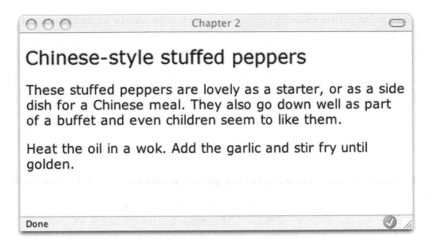

Figure 2.14. The default heading and paragraph spacing

Solution

To remove all space between a heading and the paragraph that follows it, you must remove the bottom margin from the heading as well as the top margin from the paragraph. In modern browsers—including Internet Explorer 7—we can do this through CSS, using an **adjacent selector**. However, to achieve the same effect in older browsers, we need to revert to other techniques that are better supported.

Using an Adjacent Selector

An adjacent selector lets you target an element that follows another element, as long as both share the same parent. In fact, you can use adjacent selectors to specify an element that follows several other elements, not just one—the element to which the style is applied is always the *last element in the chain*. If you're confused, don't worry: this concept will become a lot clearer once we've seen it in action.

The following style rules remove the top margin from any paragraph that immediately follows a level-one heading. Note that the top margin is not removed from the h1—just the paragraph that follows it:

headingnospace.css *(excerpt)*

```
h1 {
  font: 1.6em Verdana, Geneva, Arial, Helvetica, sans-serif;
  margin-bottom: 0;
```

```
}
h1+p {
  margin-top: 0;
}
```

Figure 2.15 shows the display of the original page once this rule is applied.

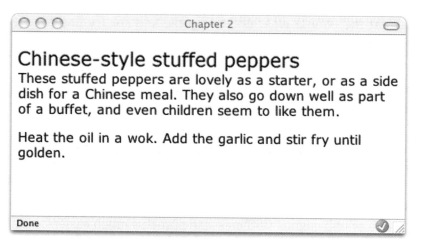

Figure 2.15. Using an adjacent selector to change the heading display

As you can see, the first paragraph that follows the h1 no longer has a top margin; all subsequent paragraphs, however, retain their top margins.

As I mentioned, adjacent selectors only work with newer browsers—for example, the only version of Internet Explorer that includes support for the adjacent selector is Internet Explorer 7. In some cases, you might decide that it's acceptable for users of older browsers to see a gap between the heading and the text. But if this isn't the case, and you want to remove the margins from the page that's seen by users of older browsers, you have a couple of options.

You can make use of class selectors, as we did in "How do I display two different styles of link on one page?", to apply a margin of 0 to that class. If you've read that solution, you should find it fairly straightforward to implement this approach. Another option is to apply a negative margin to the heading, which I'll explain next.

Applying a Negative Margin

In CSS, margins can take either a positive or a negative value. Padding, however, can only take a positive value.

Applying a negative margin to the heading is another way to remove the space between the heading and the first paragraph. The style rule below produces a similar effect to the one we saw in Figure 2.15:

```
h1 {
    font: 1.6em Verdana, Geneva, Arial, Helvetica, sans-serif;
    margin-bottom: -0.6em;
}
```

How do I highlight text on the page?

Before CSS came along, we might have used `<font>` tags to highlight an important term on a page, or to identify the search terms visitors had used to locate our document through a search engine. CSS makes the process much easier.

Solution

CSS allows you to create a class for the highlighting style, and apply it by wrapping the highlighted text with `<span>` tags that apply the class. For example, in the following paragraph, we've wrapped a phrase in `<span>` tags that apply the class `hilite`:

hilite.html *(excerpt)*

```
<p>These <span class="hilite">stuffed peppers</span> are lovely
    as a starter, or as a side dish for a Chinese meal. They also
    go down well as part of a buffet, and even children seem to
    like them.</p>
```

The `hilite` class is shown overleaf; the highlighted section will display as shown in Figure 2.16:

```
                                                    hilite.css (excerpt)
.hilite {
  background-color: #FFFFCC;
  color: #B22222;
}
```

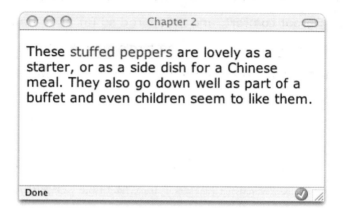

Figure 2.16. Highlighting text with CSS

How do I alter the line height (leading) on my text?

One of the great advantages of using CSS rather than <font> tags is that it gives you far more control over the way text looks on the page. In this solution, we'll alter the leading of the text in your document.

Solution

If the default spacing between the lines of text on your page looks a little narrow, you can change it with the line-height property:

```
                                                            leading.css
p {
  font: 0.9em Verdana, Geneva, Arial, Helvetica, sans-serif;
  line-height: 2.0;
}
```

The result is shown in Figure 2.17.

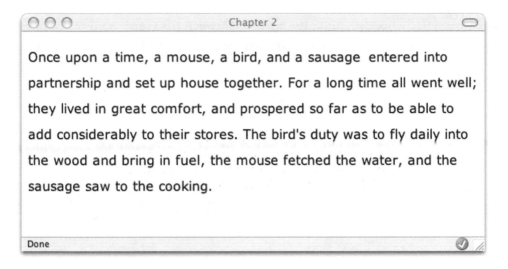

Figure 2.17. Altering leading using the `line-height` property

Easy! Just be careful not to space the text out so much that it becomes difficult to read.

 No Units?

You'll notice that we haven't specified any units of measurement in this example—the value of 2.0 is a ratio. You *can* specify a value for `line-height` using standard CSS units of measurement, such as ems or pixels, but doing so breaks the link between the line height and the font size for child elements.

For example, if the example above contained a `span` that set a large `font-size`, the line height would scale up proportionally, maintaining the same ratio, because the `line-height` of the paragraph was set to the numerical value `2.0`. If, however, `line-height` was set to `2em` or `200%`, the `span` would inherit the actual line height, not the ratio, and the large font size would not affect the line height of the span. Depending on the effect you're going for, this may actually be a desirable result.

How do I justify text?

When you justify text, you alter the spacing between the words so that both the right and left margins are straight. You can create this effect easily using CSS.

Solution

You can justify paragraph text with the help of the `text-align` property, like so:

justify.css

```
p {
  text-align: justify;
  font: 1em Verdana, Geneva, Arial, Helvetica, sans-serif;
  line-height: 2.0;
}
```

Figure 2.18 shows the effect of setting `text-align` to `justify`.

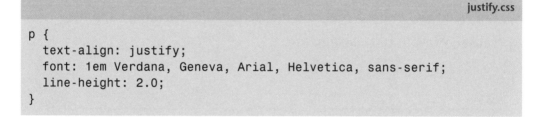

Figure 2.18. Justifying text using `text-align`

Discussion

The other values for `text-align` are:

`right`   aligns the text to the right of the container

`left`   aligns the text to the left of the container

`center`   centers the text in the container

How do I style a horizontal rule?

In general, you should avoid including in your markup elements that are purely presentational, such as the horizontal rule (`hr`). A document that is structured semantically is easier to maintain, loads faster, and is optimized for search engine indexing. A similar effect to that produced by the `hr` element can usually be achieved by applying borders to existing elements.

However, there are occasions when using an `hr` is either the best way to achieve the desired effect, or is necessary to serve unstyled content to an older browser that doesn't support CSS.

Solution

You can change the color, height, and width of a horizontal rule with CSS. However, you'll need to watch out for some inconsistencies between browsers. For instance, in the example below, I've used the same values for `color` and `background-color` because Mozilla-based browsers color the rule using `background-color`, while Internet Explorer uses `color`:

hrstyle.css *(excerpt)*

```
hr {
  border: none;
  background-color: #ADD8E6;
  color: #ADD8E6;
  height: 1px;
  width: 80%;
}
```

The result of this rule can be seen in Figure 2.19.

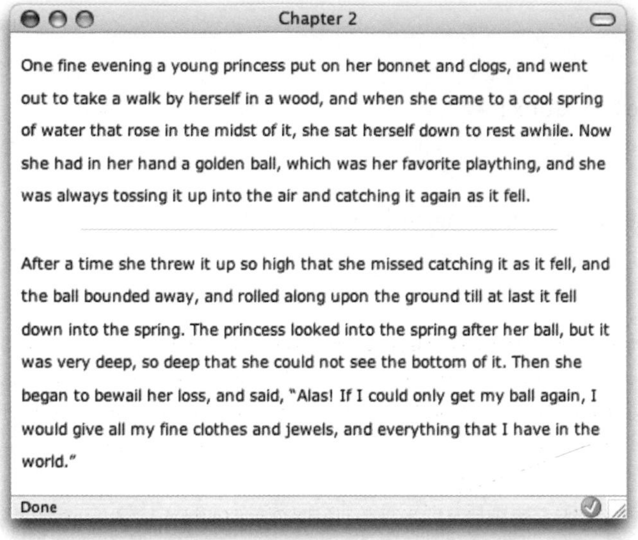

One fine evening a young princess put on her bonnet and clogs, and went out to take a walk by herself in a wood, and when she came to a cool spring of water that rose in the midst of it, she sat herself down to rest awhile. Now she had in her hand a golden ball, which was her favorite plaything, and she was always tossing it up into the air and catching it again as it fell.

After a time she threw it up so high that she missed catching it as it fell, and the ball bounded away, and rolled along upon the ground till at last it fell down into the spring. The princess looked into the spring after her ball, but it was very deep, so deep that she could not see the bottom of it. Then she began to bewail her loss, and said, "Alas! If I could only get my ball again, I would give all my fine clothes and jewels, and everything that I have in the world."

Figure 2.19. Changing the color, height, and width of a horizontal rule

How do I indent text?

Solution

To indent text, we apply to its container a rule that sets a `padding-left` value, like this:

indent.html (excerpt)

```
<p>After a time she threw it up so high that she missed catching
it as it fell, and the ball bounded away, and rolled along upon
the ground till at last it fell down into the spring.</p>

<p class="indent">The princess looked into the spring after her
ball, but it was very deep, so deep that she could not see the
bottom of it. Then she began to bewail her loss, and said, "Alas!
If I could only get my ball again, I would give all my fine
clothes and jewels, and everything that I have in the world."</p>
```

```
                                                          indent.css (excerpt)
.indent {
  padding-left: 30px;
}
```

You can see the indented paragraph in Figure 2.20.

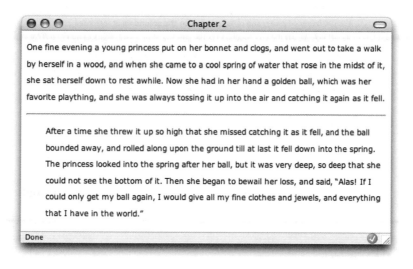

Figure 2.20. Indenting text using CSS

Discussion

You shouldn't use the HTML tag `<blockquote>` to indent text, unless the text is actually a quote. Although visual editing environments such as Macromedia Dreamweaver implement text indentation by applying a `blockquote`, resist the temptation to use it for this purpose; instead, set up a CSS rule to indent the appropriate blocks as shown above.

The `<blockquote>` tag is designed to mark up a quote, and devices such as screen readers used by the visually impaired will read this text in a way that helps those users understand that what they're hearing is a quote. If you use `<blockquote>` to indent regular paragraphs, it will be very confusing for users who hear the content read as a quote.

A One-liner

A related technique enables us to indent just the first line of each paragraph. Simply apply the CSS property `text-indent` either to the paragraph, or to a class that's applied to the paragraphs you wish to display in this way:

indent2.css

```
p {
   text-indent: 20px;
}
```

How do I center text?

Solution

You can center text, or any other element, using the `text-align` property with a value of `center`:

center.html (excerpt)

```
<p>After a time she threw it up so high that she missed catching
it as it fell, and the ball bounded away, and rolled along upon
the ground till at last it fell down into the spring.</p>

<p class="centered">The princess looked into the spring after her
ball, but it was very deep, so deep that she could not see the
bottom of it. Then she began to bewail her loss, and said, "Alas!
If I could only get my ball again, I would give all my fine
clothes and jewels, and everything that I have in the world."</p>
```

center.css (excerpt)

```
.centered {
   text-align: center;
}
```

The result of this rule can be seen in Figure 2.21.

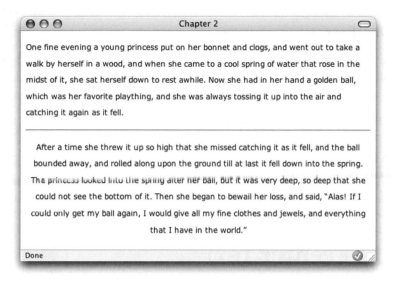

Figure 2.21. Centering text using `text-align`

How do I change text to all capitals using CSS?

Solution

You can change text to all capitals, and perform other transformations, using the `text-transform` property:

uppercase.html *(excerpt)*

```
<p>After a time she threw it up so high that she missed catching
it as it fell, and the ball bounded away, and rolled along upon
the ground till at last it fell down into the spring.</p>

<p class="transform">The princess looked into the spring after her
ball, but it was very deep, so deep that she could not see the
bottom of it. Then she began to bewail her loss, and said, "Alas!
If I could only get my ball again, I would give all my fine
clothes and jewels, and everything that I have in the world."</p>
```

uppercase.css (excerpt)

```
.transform {
  text-transform: uppercase;
}
```

Note the uppercase text in Figure 2.22.

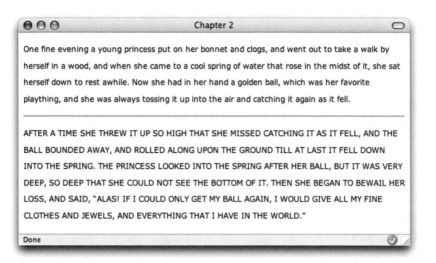

One fine evening a young princess put on her bonnet and clogs, and went out to take a walk by herself in a wood, and when she came to a cool spring of water that rose in the midst of it, she sat herself down to rest awhile. Now she had in her hand a golden ball, which was her favorite plaything, and she was always tossing it up into the air and catching it again as it fell.

AFTER A TIME SHE THREW IT UP SO HIGH THAT SHE MISSED CATCHING IT AS IT FELL, AND THE BALL BOUNDED AWAY, AND ROLLED ALONG UPON THE GROUND TILL AT LAST IT FELL DOWN INTO THE SPRING. THE PRINCESS LOOKED INTO THE SPRING AFTER HER BALL, BUT IT WAS VERY DEEP, SO DEEP THAT SHE COULD NOT SEE THE BOTTOM OF IT. THEN SHE BEGAN TO BEWAIL HER LOSS, AND SAID, "ALAS! IF I COULD ONLY GET MY BALL AGAIN, I WOULD GIVE ALL MY FINE CLOTHES AND JEWELS, AND EVERYTHING THAT I HAVE IN THE WORLD."

Figure 2.22. Using `text-transform` to display the text in uppercase letters

Discussion

The `text-transform` property has other useful values. The value `capitalize` will capitalize the first letter of each word, as illustrated in Figure 2.23:

capitalize.css (excerpt)

```
.transform {
  text-transform: capitalize;
}
```

The other values that the `text-transform` property can take are:

- `lowercase`
- `none` (the default)

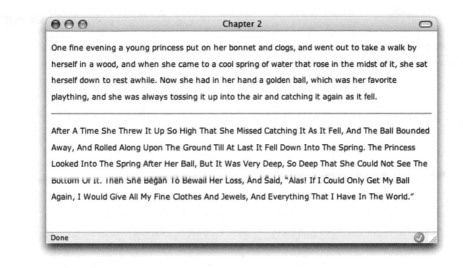

Figure 2.23. Applying `text-transform` to capitalize the first letter of every word

How do I change or remove the bullets on list items?

Solution

You can change the style of bullets displayed on an unordered list by altering the `list-style-type` property. First, here's the markup for the list:

```
listtype.html (excerpt)
<ul>
  <li>list item one</li>
  <li>list item two</li>
  <li>list item three</li>
</ul>
```

To display square bullets, like the ones shown in Figure 2.24, set the `list-style-type` property to `square`:

listtype.css

```
ul {
  list-style-type: square;
}
```

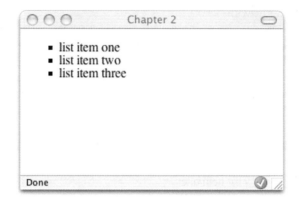

Figure 2.24. Using square bullets for list items

Discussion

Other values that the list-style-type property can take are:

- disc
- circle
- decimal-leading-zero
- decimal
- lower-roman
- upper-roman
- lower-greek
- lower-alpha
- lower-latin
- upper-alpha
- upper-latin
- Hebrew
- Armenian
- Georgian
- none

Not all of these values are supported by all browsers; those browsers that don't support a particular bullet type will display the default type instead. You can see the different types, and check the support your browser provides for them, at the CSS Test Suite for list style type.[1] Setting `list-style-type` to `none` will remove bullets from the display, although the list will still be indented as if the bullets were there, as Figure 2.25 shows:

listtype2.css

```
ul {
  list-style-type: none;
}
```

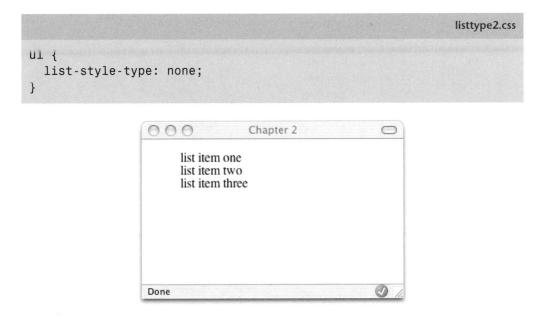

Figure 2.25. Displaying a list without bullets

How do I use an image for a list-item bullet?

Solution

To use an image for a bullet, create your image, then use the `list-style-image` property, instead of `list-style-type`, to set your bullets. This property accepts a URL, which can incorporate the path to your image file as a value:

---

[1] http://www.meyerweb.com/eric/css/tests/css2/sec12-06-02a.htm

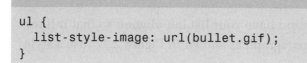

```
ul {
    list-style-image: url(bullet.gif);
}
```

Figure 2.26 shows how this effect can be used to spruce up a list.

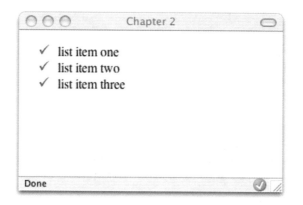

Figure 2.26. Using an image as a list bullet

 Setting Bullets on Individual List Items

The `list-style-image` property actually applies to the list item (`li`) elements in the list. However, if you apply `list-style-image` to the list as a whole (the `ul` or `ol` element), each individual list item will inherit it. You do, however, have the option of setting the property on individual list items (by assigning a `class` or `id` to each), giving individual items their own unique bullet images.

How do I remove the indented left-hand margin from a list?

If you've set `list-style-type` to `none`, you may also wish to remove or decrease the default left-hand margin that the browser sets on a list.

Solution

To remove the indentation entirely and have your list left-aligned so that it lines up with, for example, a preceding paragraph as shown in Figure 2.27, use a style rule similar to this:

listnomargin.css

```
ul {
  list-style-type: none;
  padding-left: 0;
  margin-left: 0;
}
```

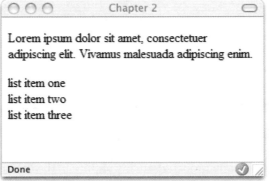

Figure 2.27. A list without indentation or bullets

Discussion

You can apply new indentation values to the list items if you wish. To indent the content by a few pixels, try this:

listsmallmargin.css

```
ul {
  list-style-type: none;
  padding-left: 5px;
  margin-left: 0;
}
```

How do I display a list horizontally?

By default, list items display as block elements; therefore, each new item will display on a new line. However, there may be times when some content on your page is, structurally speaking, a list, even though you mightn't want to display it as such—a collection of navigation links is a good example. How can you display these list items horizontally?

Solution

You can set a list to display horizontally by altering the `display` property of the `li` element to `inline`, like so:

listinline.html *(excerpt)*

```
<ul class="horiz">
  <li>list item one</li>
  <li>list item two</li>
  <li>list item three</li>
</ul>
```

listinline.css

```
ul.horiz li {
  display: inline;
}
```

The result of this style rule is depicted in Figure 2.28.

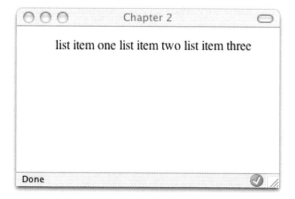

Figure 2.28. Displaying a list horizontally

How do I add comments to my CSS file?

You can, and should, add comments to your CSS file. CSS files that are very simple—containing just a few rules for text styling purposes, for instance—may not require commenting. However, once you start to use a large number of style rules and multiple style sheets on a site, comments come in very handy! Without them, you can spend a lot of time hunting around for the right classes, pondering which class does what, and trying to find the style sheet in which it lives.

Solution

CSS supports multiline C-style comments, just like JavaScript. So, to comment out an area, use the following sequence of characters:

```
/*
   ⋮
*/
```

At the very least, you should add a comment at the top of each style sheet to explain what's in that style sheet, like so:

```
/* This is the default style sheet for all text on the site */
```

How do I remove page margins without adding attributes to the <body> tag?

Before CSS support was widespread, web designers would often remove the default gutter between the document and the browser window by adding attributes to the <body> tag, like this:

```
<body topmargin="0" leftmargin="0" marginheight="0"
    marginwidth="0">
```

Solution

The above attributes of the `<body>` tag are now deprecated. They should be replaced by the following style rules, which have been defined for the `body` element:

```
body {
  margin: 0;
  padding: 0;
}
```

 Cleaning All of the Gutters

Some browsers (such as older versions of Opera) apply `margin` and `padding` to the `html` element instead of the `body` tag.[2] So, to ensure that you've covered all your bases, you should also include the `html` element in your style rule:

zeropagegutter.css (excerpt)

```
html, body {
  margin: 0;
  padding: 0;
}
```

How can I remove browsers' default padding and margins from all elements?

The display that you see in a browser when you view an unstyled document is the result of the browser's internal style sheet. Often, the differences that arise in the way various browsers display an unstyled page occur because those browsers have slightly different internal style sheets.

Solution

One way to solve this problem is to remove the default margins and padding from all elements before you create your styles.

---

[2] http://archivist.incutio.com/viewlist/css-discuss/46074/

The following rule will set the padding and margins on *all* elements to zero. It will have the effect of causing every element on the page—paragraphs, headings, lists, and more—to display without leaving any space between itself and its neighbors, as Figure 2.29 demonstrates:

zeropagemargin.css *(excerpt)*

```
* {
  margin: 0;
  padding: 0
}
```

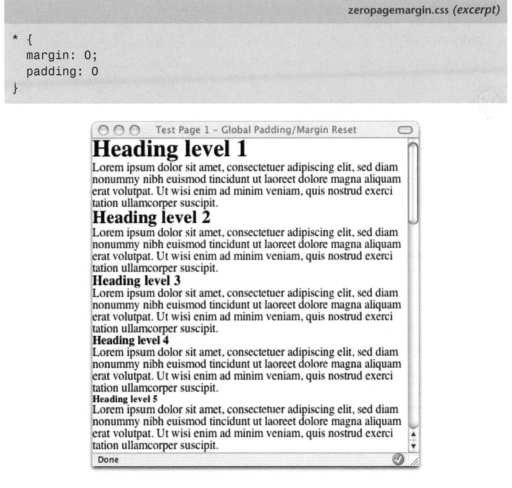

Figure 2.29. Removing the default margins and padding from all elements on a page

Discussion

This style rule uses the universal selector—*—to remove the margins and padding from *everything*, a technique known as **performing a global whitespace reset.**[3] If

---

[3] http://leftjustified.net/journal/2004/10/19/global-ws-reset/

you're working on a particularly complex design, this may well be the best way to start.

However, once you've done it, you'll need to go back and add margins and padding to every element that you use. This is particularly important for some form elements, which may be rendered unusable by this style rule!

However, for simpler designs, removing the whitespace from every element is usually overkill, and will simply generate more work, as you'll need to go back and add padding and margins to elements such as paragraphs, blockquotes, and lists. A viable alternative for simple designs is to remove the margins and padding from a select set of elements only. The following style rule shows how this works; it removes whitespace from heading and list elements:

```
h1, h2, h3, h4, h5, h6, ul, ol {
   margin: 0;
   padding: 0;
}
```

Summary

This chapter has covered some of the more common questions asked by those who are relatively new to CSS—questions that relate to styling and manipulating text on the page. By combining these techniques, you can create attractive effects that will degrade appropriately for those who aren't using a browser that supports CSS.

Chapter

CSS and Images

Given many of the designs favored by CSS purists, you'd be forgiven for thinking that the image is soon to be a thing of the past, eschewed in favor of clean, standards-compliant, CSS-formatted, text-based design. However, while sites that rely entirely on sliced-up images are beginning to look a little dated in comparison with the clean simplicity of the CSS layout "style," well-placed images can bring an otherwise commonplace design to life. And, as designers begin to push the boundaries of what can be achieved with standards-compliant semantic markup, sites whose designs manage to integrate semantics with beauty are becoming much more commonplace.

To work with images in CSS requires just a few simple skills—once you've learned them, you can combine them to create countless interesting effects. The solutions in this chapter demonstrate the basic concepts of working with images while answering some common questions. We'll be using images more in the other chapters, but, as with most of the solutions in this book, don't be afraid to experiment to see what unique effects you can create.

How do I add borders to images?

Photographic images, which might be used to illustrate an article, or displayed in a photo album, look neat when they're bordered with a thin line. However, opening each shot in a graphics program to add borders is a time-consuming process and, if you ever need to change that border's color or thickness, you'll need to go through the same arduous process all over again. Fortunately, CSS makes this chore a whole lot easier.

Solution

Adding a border to an image is a simple procedure using CSS. There are two images in the document displayed in Figure 3.1.

Figure 3.1. Displaying images in a web browser

The following rule adds a single black border to our images:

```
img {
   border-width: 1px;
   border-style: solid;
   border-color: #000000;
}
```

The rule could also be written like this:

borderbasic.css (excerpt)

```
img {
  border: 1px solid #000000;
}
```

Figure 3.2 shows the effect this rule has on the images.

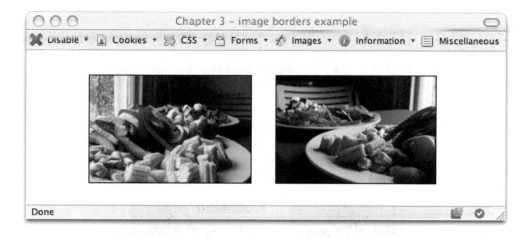

Figure 3.2. Applying a CSS border to make the images look neater

Now, this is all well and good, but your layout probably contains other images to which you *don't* want to apply a permanent black border. The solution to this problem is to create a CSS class for the border, and apply it to selected images as required:

borderclass.css (excerpt)

```
.imgborder {
  border: 1px solid #000000;
}
```

```
<img src="myfish.jpg" alt="My Fish" class="imgborder" />
```

If you're displaying a selection of images—such as a photograph album—on the page, you could set borders on all the images within a particular container, such as a div that has a unique ID:

```
                                              borderalbum.css (excerpt)
#album img {
  border: 1px solid #000000;
}
```

This approach will save you from having to add the class to each individual image within the container.

How do I use CSS to replace the deprecated HTML border attribute on images?

If you're anything like me, you used to use the border attribute of the <img> tag to achieve certain effects—to ensure, for example, that an ugly blue border didn't appear around your navigation buttons. However, the border attribute has been deprecated in the current versions of HTML and XHTML.

Solution

Just as you can create a border, so you can remove one. Setting an image's border property to none will remove those ugly borders:

```
                                               bordernone.css (excerpt)
img {
  border: none;
}
```

How do I set a background image for my page using CSS?

Before CSS, we added backgrounds to pages using the background attribute of the <body> tag. This attribute is now deprecated and has been replaced by CSS properties.

Solution

This style rule adds the image **background-norepeat.jpg** as a background to any page to which this style sheet is attached:

```
                                                          backgrounds.css
body {
    font: 0.9em Verdana, Geneva, Arial, Helvetica, sans-serif;
    background-color: #d2d7e4;
    color: #000000;
    background-image: url(background-norepeat.jpg);
    background-repeat: no-repeat;
}
```

The effects of this style are shown in Figure 3.3.

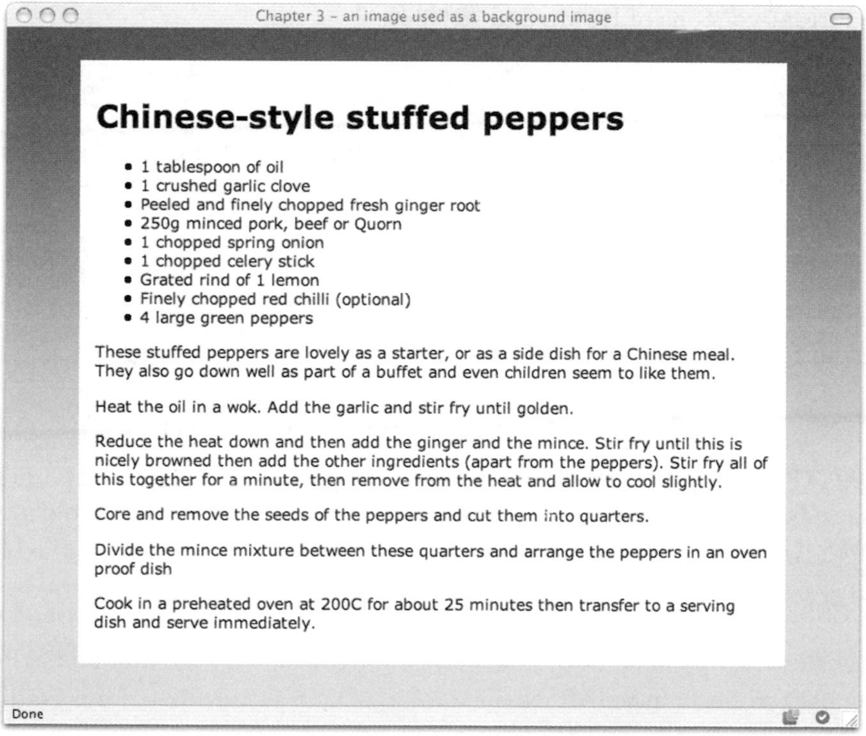

Figure 3.3. Displaying an image as a background image

Discussion

The CSS property `background-image` enables you to specify within the style sheet the location of a background image. To apply a background to the entire document, we'd set this property for the `body` element, but, as we'll see in a solution later in this chapter, a background image can be applied to any element on the page.

By default, the background will tile, repeating both vertically and horizontally to fill the space required for the content. The effect shown in Figure 3.3 was achieved using the image in Figure 3.4, with the `background` property set to `no-repeat`.

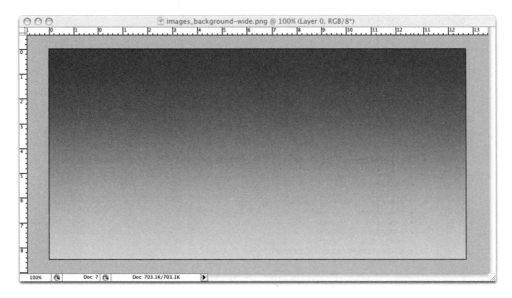

Figure 3.4. Creating a background effect using a (rather wide) image that does not repeat

The image is only 400 pixels tall—not as tall as a typical web page—so I've given the page a background color that's the same as the color of the bottom row of pixels in the gradient image. In this way, the gradient merges seamlessly into the background color.

There is a better way to achieve this effect, though—using a smaller and faster-loading background image. All we need to do is take a thin slice of our gradient image, like the one shown in Figure 3.5.

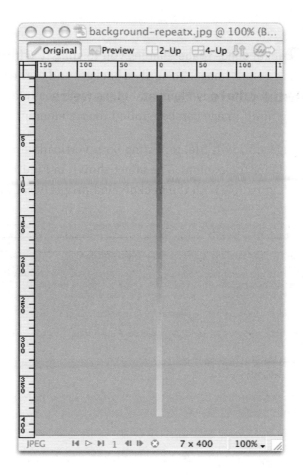

Figure 3.5. A slice of the larger background image

By setting the `background-image` property for this new image to `repeat-x`, we can achieve exactly the same visual effect that we saw in the first example, while using a much smaller image file. Again, we specify a background color that matches the bottom of the gradient image, to ensure that the gradient effect covers the whole of the area exposed in the user's browser.

If the gradient ran from left to right, rather than from top to bottom, we could use the same approach to create the background—we'd simply need to rotate the effect by 90 degrees. Taking a horizontal slice of the image and setting the `background-repeat` to `repeat-y` causes our gradient to repeat *down* the page, as Figure 3.6 shows.

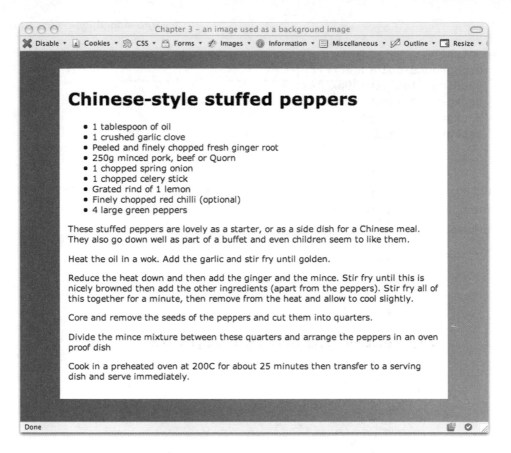

Figure 3.6. A gradient image set to repeat-y

How do I position my background image?

By default, if you add a single, non-repeating background image to the page, it will appear in the top-left corner of the viewport. If you've set the background to tile in any direction, the first image will appear at that location, and will tile from that point. However, it's also possible to display the image at other locations on the page.

Solution

We use the CSS property background-position to position the image on the page:

```
                                    backgroundposition.css (excerpt)
#content {
  background-color: #FFFFFF;
  padding: 1em 1em 40px 1em;
  background-image: url(tick.gif);
  background-repeat: no-repeat;
  background-position: bottom right;
}
```

The above style rule will display a tick graphic at the bottom right of the white content area, as shown in Figure 3.7. To prevent the text in this container from overlapping the image, I've applied some padding to the container.

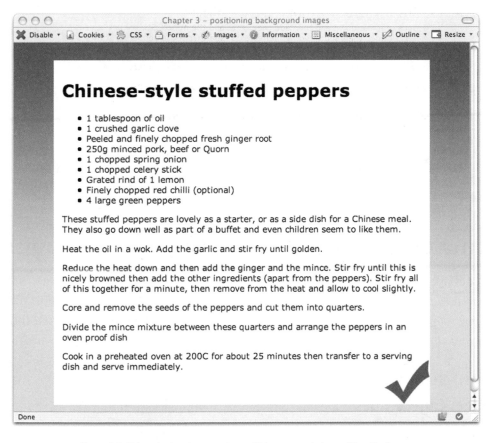

Figure 3.7. Using the background-position property to position the image

Discussion

The background-position property can take as its value keywords, percentage values, or values in units, such as pixels.

Keywords

In the example above, we used keywords to specify that the background image should be displayed at the bottom right of the content div:

backgroundposition.css *(excerpt)*

```
background-position: bottom right;
```

You can use any of these keyword combinations:

- top left
- top center
- top right
- center left
- center center
- center right
- bottom left
- bottom center
- bottom right

If you only specify one of the values, the other will default to center:

```
background-position: top;
```

The style declaration above is the same as the following:

```
background-position: top center;
```

Percentage Values

To achieve more accurate image placement, you can specify the values as percentages. This approach is particularly useful in a liquid layout where other page elements are specified in percentages so that they resize in accordance with the user's screen resolution and dimensions:

```
background-position: 30% 80%;
```

The first of the percentages included here refers to the background's horizontal position; the second dictates its vertical position. Percentages are taken from the top-left corner of the display, with 0% 0% placing the top-left corner of the image against the top-left corner of the browser window, and 100% 100% placing the bottom-right corner of the image against the bottom-right corner of the window.

As with keywords, a default percentage value comes into play if you only specify one value. That default is 50%. Take a look at the following declaration:

```
background-position: 30%;
```

The above style declaration creates the same effect as that shown below:

```
background-position: 30% 50%;
```

Unit Values

You can set positioning values using any CSS units, such as pixels or ems:

```
background-position: 20px 20px;
```

As with percentages, the first of the specified values dictates the horizontal position, while the second dictates the vertical. But unlike percentages, the measurements directly control the position of the top-left corner of the background image.

You can mix units with percentages and, if you only specify one value, the second will default to 50%.

How do I fix my background image in place when the page is scrolled?

You've probably seen sites on which the background image remains static while the content scrolls over it. This effect is achieved using the `background-attachment` property.

Solution

We can use the `background-attachment` property with a value of `fixed` to fix the background so that it doesn't move with the content, as illustrated in Figure 3.8.

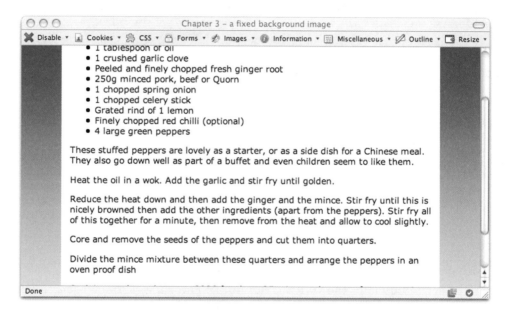

Figure 3.8. A fixed background image that doesn't scroll off the page with the content

backgroundfixed.html *(excerpt)*

```
body {
    font: 0.9em Verdana, Geneva, Arial, Helvetica, sans-serif;
    background-color: #d2d7e4;
    color: #000000;
    background-image: url(background-repeatx.jpg);
    background-repeat: repeat-x;
```

```
    background-attachment: fixed;
}
```

Discussion

In this solution, we're using several CSS properties to add our image to the background, position it, and dictate how it behaves when the document is scrolled.

Alternatively, we could use a shorthand method to supply this information—the CSS background property. This property allows you to declare background-color, background-image, background repeat, background-attachment, and background-position in a single property declaration. Take, for example, the CSS rule shown below:

backgroundfixed.css *(excerpt)*

```
body {
  background-color: #d2d7e4;
  background-image: url(background-repeatx.jpg);
  background-repeat: repeat-x;
  background-attachment: fixed;
  background-position: 0 0;
}
```

These declarations could be written more succinctly as follows:

```
body {
  background: #d2d7e4 url(background-repeatx.jpg) repeat-x fixed 0 0;
}
```

A final note on background-attachment: fixed: as is often the case with CSS styles, support for this declaration is limited among the Internet Explorer family. Internet Explorer 7 implements it correctly, but earlier versions of the browser do not. Though workarounds involving JavaScript are available, they may be more trouble than they're worth.[1] By default, users of older versions of Internet Explorer that don't support background-attachment: fixed will see a scrolling background

---

[1] http://www.howtocreate.co.uk/fixedBackground.html

image—an outcome that's generally considered an acceptable compromise (and may even entice these users to upgrade their browsers).

Can I set a background image on any element?

In this chapter, we've already looked at setting background images for the document and for the main content area of the page. However, background images can be used on other elements, too.

Solution

This style rule creates the effect that displays on the Ingredients box in Figure 3.9.

backgrounds2.css (excerpt)

```
#smallbox {
  background-image: url(boxbg.gif);
  background-repeat: repeat-x;
  float: left;
  margin-right: 20px;
  width: 220px;
  border:1px solid #d2d7e4;
}
```

The gradient background on the Ingredients box shown in Figure 3.9 comprises a background image that's very similar to the one I've used for the background on the body, except that the Ingredients box coloring graduates from light blue to white. I've also added a border that's the same as the color at the darkest part of the gradient.

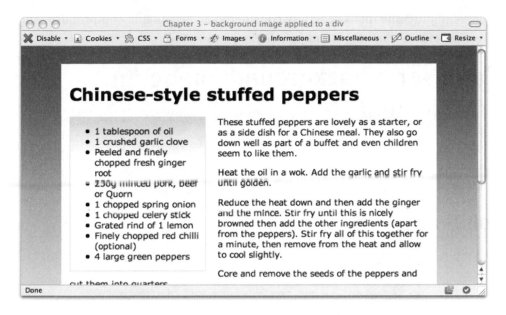

Figure 3.9. Using a background image to create a gradient behind the Ingredients box

Discussion

Background images can be applied to any page element, including headings, as Figure 3.10 shows. There, I've used a repeated image to display a dotted border beneath the heading. The image is positioned at the bottom left of the heading, and I've given the heading six pixels of bottom padding so that the text doesn't appear to sit on top of the background image:

backgrounds2.html *(excerpt)*

```
<h1>Chinese-style stuffed peppers</h1>
```

backgrounds2.css *(excerpt)*

```
h1 {
  background-image: url(dotty.gif);
  background-repeat: repeat-x;
  background-position: bottom left;
  padding: 0 0 6px 0;
  color: #41667f;
  font-size: 160%;
  font-weight: normal;
```

```
    background-color: transparent;
}
```

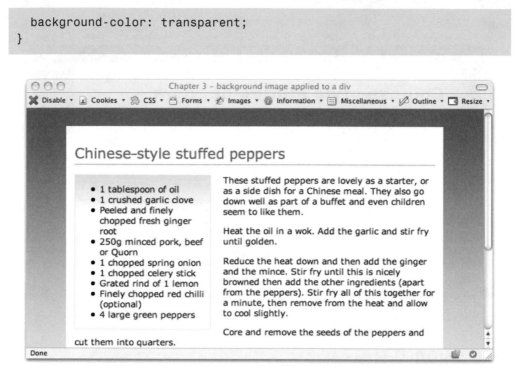

Figure 3.10. Applying a background image to the heading to create an underline

You can even apply backgrounds to links, which can give you the ability to make some interesting effects, as Figure 3.11 shows:

backgrounds2.css *(excerpt)*

```
a:link, a:visited {
  color: #41667f;
  background-color: transparent;
  padding-right: 10px;
}
a:hover {
  background-image: url(arrow.gif);
  text-decoration: none;
  background-position: center right;
  background-repeat: no-repeat;
}
```

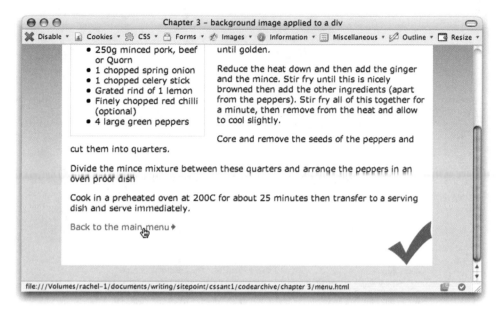

Figure 3.11. Applying a background image to the link on hover

How do I place text on top of an image?

In the bad old pre-CSS days, the only way to overlay text on an image was to add the text via your graphics program! CSS provides far better means to achieve this effect.

Solution

The easiest way to layer text over of an image is to set the image to be a background image. The image that appears beneath the heading on the Ingredients box in Figure 3.12 was added using the following style rule:

backgrounds3.css (excerpt)

```
#smallbox h2 {
  margin: 0;
  padding: 0.2em;
  background-image: url(boxheaderbg.jpg);
  background-repeat: no-repeat;
  color: #FFFFFF;
  background-color: red;
  font-size: 140%;
```

```
    font-weight: normal;
}
```

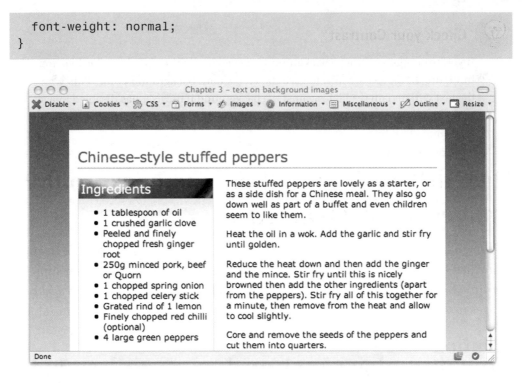

Figure 3.12. Applying a background image to the Ingredients box heading

Discussion

Using CSS to place text on top of an image offers many advantages over the approach of simply adding text to the image through a graphics program.

First, it's harder to change text that's part of a graphic—to do so, you need to find the original graphic, re-edit it in a graphics program, and upload it again every time you want to change the text.

Second, text is far more accessible if it's included on the page as text content rather than as part of an image. Browsers that don't support images will be able to read text that has been added using CSS, and such text can also be resized by the user. Including image text via CSS can also benefit your search engine rankings—though search engines can't index text that's part of an image, they can see regular text that has been placed on top of an image, and index it accordingly.

Check your Contrast!

If you're going to overlay a background image with light-colored text (as I've done in Figure 3.12), be sure also to give the area a dark background color. This way, the text will remain readable against the background if the user has disabled images in the browser, or are browsing on a slow connection over which the images don't load immediately.

How do I add more than one background image to my document?

Although it's detailed in the CSS2 specification, it's not currently possible to apply more than one background image to your document (only the Safari browser supports multiple backgrounds at present). So, what should you do if you want to add two images to the document—for example, one that repeats, and one that stands alone?

Solution

It is possible to give the effect of multiple background images by applying different backgrounds to various nested elements, such as the `html` and `body` elements:

backgrounds4.css *(excerpt)*

```
html {
  background-image: url(background-repeatx.jpg);
  background-repeat: repeat-x;
  background-color: #d2d7e4;
}

body {
  font: 0.9em Verdana, Geneva, Arial, Helvetica, sans-serif;
  color: #000000;
  background-image: url(recipes.gif);
  background-repeat: no-repeat;
  background-position:98% 2%;
  margin: 0;
  padding: 46px 0 0 0;
}
```

The effects of these styles can be seen in Figure 3.13.

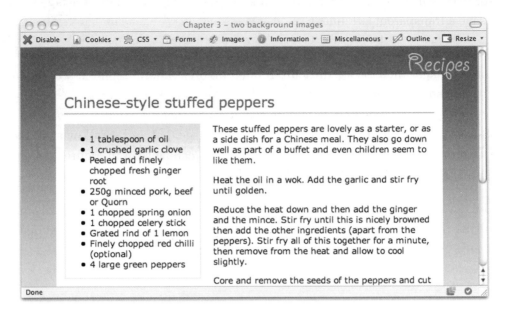

Figure 3.13. Applying background images to the `html` and `body` elements

Discussion

This simple example can form the basis of more complex effects using multiple background images. As you've seen through the examples in this chapter, a background image can be applied to any element on the page. The careful and creative use of images in this way can achieve many interesting visual effects while maintaining the accessibility of the document (as the background images will not interfere with the document's structure).

Many of the entries in the CSS Zen Garden rely on such careful use of background images to achieve their layouts.[2]

How can I use transparency in my pages?

Achieving real transparency using images is possible with the PNG image format—by saving your images as a 24-bit PNG, you can achieve opacity and true transparency.

---

[2] http://www.csszengarden.com/

While GIF images also support transparency, the format requires us to use a **matte**—a color that's similar to the background upon which the image will be placed—when we save a transparent GIF image.

This technicality means that creating a transparent GIF image that spans differently colored backgrounds is very difficult. It often involves chopping the image in two, saving each part separately, then reassembling the image pieces on the page—a process that reeks of old-school methods, and is one that we usually try to avoid in CSS-based layouts. Using the GIF format for an image that will scroll over a fixed background results in an ugly "halo effect," which can be seen in Figure 3.14 and Figure 3.15.

Figure 3.14. Using blue as a matte color behind the Recipes GIF image

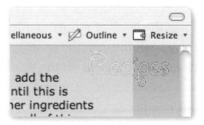

Figure 3.15. Scrolling down the page causing the GIF's matte pixels to display as a halo

Solution

The example in Figure 3.16 uses two PNG images. The first replaces the white background of #content with a ten-pixel PNG image. I developed this image in Photoshop by creating a new transparent image, then placing a solid white layer over the top of the transparent background. I then reduced the opacity of this layer to 40% and saved the file as a 24-bit PNG, giving it the name **opaque.png**.

The second image is a replacement for the background image **recipes.gif**; it's a 24-bit PNG with a transparent background. I'd like to fix the image in the top right of the viewport (using `background-attachment: fixed`), so that it remains in that location when the user scrolls the page. If I were to use a GIF image (with a dark blue as the matte), we'd see the halo effect mentioned above when the background moves and the image appears above the lighter page background.

Here's the CSS that creates the effect shown in Figure 3.16:

background5.css (excerpt)

```
body {
  font: 0.9em Verdana, Geneva, Arial, Helvetica, sans-serif;
  color: #000000;
  background-image: url(recipes.png);
  background-repeat: no-repeat;
  background-position:98% 2%;
  background-attachment:fixed;
  margin: 0;
  padding: 46px 0 0 0;
}

#content {
  margin: 0 4em 2em 4em;
  background-image: url(opaque.png);
  padding: 1em 50px 40px 1em;
}
```

Discussion

PNG images can be used to create unique and attractive effects. Unfortunately, the browser that has the largest market share at the time of writing—Internet Explorer 6—doesn't provide Alpha channel support, so it can't render transparent PNGs.

However, as long as you think carefully through your layout, it's often possible to include this kind of effect in your pages for visitors using other modern browsers, including Firefox, Safari, Opera, and Internet Explorer 7. Another alternative is to use JavaScript to work around this limitation of Internet Explorer 6 and earlier. I'll outline a method for doing this in Chapter 7.

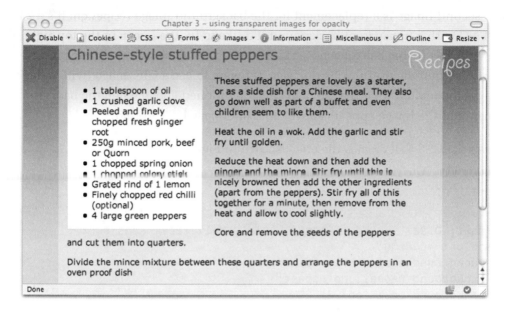

Figure 3.16. Displaying an opaque background without the halo effect on the Recipes image

Summary

This chapter has explained the answers to some common image-related questions. We've concentrated mainly on background images, as these really are the building blocks with which we create image-rich design in CSS. Keeping images in the background enables you to more easily offer alternative style sheets and change the look of your pages, as well as to create interesting effects.

There will, of course, be image-related questions all through this book. In particular, Chapter 9 will explore the positioning of images along with other elements on the page, and the use of images in more complex layouts than the one we've seen here.

Navigation

Unless you limit yourself to one-page web sites, you'll need to design navigation. In fact, navigation is among the most important parts of any web design, and requires a great deal of thought if visitors are to get around your site easily.

Making site navigation easy is one area in which CSS really comes into its own. Older methods of creating navigation tended to rely on lots of images, nested tables and JavaScript—all of which can seriously affect the usability and accessibility of a site. If your site cannot be navigated using a device that doesn't support JavaScript, for example, not only are you blocking users who have turned JavaScript off, but you're also locking out text-only devices such as screen readers and search engine robots—they'll never get past your home page to index the content of your site. If your design clients don't care about accessibility, tell them their clunky menu is stopping them from achieving a decent search engine ranking!

CSS allows you to create attractive navigation that, in reality, is no more than text—text that can be marked up in such a way as to ensure that it's both accessible and understandable by all those who can't physically see your design, but still want to get to your content. In this chapter, we'll look at a variety of solutions for creating

CSS-based navigation. Some are suited to implementation on an existing site, to make it load more quickly, and boost its accessibility by replacing an old-fashioned, image-based navigation. Others are more suited to incorporation within a pure CSS layout.

How do I replace image-based navigation with CSS?

Creating an image as a navigation "button" is still a common way to develop the navigation for a site. The images usually contain text that shows where each navigation item leads. A variety of problems are associated with using images for navigation buttons:

- In order to add a new item to the navigation, we must first create a new image. If, at this point, you discover that you've lost the original Photoshop file you used for the navigation buttons, you'll need to recreate the whole navigation from scratch!

- Imagine your navigation is created dynamically, perhaps using database content. While it's possible to create new images on the fly, someone will have to write a whole lot more code to integrate them onto every page!

- Users who have turned images off, or who use devices such as screen readers, will be unable to read the text within the button.

- Additional images extend page load times.

Solution

Old-school navigation systems are often implemented using layout tables and images. You can replace such image-based navigation with text that's styled using CSS.

The following CSS and HTML creates a simple navigation menu by styling the cells of a table and the links within them.

Lists are Usually Best!

I've used a table in this example only in the hope that it may be helpful if you're trying to retrofit an older site without completely rebuilding the page. If you're building your navigation from scratch, you should mark up your navigation items as an unordered list—the topic of the following solution, "How do I style a structural list as a navigation menu?"

replaceimages.html

```
<!DOCTYPE html PUBLIC "-//W3C//DTD XHTML 1.0 Strict//EN"
    "http://www.w3.org/TR/xhtml1/DTD/xhtml1-strict.dtd">
<html xmlns="http://www.w3.org/1999/xhtml" lang="en-US">
<head>
<title>Replace images</title>
<meta http-equiv="content-type"
    content="text/html; charset=utf-8" />
<link rel="stylesheet" type="text/css" href="replaceimages.css" />
</head>
<body>
<table id="navigation">
  <tr>
    <td>
      <a href="#">Recipes</a>
    </td>
  </tr>
  <tr>
    <td>
      <a href="#">Contact Us</a>
    </td>
  </tr>
  <tr>
    <td>
      <a href="#">Articles</a>
    </td>
  </tr>
  <tr>
    <td>
      <a href="#">Buy Online</a>
    </td>
  </tr>
</table>
```

```
</body>
</html>
```

replaceimages.css

```css
#navigation {
  width: 180px;
  padding: 0;
  margin: 0;
  border-collapse: collapse;
}
#navigation td {
  border-bottom: 2px solid #460016;
  background-color: #FFDFEA;
  color: #460016;
}
#navigation a:link, #navigation a:visited {
  display: block;
  margin: 0.4em 0 0.4em 1em;
  color: #460016;
  background-color: transparent;
  font-size: 90%;
  text-decoration: none;
  font-weight: bold;
}
* html #navigation a {
  width: 100%;
}
```

This technique could be used to ease the maintenance of an existing site in two ways: first, by allowing us to add new menu items without needing to create new images, and second, by reducing load times.

Discussion

CSS can be used to create attractive navigation systems through the simple styling of plain text. Figure 4.1 shows a menu that was created by inserting images into table cells—a common way to create a site menu.

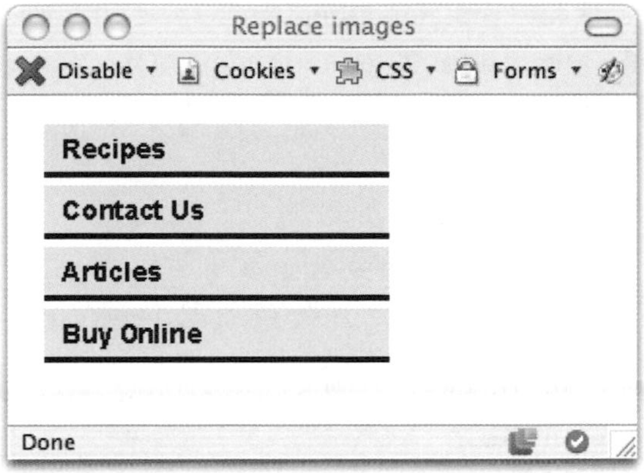

Figure 4.1. Using images to create navigation

Here's the markup for this table:

```
<table width="180" cellpadding="0" cellspacing="0">
  <tr>
    <td>
      <a href="#"><img src="images/nav1.gif" width="180"
          height="28" alt="Recipes" border="0" /></a>
    </td>
  </tr>
  <tr>
    <td>
      <a href="#"><img src="images/nav2.gif" width="180"
          height="28" alt="Contact Us" border="0" /></a>
    </td>
  </tr>
  <tr>
    <td>
      <a href="#"><img src="images/nav3.gif" width="180"
          height="28" alt="Articles" border="0" /></a>
    </td>
  </tr>
  <tr>
    <td>
      <a href="#"><img src="images/nav4.gif" width="180"
          height="28" alt="Buy Online" border="0" /></a>
    </td>
  </tr>
</table>
```

By removing the images and replacing them with the text for each navigation item, we immediately make our code smaller and the page more accessible. However, plain text doesn't do much for the appearance of the page, as you can see in Figure 4.2.

Figure 4.2. A bland navigation system without images

We can use CSS to recreate the look of this menu without the images. First, let's give the navigation table an ID—this will enable us to identify it within the document, and create CSS selectors for the elements within that table. We'll also be able to create some style rules for the ID navigation, which will allow us to remove the other attributes from the <table> tag:

replaceimages.html *(excerpt)*

```
<table id="navigation">
```

Here's the CSS that controls how the table looks:

replaceimages.css *(excerpt)*

```
#navigation {
  width: 180px;
  padding: 0;
  margin: 0;
  border-collapse: collapse;
}
```

Setting the `border-collapse` property to `collapse` causes the cells of the table to stick together, leaving only a single border between cells. By default, each table cell would have its own border, and additional margins would exist between cells.

Now we need to style the table's `td` elements. We want to give the cells the desired background color, and add a bottom border to each:

replaceimages.css *(excerpt)*

```
#navigation td {
  border-bottom: 2px solid #460016;
  background-color: #FFDFEA;
  color: #460016;
}
```

It's already looking good, as you can see in Figure 4.3.

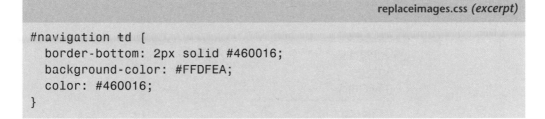

Figure 4.3. Applying the new styles to the navigation

Now we must create CSS for the links within the table cells. We need to set some padding to move the text away from the edge of the cell; we must define a color, size, font family, and weight; and we want to remove the underline from the link:

replaceimages.css *(excerpt)*

```
#navigation a:link, #navigation a:visited {
  display:block;
  padding: 0.4em 0 0.4em 1em;
  color: #460016;
```

```
  background-color: transparent;
  font-size: 90%;
  text-decoration: none;
  font-weight: bold;
}
```

Figure 4.4 shows the finished effect.

Figure 4.4. Creating the navigation using CSS instead of images

How do I style a structural list as a navigation menu?

The example titled "How do I replace image-based navigation with CSS?" illustrated the use of CSS to create navigation elements within a table. That method proves very useful where you're retrofitting an existing site to improve its accessibility and load times, but for new sites, you're likely to be trying to avoid using tables for layout, or using them only where absolutely necessary. Therefore, a navigation solution that doesn't involve tables is useful; also, by eradicating `table` elements, you'll find that your page contains far less markup.

Solution

A navigation system is simply a list of places that users can visit on the site. Therefore, an unordered list is the ideal way to mark up your navigation. The navigation in Figure 4.5 is marked up as a list, and styled using CSS, as you can see here.

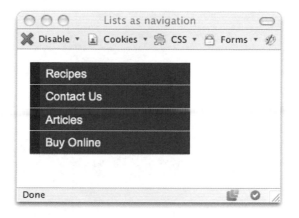

Figure 4.5. Creating navigation by styling a list

listnav1.html

```
<!DOCTYPE html PUBLIC "-//W3C//DTD XHTML 1.0 Strict//EN"
    "http://www.w3.org/TR/xhtml1/DTD/xhtml1-strict.dtd">
<html xmlns="http://www.w3.org/1999/xhtml" lang="en-US">
<head>
<title>Lists as navigation</title>
<meta http-equiv="content-type"
    content="text/html; charset=utf-8" />
<link rel="stylesheet" type="text/css" href="listnav1.css" />
</head>
<body>
<div id="navigation">
  <ul>
    <li><a href="#">Recipes</a></li>
    <li><a href="#">Contact Us</a></li>
    <li><a href="#">Articles</a></li>
    <li><a href="#">Buy Online</a></li>
  </ul>
</div>
</body>
</html>
```

listnav1.css

```
#navigation {
  width: 200px;
}
#navigation ul {
  list-style: none;
  margin: 0;
  padding: 0;
}
#navigation li {
  border-bottom: 1px solid #ED9F9F;
}
#navigation li a:link, #navigation li a:visited  {
  font-size: 90%;
  display: block;
  padding: 0.4em 0 0.4em 0.5em;
  border-left: 12px solid #711515;
  border-right: 1px solid #711515;
  background-color: #B51032;
  color: #FFFFFF;
  text-decoration: none;
}
```

Discussion

To create navigation based on an unordered list, first create your list, placing each navigation link inside a li element:

listnav1.html *(excerpt)*

```
<ul>
  <li><a href="#">Recipes</a></li>
  <li><a href="#">Contact Us</a></li>
  <li><a href="#">Articles</a></li>
  <li><a href="#">Buy Online</a></li>
</ul>
```

Next, wrap the list in a `div` with an appropriate ID:

```
                                                    listnav1.html (excerpt)

<div id="navigation">
  <ul>
    <li><a href="#">Recipes</a></li>
    <li><a href="#">Contact Us</a></li>
    <li><a href="#">Articles</a></li>
    <li><a href="#">Buy Online</a></li>
  </ul>
</div>
```

As Figure 4.6 shows, this markup looks fairly ordinary with the browser's default styles applied.

Figure 4.6. A very basic, unstyled list

The first thing we need to do is style the container in which the navigation sits—in this case, `#navigation`:

```
                                                     listnav1.css (excerpt)

#navigation {
  width: 200px;
}
```

I've given `#navigation` a width. If this navigation system were part of a CSS page layout, I'd probably add some positioning information to this ID as well.

Next, we style the list:

```
                                              listnav1.css (excerpt)

#navigation ul {
  list-style: none;
  margin: 0;
  padding: 0;
}
```

As Figure 4.7 illustrates, the above rule removes list bullets and the indented margin that browsers apply, by default, when displaying a list.

Figure 4.7. Viewing the list after indentation and bullets are removed

The next step is to style the li elements within #navigation, to give them a bottom border:

```
                                              listnav1.css (excerpt)

#navigation li {
  border-bottom: 1px solid #ED9F9F;
}
```

Finally, we style the link itself:

listnav1.css *(excerpt)*

```
#navigation li a:link, #navigation li a:visited  {
  font-size: 90%;
  display: block;
  padding: 0.4em 0 0.4em 0.5em;
  border-left: 12px solid #711515;
  border-right: 1px solid #711515;
  background-color: #B51032;
  color: #FFFFFF;
  text-decoration: none;
}
```

Most of the work is done here, creating CSS rules to add left and right borders, removing the underline, and so on. The first property declaration in this rule sets the `display` property to `block`. This causes the link to display as a block element, meaning that the whole area of each navigation "button" is active when you move the cursor over it—the same effect you'd see if you used an image for the navigation.

How do I use CSS to create rollover navigation without images or JavaScript?

Site navigation often features a rollover effect: when a user holds the cursor over a menu button, a new button image displays, creating a highlighting effect. To achieve this effect using image-based navigation, you need to use two images and JavaScript.

Solution

Using CSS to build your navigation makes the creation of attractive rollover effects far simpler than it would be if you used images. The CSS rollover is created using the `:hover` pseudo-class selector—the same selector you'd use to style a hover state for your links.

Let's take the above list navigation example and add the following rule to create a rollover effect:

listnav2.css *(excerpt)*

```
#navigation li a:hover {
  background-color: #711515;
```

```
    color: #FFFFFF;
}
```

Figure 4.8 shows what the menu looks like when the cursor is positioned over the first menu item.

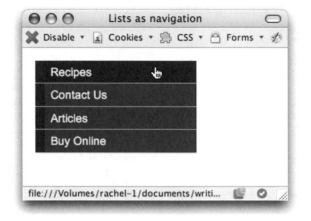

Figure 4.8. The CSS navigation showing a rollover effect

Hover Here? Hover There!

In Mozilla, and Internet Explorer 7, you can apply the `:hover` pseudo-selector to *any* element you like, but in Internet Explorer 6 and below, you can apply it only to links.

Older versions of Internet Explorer allow only the anchor text to be made clickable, because the link doesn't expand to fill its container (in this case, the list item). This means that the user is forced actually to click on the text, rather than the red background, to select the menu item.

One way to rectify this issue is to use a CSS hack that expands the width of the link—but only in Internet Explorer version 6 and earlier. Here's the rule that does just that:

```
* html #navigation li a {
  width: 100%;
}
```

We'll cover cross-browser techniques in more detail in Chapter 7.

Discussion

The CSS we've used to create this effect is very simple. You can create hover states for heavily styled links just as you can for standard links. In this example, I simply changed the background color to make it the same as the left-hand border; however, you could alter the background, text, and border color to create interesting effects for the navigation.

Can I use CSS and lists to create a navigation system with subnavigation?

The examples we've seen so far in this chapter have assumed that you only have one navigation level to display. Sometimes, more than one level is necessary—but is it possible to create multi-leveled navigation using styled lists in CSS?

Solution

The perfect way to display subnavigation within a navigation system is to create a sublist within a list. The two levels of navigation will be easy to understand when they're marked up in this way—even in browsers that don't support CSS.

To produce multi-level navigation, we can edit the example we saw in Figure 4.8, adding a nested list and styling the colors, borders, and link properties of the new list's items:

listnav_sub.html

```
<!DOCTYPE html PUBLIC "-//W3C//DTD XHTML 1.0 Strict//EN"
    "http://www.w3.org/TR/xhtml1/DTD/xhtml1-strict.dtd">
<html xmlns="http://www.w3.org/1999/xhtml" lang="en-US">
<head>
<title>Lists as navigation</title>
<meta http-equiv="content-type"
    content="text/html; charset=utf-8" />
<link rel="stylesheet" type="text/css" href="listnav_sub.css" />
</head>
<body>
<div id="navigation">
  <ul>
    <li><a href="#">Recipes</a>
```

```
      <ul>
        <li><a href="#">Starters</a></li>
        <li><a href="#">Main Courses</a></li>
        <li><a href="#">Desserts</a></li>
      </ul>
    </li>
    <li><a href="#">Contact Us</a></li>
    <li><a href="#">Articles</a></li>
    <li><a href="#">Buy Online</a></li>
  </ul>
</div>
</body>
</html>
```

listnav_sub.css

```
#navigation {
  width: 200px;
}
#navigation ul {
  list-style: none;
  margin: 0;
  padding: 0;
}
#navigation li {
  border-bottom: 1px solid #ED9F9F;
}
#navigation li a:link, #navigation li a:visited  {
  font-size: 90%;
  display: block;
  padding: 0.4em 0 0.4em 0.5em;
  border-left: 12px solid #711515;
  border-right: 1px solid #711515;
  background-color: #B51032;
  color: #FFFFFF;
  text-decoration: none;
}
#navigation li a:hover {
  background-color: #711515;
  color: #FFFFFF;
}
#navigation ul ul {
  margin-left: 12px;
}
```

```
#navigation ul ul li {
  border-bottom: 1px solid #711515;
  margin:0;
}
#navigation ul ul a:link, #navigation ul ul a:visited {
  background-color: #ED9F9F;
  color: #711515;
}
#navigation ul ul a:hover {
  background-color: #711515;
  color: #FFFFFF;
}
```

The result of these additions is shown in Figure 4.9.

Figure 4.9. The CSS list navigation containing subnavigation

Discussion

Nested lists are a perfect way to describe the navigation system that we're working with here. The first list contains the main sections of the site; the sublist under **Recipes** shows the subsections within the **Recipes** category. Even without any CSS styling, the structure of the list is still clear and comprehensible, as you can see in Figure 4.10.

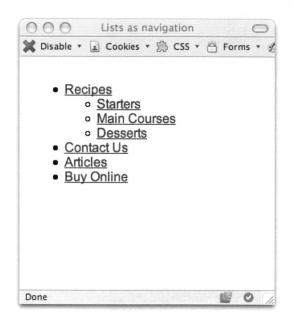

Figure 4.10. The navigation remaining logical without the CSS

The HTML that we use to mark up this list simply nests the sublist inside the li element of the appropriate main item:

```
<ul>
  <li><a href="#">Recipes</a>
    <ul>
      <li><a href="#">Starters</a></li>
      <li><a href="#">Main Courses</a></li>
      <li><a href="#">Desserts</a></li>
    </ul>
  </li>
  <li><a href="#">Contact Us</a></li>
  <li><a href="#">Articles</a></li>
  <li><a href="#">Buy Online</a></li>
</ul>
```

With this HTML, and without any changes to the CSS, the menu will display as shown in Figure 4.11, where the li elements inherit the styles of the main menu.

Figure 4.11. The sublist taking on the styles of the main navigation

Let's add a style rule for the nested list to communicate visually that it's a submenu, and not part of the main navigation:

```
                                                  listnav_sub.css (excerpt)

#navigation ul ul {
  margin-left: 12px;
}
```

This rule will indent the nested list so that it's in line with the right edge of the border for the main menu, as demonstrated in Figure 4.12.

Figure 4.12. The indented subnavigation

Let's add some simple styles to the li and a elements within the nested list to complete the effect:

```
                                                        listnav_sub.css (excerpt)
#navigation ul ul li {
  border-bottom: 1px solid #711515;
  margin: 0;
}
#navigation ul ul a:link, #navigation ul ul a:visited {
  background-color: #ED9F9F;
  color: #711515;
}
#navigation ul ul a:hover {
  background-color: #711515;
  color: #FFFFFF;
}
```

How do I make a horizontal menu using CSS and lists?

All the examples we've seen in this chapter have dealt with vertical navigation—the kind of navigation that will most likely be found in a column to the left or right of a site's main content area. However, site navigation is also commonly found as a horizontal menu close to the top of the document.

Solution

As Figure 4.13 shows, this type of menu can be created using styled lists in CSS. The `li` elements must be set to display inline so that each list item does not display on its own line.

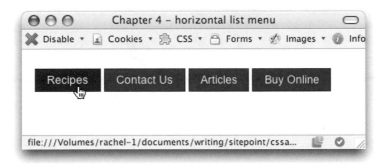

Figure 4.13. Using CSS to create horizontal list navigation

Here's the HTML and CSS that creates this display:

listnav_horiz.html

```
<!DOCTYPE html PUBLIC "-//W3C//DTD XHTML 1.0 Strict//EN"
    "http://www.w3.org/TR/xhtml1/DTD/xhtml1-strict.dtd">
<html xmlns="http://www.w3.org/1999/xhtml" lang="en-US">
<head>
<title>Lists as navigation</title>
<meta http-equiv="content-type"
    content="text/html; charset=utf-8" />
<link rel="stylesheet" type="text/css" href="listnav_horiz.css" />
</head>
<body>
<div id="navigation">
```

```
  <ul>
    <li><a href="#">Recipes</a></li>
    <li><a href="#">Contact Us</a></li>
    <li><a href="#">Articles</a></li>
    <li><a href="#">Buy Online</a></li>
  </ul>
</div>
</body>
</html>
```

listnav_horiz.css

```
body {
  padding: 1em;
}
#navigation {
  font-size: 90%;
}
#navigation ul {
  list-style: none;
  margin: 0;
  padding: 0;
  padding-top: 1em;
}
#navigation li {
  display: inline;
}
#navigation a:link, #navigation a:visited {
  padding: 0.4em 1em 0.4em 1em;
  color: #FFFFFF;
  background-color: #B51032;
  text-decoration: none;
  border: 1px solid #711515;
}
#navigation a:hover {
  color: #FFFFFF;
  background-color: #711515;
}
```

Discussion

To create the horizontal navigation, we start with a list that's identical to the one we created for our vertical list menu:

listnav_horiz.html *(excerpt)*

```
<div id="navigation">
  <ul>
    <li><a href="#">Recipes</a></li>
    <li><a href="#">Contact Us</a></li>
    <li><a href="#">Articles</a></li>
    <li><a href="#">Buy Online</a></li>
  </ul>
</div>
```

We style the #navigation container to apply some basic font information, as we did with the vertical navigation. In a CSS layout, this ID would probably also contain some additional styles that determine the navigation's position on the page:

listnav_horiz.css *(excerpt)*

```
#navigation {
  font-size: 90%;
}
```

In styling the ul element, we remove the list bullets and default indentation applied to the list by the browser:

listnav_horiz.css *(excerpt)*

```
#navigation ul {
  list-style: none;
  margin: 0;
  padding: 0;
  padding-top: 1em;
}
```

The property that transforms our list from a vertical to a horizontal display is applied to the li element. After we set the display property to inline, the list looks like Figure 4.14:

listnav_horiz.css *(excerpt)*

```
#navigation li {
  display: inline;
}
```

Figure 4.14. Displaying the list menu horizontally

All that's left for us to do is to style the links for our navigation:

listnav_horiz.css *(excerpt)*

```
#navigation a:link, #navigation a:visited {
  padding: 0.4em 1em 0.4em 1em;
  color: #FFFFFF;
  background-color: #B51032;
  text-decoration: none;
  border: 1px solid #711515;
}
#navigation a:hover {
  color: #FFFFFF;
  background-color: #711515;
}
```

If you're creating boxes around each link, as I have here, remember that, in order to make more space between the text and the edge of its container, you'll need to add more left and right padding to the links. To create more space between the navigation items, add left and right margins to the links.

How do I create button-like navigation using CSS?

Navigation that appears to be composed of clickable buttons is a feature of many web sites. This kind of navigation is often created using images to which effects are applied to make the edges look beveled and button-like. Often, some JavaScript code is used to swap in another image, so the button appears to depress when the user holds the cursor over it or clicks on the image.

Is it possible to create such button-like navigation systems using only CSS? Absolutely!

Solution

Creating a button effect like that shown in Figure 4.15 is possible, and fairly straightforward, using CSS. The effect's success hinges on your use of the CSS border properties.

Figure 4.15. Building button-like navigation with CSS

Here's the code you'll need:

```
                                                           listnav_button.html
<!DOCTYPE html PUBLIC "-//W3C//DTD XHTML 1.0 Strict//EN"
    "http://www.w3.org/TR/xhtml1/DTD/xhtml1-strict.dtd">
<html xmlns="http://www.w3.org/1999/xhtml" lang="en-US">
<head>
<title>Lists as navigation</title>
<meta http-equiv="content-type"
    content="text/html; charset=utf-8" />
<link rel="stylesheet" type="text/css" href="listnav_button.css"
    />
</head>
<body>
<div id="navigation">
  <ul>
    <li><a href="#">Recipes</a></li>
```

```
      <li><a href="#">Contact Us</a></li>
      <li><a href="#">Articles</a></li>
      <li><a href="#">Buy Online</a></li>
   </ul>
</div>
</body>
</html>
```

listnav_button.css

```css
#navigation {
  font-size:90%
}
#navigation ul {
  list-style: none;
  margin: 0;
  padding: 0;
  padding-top: 1em;
}
#navigation li {
  display: inline;
}
#navigation a:link, #navigation a:visited {
  margin-right: 0.2em;
  padding: 0.2em 0.6em 0.2em 0.6em;
  color: #A62020;
  background-color: #FCE6EA;
  text-decoration: none;
  border-top: 1px solid #FFFFFF;
  border-left: 1px solid #FFFFFF;
  border-bottom: 1px solid #717171;
  border-right: 1px solid #717171;
}
#navigation a:hover {
  border-top: 1px solid #717171;
  border-left: 1px solid #717171;
  border-bottom: 1px solid #FFFFFF;
  border-right: 1px solid #FFFFFF;
}
```

Discussion

To create this effect, we'll use the horizontal list navigation described in "How do I make a horizontal menu using CSS and lists?". However, to create the button look, we'll use different colored borders at the top and left than we use for the bottom and right sides of each button. By giving the top and left edges of the button a lighter colored border than we assign to the button's bottom and right edges, we create a slightly beveled effect:

listnav_button.css (excerpt)

```css
#navigation a:link, #navigation a:visited {
  margin-right: 0.2em;
  padding: 0.2em 0.6em 0.2em 0.6em;
  color: #A62020;
  background-color: #FCE6EA;
  text-decoration: none;
  border-top: 1px solid #FFFFFF;
  border-left: 1px solid #FFFFFF;
  border-bottom: 1px solid #717171;
  border-right: 1px solid #717171;
}
```

We reverse the border colors for the hover state, which creates the effect of the button being pressed:

listnav_button.css (excerpt)

```css
#navigation a:hover {
  border-top: 1px solid #717171;
  border-left: 1px solid #717171;
  border-bottom: 1px solid #FFFFFF;
  border-right: 1px solid #FFFFFF;
}
```

Try using heavier borders, and changing the background images on the links, to create effects that suit your design.

How do I create tabbed navigation with CSS?

Navigation that appears as tabs across the top of the page is a popular navigation choice. Many sites create tabs using images. However, this approach suffers from the problems associated with text contained in images, which we discussed in "How do I replace image-based navigation with CSS?". However, it is possible to create a tab effect by combining background images and text styled with CSS.

Solution

The tabbed navigation shown in Figure 4.16 can be created by styling a horizontal list.

Figure 4.16. Using CSS to create tabbed navigation

Here's the HTML and CSS that creates this effect:

tabs.html

```
<!DOCTYPE html PUBLIC "-//W3C//DTD XHTML 1.0 Strict//EN"
    "http://www.w3.org/TR/xhtml1/DTD/xhtml1-strict.dtd">
<html xmlns="http://www.w3.org/1999/xhtml" lang="en-US">
<head>
<title>Lists as navigation</title>
<meta http-equiv="content-type"
    content="text/html; charset=utf-8" />
<link rel="stylesheet" type="text/css" href="tabs.css" />
</head>
<body id="recipes">
<div id="header">
<ul id="tabnav">
  <li class="recipes"><a href="#">Recipes</a></li>
  <li class="contact"><a href="#">Contact Us</a></li>
  <li class="articles"><a href="#">Articles</a></li>
  <li class="buy"><a href="#">Buy Online</a></li>
</ul>
</div>
<div id="content">
<h1>Recipes</h1>
<p>Lorem ipsum dolor sit amet, …</p>
</div>
</body>
</html>
```

tabs.css

```
body {
  font: .8em/1.8em verdana, arial, sans-serif;
  background-color: #FFFFFF;
  color: #000000;
  margin: 0 10% 0 10%;
}

#header {
  float: left;
  width: 100%;
  border-bottom: 1px solid #8DA5FF;
  margin-bottom: 2em;
}

#header ul {
```

```css
    margin: 0;
    padding: 2em 0 0 0;
    list-style: none;
}

#header li {
    float: left;
    background-image: url("images/tab_left.gif");
    background-repeat: no-repeat;
    margin: 0 1px 0 0;
    padding: 0 0 0 8px;
}

#header a {
    float: left;
    display: block;
    background-image: url("images/tab_right.gif");
    background-repeat: no-repeat;
    background-position: right top;
    padding: 0.2em 10px 0.2em 0;
    text-decoration: none;
    font-weight: bold;
    color: #333366;
}

#recipes #header li.recipes,
#contact #header li.contact,
#articles #header li.articles,
#buy #header li.buy {
    background-image: url("images/tab_active_left.gif");
}

#recipes #header li.recipes a,
#contact #header li.contact a,
#articles #header li.articles a,
#buy #header li.buy a {
    background-image: url("images/tab_active_right.gif");
    background-color: transparent;
    color:#FFFFFF;
}
```

Discussion

The tabbed navigation approach I've used here is a basic version of Douglas Bowman's Sliding Doors of CSS method, which is a tried and tested technique for creating a tabbed interface.[1] The structure that I've given to the navigation menu is the same kind of simple unordered list that we've worked with throughout this chapter, except that each list item is assigned a `class` attribute that describes the link it contains. We've also wrapped the entire list in a `div` with an `id` of `header`. The technique takes its name from the two images used to implement it—one overlaps the other, and the images slide apart as the text size increases.

You'll need four images to create this effect: two to create the regular tab color, and two to use when the tab is the currently selected (highlighted) tab. The images I've used in this example are shown in Figure 4.17. As you can see, they're far wider and taller than would generally be necessary for a tab—this provides plenty of space for the tab to "grow" if the user's browser is configured to display text at a very large size.

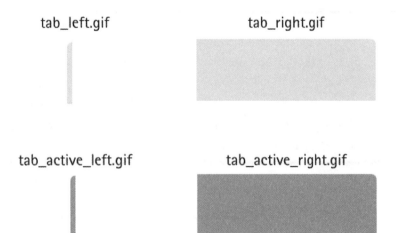

Figure 4.17. The image files used to create the tabs

---

[1] http://www.alistapart.com/articles/slidingdoors/

Here's the basic list of navigation items:

```html
<div id="header">
<ul id="tabnav">
  <li class="recipes"><a href="#">Recipes</a></li>
  <li class="contact"><a href="#">Contact Us</a></li>
  <li class="articles"><a href="#">Articles</a></li>
  <li class="buy"><a href="#">Buy Online</a></li>
</ul>
</div>
```

The first step is to style the container that surrounds the navigation. We're going to give our header a simple bottom border for the purposes of this exercise, but on a real-world site this container may hold other elements in addition to our tabs (such as a logo or search field):

```css
#header {
  float: left;
  width: 100%;
  border-bottom: 1px solid #8DA5FF;
  margin-bottom: 2em;
}
```

As you'll have noticed, we float the header to the left. We'll also float the individual list items; floating the container that houses them ensures that they remain contained once they're floated, and that the border will display below them.

Next, we create a style rule for the ul element inside the header:

```css
#header ul {
  margin: 0;
  padding: 2em 0 0 0;
  list-style: none;
}
```

This rule removes the bullets and alters the margin and padding on our list—we've added two ems of padding to the top of the `ul` element. Figure 4.18 shows the results of our work so far.

Figure 4.18. Displaying the navigation after styling the `ul` element

Now we need to style the list items:

```
                                                        tabs.css (excerpt)
#header li {
  float: left;
  background-image: url("images/tab_left.gif");
  background-repeat: no-repeat;
  margin: 0 1px 0 0;
  padding: 0 0 0 8px;
}
```

This rule uses the `float` property to position the list items horizontally while maintaining the block-level status of each. We then add the first of our "sliding door" images—the thin left-hand side of the tab—as a background image. A single-pixel right margin on the list item creates a gap between one tab and the next. Figure 4.19 shows that the left-hand tab image now appears for each tab.

Figure 4.19. The navigation tabs reflecting the new styles

Next, we style the links, completing the look of our tabs in their unselected state. The image that forms the right-hand side of the tab is applied to each link, completing the tab effect:

tabs.css *(excerpt)*

```
#header a {
  float: left;
  display: block;
  background-image: url("images/tab_right.gif");
  background-repeat: no-repeat;
  background-position: right top;
  padding: 0.2em 10px 0.2em 0;
  text-decoration: none;
  font-weight: bold;
  color: #333366;
}
```

The results are shown in Figure 4.20.

Figure 4.20. Styling the navigation links

If you increase the text size in the browser, you can see that the tabs neatly increase in size too. In fact, they do so without overlapping and without the text protruding out of the tab—this is because we have used images that allow plenty of room for growth.

To complete the tab navigation, we need to highlight the tab that corresponds to the currently displayed page. You'll recall that each list item has been assigned a unique class name. If we assign to the body element an ID that has a value equal to the value of each list item class, CSS can do the rest of the work:

tabs.html *(excerpt)*

```
<body id="recipes">
```

Although it looks like a lot of code, the CSS code that styles the tab matching the body ID is relatively straightforward. The images I've used are exact copies of the left and right images that we applied to the tabs, but they're a different color, which produces the effect of one tab appearing to be highlighted.

Here's the CSS:

tabs.css (excerpt)

```css
#recipes #header li.recipes,
#contact #header li.contact,
#articles #header li.articles,
#buy #header li.buy {
  background-image: url("images/tab_active_left.gif");
}

#recipes #header li.recipes a,
#contact #header li.contact a,
#articles #header li.articles a,
#buy #header li.buy a {
  background-image: url("images/tab_active_right.gif");
  background-color: transparent;
  color: #FFFFFF;
}
```

With these rules in place, specifying an ID of `recipes` to our `body` will cause the **Recipes** tab to be highlighted, specifying `contact` will cause the **Contact Us** tab to be highlighted, and so on. The results of this work are shown in Figure 4.21.

Identifying a Useful Technique

The technique of adding an ID to the `body` element can be very useful. For example, you may have different color schemes for different sections of your site, to help the user identify which section they're using. You can simply add the section name to the `body` element and make use of it within the style sheet, as we did in this example.

Figure 4.21. Highlighting the **Contact Us** tab by specifying `contact` as the ID of the body element

How do I change the cursor type?

It's common for the cursor to change to a hand icon when the cursor's moved over a link on any part of the page. Occasionally—perhaps to fit in with a particular interface—you might want to change the cursor to represent something else.

Solution

We change the cursor using the CSS `cursor` property. Table 4.1 identifies the properties that are available in CSS 2, and how they appear in Internet Explorer 6; Figure 4.22 shows this property in action.

Table 4.1. The CSS2.1 standard cursors

cursor value	Appearance (in IE 6)
auto	n/a
crosshair	╋
default	▷
e-resize	↔
help	▷?
move	✛
n-resize	↕
ne-resize	↗
nw-resize	↖
pointer	🖑
s-resize	↕
se-resize	↖
sw-resize	↗
text	I
w-resize	↔
wait	⧗

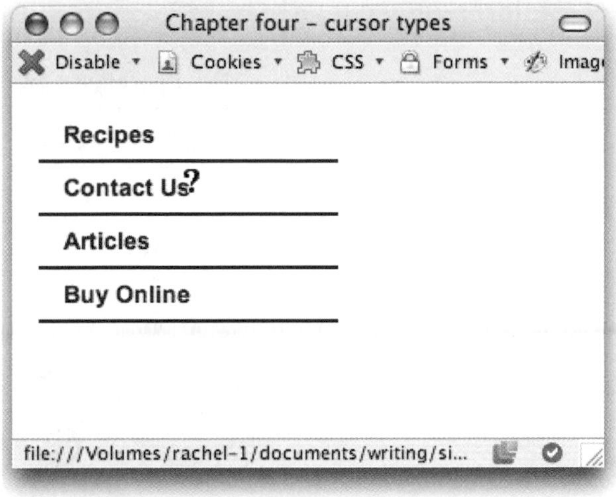

Figure 4.22. The `cursor: help` property causing the cursor to display as a question mark

Discussion

The `cursor` property can take a range of values. Changing the cursor display can be a useful way for web applications with friendly interfaces to provide valuable user feedback. For example, you might decide to use a question mark cursor to indicate help text.

Changing the Cursor Can Cause Confusion!

You should use this effect with care, and keep in mind the fact that people are generally used to standard browser behavior. For instance, users are used to seeing the cursor represent a pointing hand icon when it's hovered over a link.

Table 4.1 lists the various properties that are available in the CSS standard; these are supported by most modern browsers, including Internet Explorer 6+, Safari, Opera, and Firefox. Table 4.2 lists additional values that are supported only by Internet Explorer browsers (although with each new release of Firefox comes improved support for these extra values).

Table 4.2. Internet Explorer–only cursors

cursor value	Appearance (as in IE6)
all-scroll	
col-resize	
hand	
no-drop	
not-allowed	
progress	
row-resize	
url("*url*")	custom image[a]
vertical-text	

[a] At the time of writing, displaying a custom image for a cursor on a web page is only supported by Firefox on Windows.

How do I create rollovers in CSS without using JavaScript?

CSS-based navigation can provide some really interesting effects, but there are still some effects that require the use of images. Is it possible to enjoy the advantages of text-based navigation and still use images?

Solution

It is possible to combine images and CSS to create JavaScript-free rollovers. This solution is based on a technique described at WellStyled.com.[2] Here's the code you'll need:

---

[2] http://wellstyled.com/css-nopreload-rollovers.html

images.html

```
<!DOCTYPE html PUBLIC "-//W3C//DTD XHTML 1.0 Strict//EN"
    "http://www.w3.org/TR/xhtml1/DTD/xhtml1-strict.dtd">
<html xmlns="http://www.w3.org/1999/xhtml" lang="en-US">
<head>
<title>Lists as navigation</title>
<meta http-equiv="content-type"
    content="text/html; charset=utf-8" />
<link rel="stylesheet" type="text/css" href="images.css" />
</head>
<body>
<ul id="nav">
  <li><a href="#">Recipes</a></li>
  <li><a href="#">Contact Us</a></li>
  <li><a href="#">Articles</a></li>
  <li><a href="#">Buy Online</a></li>
</ul>
</body>
</html>
```

images.css

```
ul#nav {
  list-style-type: none;
  padding: 0;
  margin: 0;
}
#nav a:link, #nav a:visited {
  display: block;
  width: 150px;
  padding: 10px 0 16px 32px;
  font: bold 80% Arial, Helvetica, sans-serif;
  color: #FF9900;
  background: url("peppers.gif") top left no-repeat;
  text-decoration: none;
}
#nav a:hover {
  background-position: 0 -69px;
  color: #B51032;
}
#nav a:active {
  background-position: 0 -138px;
```

```
  color: #006E01;
}
```

The results can be seen in Figure 4.23, but to enjoy the full effect I suggest you try it for yourself. Don't forget to click on a link or two!

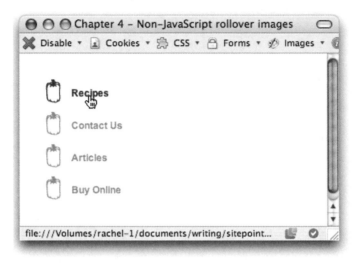

Figure 4.23. Using images to advantage in the completed menu

Discussion

This solution offers a means of using images in your navigation without having to resort to preloading lots of separate files.

The navigation has three states, but these states aren't depicted using three separate images. Instead, we use one large image that contains images for all three states, as shown in Figure 4.24.

Figure 4.24. The pepper image containing images for all three rollover states

The navigation is marked up as a simple list:

```
images.html (excerpt)

<ul id="nav">
  <li><a href="#">Recipes</a></li>
  <li><a href="#">Contact Us</a></li>
  <li><a href="#">Articles</a></li>
  <li><a href="#">Buy Online</a></li>
</ul>
```

We control the display of the background image within the declaration block for the navigation links. However, because the image is far bigger than the area required for this element, we only see the yellow pepper at first:

```
images.css (excerpt)

#nav a:link, #nav a:visited {
  display: block;
  width: 150px;
  padding: 10px 0 16px 32px;
  font: bold 80% Arial, Helvetica, sans-serif;
  color: #FF9900;
  background: url("peppers.gif") top left no-repeat;
  text-decoration: none;
}
```

When the :hover state is activated, the background image moves up the exact number of pixels required to reveal the red pepper. In this example, I had to move it by 69 pixels, but this figure will vary depending on the image that you use. You could probably work it out mathematically, or you could do as I do and simply increment the background position a few pixels at a time, until it appears in the right location on hover:

images.css *(excerpt)*

```
#nav a:hover {
  background-position: 0 -69px;
  color: #B51032;
}
```

When the :active state is activated, the background image shifts again, this time to display the green pepper when the link is clicked:

images.css *(excerpt)*

```
#nav a:active {
  background-position: 0 -138px;
  color: #006E01;
}
```

That's all there is to it! The effect can fall apart if the user resizes the text in the browser to a larger font, which allows the edges of the hidden images to display. You can anticipate this eventuality to some degree by leaving quite a large space between each of the three images—keep this in mind when preparing your images.

Image Flickering in Internet Explorer

This technique sometimes causes the navigation to "flicker" in Internet Explorer. In my tests, this only tends to be a problem when the image is larger than the ones we've used here; however, if your navigation items flicker, a well-documented remedy is available.[3]

How can I create pure CSS drop-down menus?

In "How do I replace image-based navigation with CSS?", we learned to create image- and JavaScript-free rollovers. Can the same be achieved for drop-down menus?

---

[3] http://wellstyled.com/css-nopreload-rollovers.html

Solution

The answer is yes … but the resulting menus don't work in Internet Explorer 6!
Nevertheless, Figure 4.25 illustrates this interesting technique, which will become
more useful as Internet Explorer 7 gains market share.

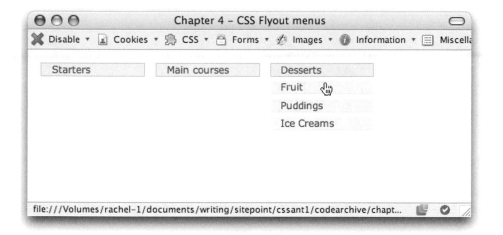

Figure 4.25. Creating a CSS-only drop-down menu

Here's the markup used for this example:

```
                                                                    menus.html
<!DOCTYPE html PUBLIC "-//W3C//DTD XHTML 1.0 Strict//EN"
  "http://www.w3.org/TR/xhtml1/DTD/xhtml1-strict.dtd">
<html xmlns="http://www.w3.org/1999/xhtml" lang="en-US">
<head>
<title>CSS Flyout menus</title>
<meta http-equiv="content-type"
    content="text/html; charset=utf-8" />
<link rel="stylesheet" type="text/css" href="menus.css" />
</head>
<body>
<ul id="nav">
  <li><a href="#">Starters</a>
    <ul>
      <li><a href="">Fish</a></li>
      <li><a href="">Fruit</a></li>
      <li><a href="">Soups</a></li>
```

```
      </ul>
    </li>
    <li><a href="#">Main courses</a>
      <ul>
        <li><a href="">Meat</a></li>
        <li><a href="">Fish</a></li>
        <li><a href="">Vegetarian</a></li>
      </ul>
    </li>
    <li><a href="#">Desserts</a>
      <ul>
        <li><a href="">Fruit</a></li>
        <li><a href="">Puddings</a></li>
        <li><a href="">Ice Creams</a></li>
      </ul>
    </li>
  </ul>
  </body>
  </html>
```

And here are the style rules to implement this effect:

menus.css

```
body {
  font: 1em Verdana, Arial, sans-serif;
  background-color: #FFFFFF;
  color: #000000;
  margin: 1em 0 0 1em;
}
#nav, #nav ul {
  padding: 0;
  margin: 0;
  list-style: none;
}
#nav li {
  float: left;
  position: relative;
  width: 10em;
  border: 1px solid #B0C4DE;
  background-color: #E7EDF5;
  color: #2D486C;
  font-size: 80%;
  margin-right: 1em;
```

```
}
#nav a:link, #nav a:visited {
  display: block;
  text-decoration: none;
  padding-left: 1em;
  color: #2D486C;
}
* html #nav a {
  width: 100%;
}
#nav ul {
  display: none;
  position: absolute;
  padding: 0;
}
#nav ul li {
  border: 0 none transparent;
  border-bottom: 1px solid #E7EDF5;
  border-top: .5em solid #FFF;
  background-color: #F1F5F9;
  font-size: 100%;
  margin-bottom: -1px;
  margin-top: 1px;
  padding: 0;
}
#nav li:hover ul {
  display: block;
}
```

Discussion

Though this attractive and easy effect will not work in Internet Explorer 6, it is supported by several other, newer browsers. This solution allows you to create a drop-down menu without using any JavaScript at all. The technique is based on the Suckerfish Dropdowns solution detailed on A List Apart.[4]

The menus themselves are based on simple unordered lists. The top-level menu items consist of one main list; the items that fall under each main item are contained in nested lists:

---

[4] http://www.alistapart.com/articles/dropdowns/

```
                                              menus.html (excerpt)

<ul id="nav">
  <li><a href="#">Starters</a>
    <ul>
      <li><a href="">Fish</a></li>
      <li><a href="">Fruit</a></li>
      <li><a href="">Soups</a></li>
    </ul>
  </li>
  ...
```

As you can see in Figure 4.26, when styles aren't applied to the menu, the page displays as a logically structured, unordered list with subsections that are easy to spot.

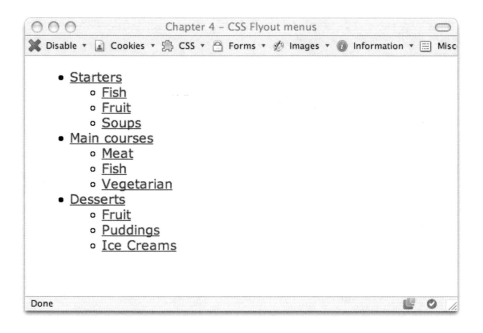

Figure 4.26. Displaying lists logically in browsers that don't support CSS

To begin with, we style the top-level menu, removing its list style. We also float the list items to the left so that they stack horizontally. The list items are given a position value of relative so that we can position our fly-out menus within them later on:

```
                                                        menus.css (excerpt)

#nav, #nav ul {
  …
  list-style: none;
}
#nav li {
  float: left;
  position: relative;
  width: 10em;
  …
  margin-right: 1em;
}
```

We coerce the links in the menu to display as blocks, so they fill the rectangular areas defined by the menu items. Internet Explorer 6 (and earlier) doesn't recognize this; however, setting the width of each link to 100% ensures that our clickable region expands to fill the containing block.

```
                                                        menus.css (excerpt)

#nav a:link, #nav a:visited {
  display: block;
  …
}
* html #nav a {
  width: 100%;
}
```

Next, we style the nested lists that constitute our fly-out menus so that, by default, they are not displayed (display: none). We do, however, specify that absolute positioning is to be used when they *are* displayed, so that they don't affect the flow of the rest of the document:

```
                                                        menus.css (excerpt)

#nav ul {
  display: none;
  position: absolute;
  …
}
```

To prevent our fly-out menu list items from being floated horizontally the way the main menu items are, we need to set their `float` property to `none`:

menus.css *(excerpt)*

```
#nav ul li {
  float: none;

  ...
}
```

Finally, we use the `:hover` pseudo-class to display the fly-out menu within any main menu item when the cursor is moved over it:

menus.css *(excerpt)*

```
#nav li:hover ul {
  display: block;
}
```

With these basic CSS rules in place, the menus display as shown in Figure 4.27.

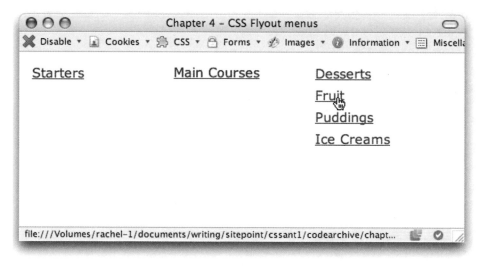

Figure 4.27. Altering the menu display with the addition of basic CSS

This code initially sets the nested lists to `display: none`. When the user hovers the cursor over a main menu list item, the property of the nested list within that list item is set to `display: block`, and the menu appears. However, this approach doesn't work in Internet Explorer, as in that browser the `:hover` pseudo-class works only on links—not on any other element.

The rest of the CSS simply applies visual styles to make the menus look good.

Falling Between the Cracks

When a fly-out menu opens, the user must move the cursor down to the fly-out menu items to select one. If, in this motion, the cursor moves outside of the list item that opened the fly-out menu, the menu will close immediately, as the `:hover` pseudo-class will no longer be in effect.

Looking at the style rules for this page, you can see that we use absolute positioning to display the nested list over the top of the rest of the page content without disturbing it.

In theory, we should be able to leave a little space between the top-level menu item and the fly-out menu simply by adding margin to the top of the list; however, in Internet Explorer 7 the fly-out menu will disappear if the cursor passes over a margin area, rendering the menu unusable. Instead, I've created the effect by applying a white border to the top of the menu.

I've also added a very small margin to the top of each list item, and a negative margin of the same amount to the bottom. This has the effect of shifting our menu down by one pixel—just enough to ensure that our white border doesn't cover up the bottom of our top-level menu item.

menus.css (excerpt)

```
#nav ul li {
   border: 0 none transparent;
   border-bottom: 1px solid #E7EDF5;
   border-top: .5em solid #FFF;
   background-color: #F1F5F9;
   font-size: 100%;
   margin-bottom: -1px;
   margin-top: 1px;
   padding: 0;
}
```

Accessibility Concerns

When you're using any drop-down menu—with or without JavaScript—make sure that users who don't see the full effect of the menus are still able to move around your site.

In the case of this example, users who don't have CSS support will see the expanded nested lists, and will be able to navigate through the site. Anyone who uses a browser that doesn't support the display of the submenus, such as Internet Explorer 6, will still be able to navigate so long as the pages to which the top-level menu items link contain links to all the pages in that section's submenu.

Any menu system that prevents users whose browsers don't support it from navigating the site is bad news.

Summary

This chapter has discussed a range of different ways in which we can create navigation using structurally sound markup, and provided examples that can be used as starting points for your own experiments.

On existing sites where a full redesign is not possible, introducing a CSS-based navigation system can be a good way to improve the site's accessibility and load speed without affecting its look and feel in a big way.

Tabular Data

Tables have had bad press of late. Originally designed to display tabular data correctly in HTML documents, they were soon misappropriated as a way to lay out web pages. Until recently, understanding how to create complex layouts using nested tables had become part of the standard skill set of the web designer. However, using tables in this way requires large amounts of markup and can cause real problems for users who are trying to access content using screen readers or other text-only devices. Thus, the Web Standards movement has pushed for the replacement of tabular layouts with CSS, which is designed for the job and is, ultimately, far more flexible, as we'll discover in Chapter 9.

But, what of the poor table? Is it to be relegated to out-of-date web-building tools gathering dust in the far corners of the Net? Not quite! It's true that tables are becoming less popular as layout tools, as designers take on the newer CSS techniques for which browser support is becoming widespread. However, tables can (and should) still be used for their true purpose—that of displaying tabular data.

This chapter will illustrate some common, correct uses of tables, incorporating elements and attributes that, though they're not used frequently, help to make your tables accessible. We'll also look at how CSS can be used to make these tables more attractive and usable for those viewing them in a web browser.

How do I lay out spreadsheet data using CSS?

Solution

The quick answer is, you don't! Spreadsheet data is tabular by nature and, therefore, should be displayed in an HTML table. However, that doesn't mean that we're resigned to the dull and uninspiring style in which tables display by default, though—we can still spruce them up using CSS, as we'll see later in this chapter. And we should still be concerned about the accessibility of our tables, even when we're using them to display the right kind of content.

Discussion

Tabular data is information that's displayed in a table, and which may logically be arranged into columns and rows.

Your accounts, stored in spreadsheet format, are a good example of tabular data. If you needed to mark up the annual accounts of an organization for which you were building a site, you might be given a spreadsheet that looked like Figure 5.1.

	A	B	C	D	E	F
1		1999	2000	2001	2002	
2	Grants	11,980	12,650	9,700	10,600	
3	Donations	4,780	4,989	6,700	6,590	
4	Investments	8,000	8,100	8,760	8,490	
5	Fundraising	3,200	3,120	3,700	4,210	
6	Sales	28,400	27,100	27,950	29,050	
7	Miscellaneous	2,100	1,900	1,300	1,760	
8	Total	58,460	57,859	58,110	60,700	

Figure 5.1. Displaying the accounts information as tabular data in Excel

Obviously, this is tabular data. We see column and row headings to which the data in each cell relates. Ideally, we'd display this data in a table, as shown in Figure 5.2, complete with table headings to ensure that the data's structured logically.

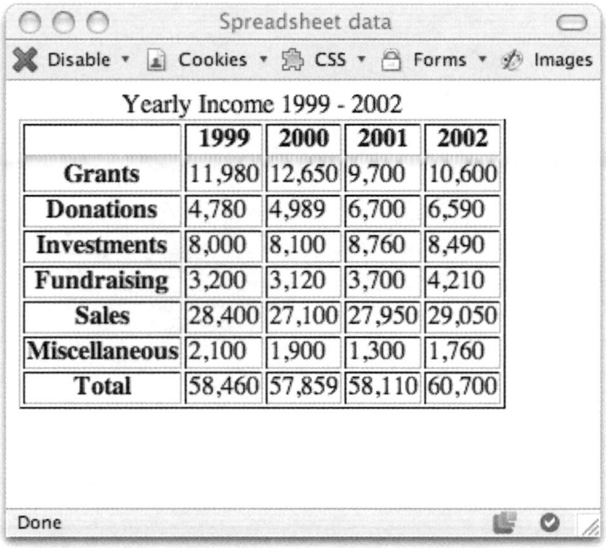

Figure 5.2. The accounts data formatted as an HTML table

How do I ensure that my tabular data is accessible as well as attractive?

Solution

The (X)HTML table specification includes elements and attributes that go beyond the basics required to achieve a certain look for tabular data. These extra parts of the table, which are often omitted by web developers, though they're easy to implement, can be used to ensure that the content of the table is clear when it's read out to visually impaired users who can't see the layout for themselves. Take a look at this example:

table.html *(excerpt)*

```
<table summary="This table shows the yearly income for years 1999
    through 2002">
```

```
<caption>Yearly Income 1999 - 2002</caption>
<tr>
  <th></th>
  <th scope="col">1999</th>
  <th scope="col">2000</th>
  <th scope="col">2001</th>
  <th scope="col">2002</th>
</tr>
<tr>
  <th scope="row">Grants</th>
  <td>11,980</td>
  <td>12,650</td>
  <td>9,700</td>
  <td>10,600</td>
</tr>
<tr>
  <th scope="row">Donations</th>
  <td>4,780</td>
  <td>4,989</td>
  <td>6,700</td>
  <td>6,590</td>
</tr>
<tr>
  <th scope="row">Investments</th>
  <td>8,000</td>
  <td>8,100</td>
  <td>8,760</td>
  <td>8,490</td>
</tr>
<tr>
  <th scope="row">Fundraising</th>
  <td>3,200</td>
  <td>3,120</td>
  <td>3,700</td>
  <td>4,210</td>
</tr>
<tr>
  <th scope="row">Sales</th>
  <td>28,400</td>
  <td>27,100</td>
  <td>27,950</td>
  <td>29,050</td>
</tr>
<tr>
```

```
    <th scope="row">Miscellaneous</th>
    <td>2,100</td>
    <td>1,900</td>
    <td>1,300</td>
    <td>1,760</td>
  </tr>
  <tr>
    <th scope="row">Total</th>
    <td>58,460</td>
    <td>57,859</td>
    <td>58,110</td>
    <td>60,700</td>
  </tr>
</table>
```

Discussion

The above markup creates a table that uses elements and attributes to explain clearly the content of each cell. Let's discuss the value that each of these elements and attributes adds.

The **summary** Attribute of the **table** Element

table.html *(excerpt)*

```
<table summary="This table shows the yearly income for years 1999
    through 2002">
```

A table's summary will not be visible to browser users, but will be read out to visitors with screen readers. We use the summary attribute to make sure that screen reader users understand the purpose and context of the table—information that, while apparent to the sighted user with a standard browser, might be less apparent when the text is being read in a linear manner by the screen reader.

The **caption** Element

table.html *(excerpt)*

```
<caption>Yearly Income 1999 - 2002</caption>
```

The `caption` element adds a caption to the table. By default, browsers generally display the caption above the table, however, you can manually set the position of the caption in relation to the table using the `caption-side` CSS property.

```
table {
  caption-side: bottom;
}
```

Why might you want to use a caption, instead of just adding a heading or paragraph text for display with the table? By using a caption, you can ensure that the text is tied to the table, and that it's recognized as the table's caption—there's no chance that the screen reader could interpret it as a separate element. If you want your table captions to display as paragraph text or level three headings in a graphical browser, no problem! You can create CSS rules for captions just as you would for any other element.

The th Element

```
<th scope="col">2000</th>
```

The `th` element identifies data that's a row or column heading. The example markup contains both row and column headings and, to ensure that this is clear, we use the `scope` attribute of the `<th>` tag. The `scope` attribute shows whether a given heading is applied to the column (`col`) or row (`row`).

Before you begin to style your tables to complement the look and feel of the site, it's good practice to ensure that those tables are accessible to users of devices such as screen readers. Accessibility is one of those things that many developers brush off, saying, "I'll check it when I'm finished." However, if you leave accessibility checks until the end of development, you may never get around to them; if you do, the problems they identify may well require time-consuming fixes, particularly in complex applications. Once you get into the habit of keeping accessibility in mind as you design, you'll find that it becomes second nature and adds very little to a project's development time.

CSS attributes make the styling of data tables simple and quick. For instance, when I begin a new site on which I know I'll have to use a lot of data tables, I create a class called `.datatable`, which contains the basic styles that I want to affect all data tables, and can easily be applied to the `<table>` tag of each. I then create rules for `.datatable th` (the heading cells), `.datatable td` (the regular cells), and `.datatable caption` (the table captions).

From that point, adding a new table is easy. All the styles are there—I just need to apply the `.datatable` class. If I decide to change the styles after I've created all the tables in my site, I simply edit my style sheet.

How do I add a border to a table without using the HTML border attribute?

Solution

The HTML `border` attribute doesn't create the prettiest of borders for tables, and it's deprecated in current versions of (X)HTML. You can replace this border with a CSS border, which will give you far more flexibility in terms of design. Here's how we'd set a border:

table.css (excerpt)

```
.datatable {
  border: 1px solid #338BA6;
}
```

This style rule will display a one-pixel, light-blue border around your table, as in Figure 5.3.

You can also add borders to individual cells:

table.css (excerpt)

```
.datatable td, .datatable th {
  border: 1px solid #73C0D4;
}
```

This style rule renders a slightly lighter border around `td` and `th` table cells that have a class of `datatable`, as Figure 5.4 shows.

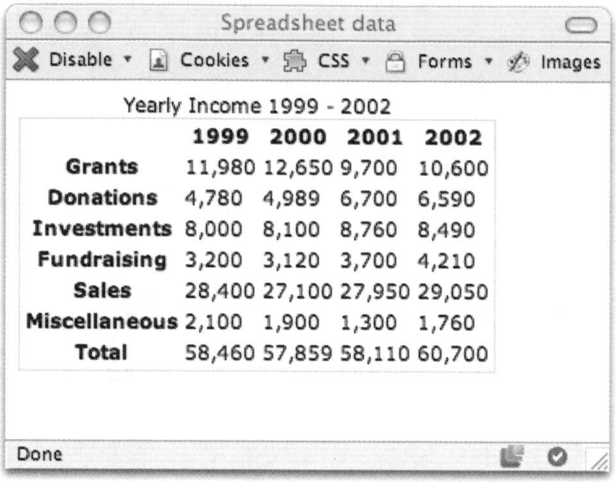

	1999	2000	2001	2002
Grants	11,980	12,650	9,700	10,600
Donations	4,780	4,989	6,700	6,590
Investments	8,000	8,100	8,760	8,490
Fundraising	3,200	3,120	3,700	4,210
Sales	28,400	27,100	27,950	29,050
Miscellaneous	2,100	1,900	1,300	1,760
Total	58,460	57,859	58,110	60,700

Figure 5.3. Applying a CSS border to the table as a whole

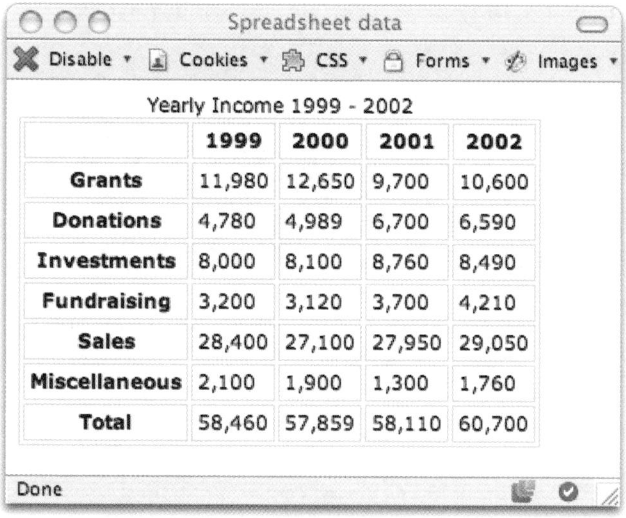

	1999	2000	2001	2002
Grants	11,980	12,650	9,700	10,600
Donations	4,780	4,989	6,700	6,590
Investments	8,000	8,100	8,760	8,490
Fundraising	3,200	3,120	3,700	4,210
Sales	28,400	27,100	27,950	29,050
Miscellaneous	2,100	1,900	1,300	1,760
Total	58,460	57,859	58,110	60,700

Figure 5.4. Applying a CSS border to individual table cells

Discussion

By experimenting with CSS borders on your tables, you can create countless attractive effects—even if the data those tables contain is thoroughly dull! You can use differently colored borders for table headings and table cells, and apply various thicknesses and styles of border to table cells. You might even try out such tricks as using one shade for top and left borders, and another for bottom and right borders, to create an indented effect.

We can apply a range of different values to the CSS `border-style` property. We've already met `solid`, which displays a solid line as the border, and this is shown along with the other available options in Table 5.1.

Table 5.1. CSS border style constants

Constant	Supporting Browsers	Sample
double	All CSS browsers	double
groove		groove
inset		inset
none		none
outset		outset
ridge		ridge
solid		solid
dashed	Safari, Opera, Firefox, IE 5.5+	dashed
dotted	Safari, Opera, Firefox, IE 7	dotted
hidden	Safari, Opera, Firefox, IE 5.5+	hidden

How do I stop spaces appearing between the cells of my table when I've added borders using CSS?

If you've ever tried to get rid of the spaces between table cells, you might have used the `table` attribute `cellspacing="0"`. This would have left you with a two-pixel border, though, because borders touch, but don't overlap. This solution explains how to create a neat, single-pixel border around all cells.

Solution

You can get rid of the spaces that appear between cells by setting the CSS `border-collapse` property for the table to `collapse`:

```
                                                            table.css
.datatable {
  border: 1px solid #338BA6;
  border-collapse: collapse;
}

.datatable td, .datatable th {
  border: 1px solid #73C0D4;
}
```

Figure 5.4 shows a table before the `border-collapse` property is applied; Figure 5.5 shows the effect of this property on the display.

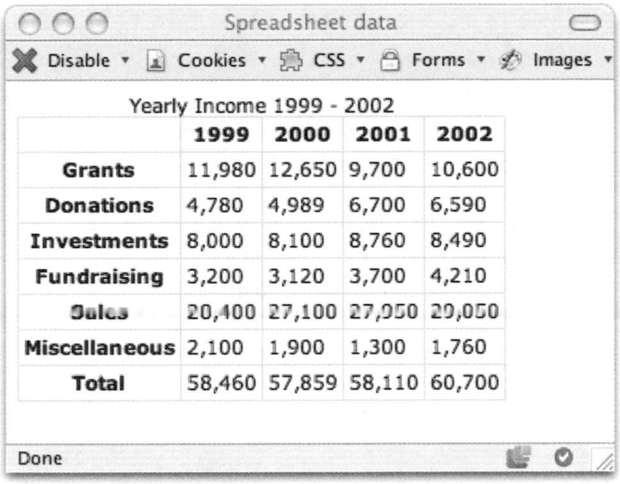

Yearly Income 1999 - 2002

	1999	2000	2001	2002
Grants	11,980	12,650	9,700	10,600
Donations	4,780	4,989	6,700	6,590
Investments	8,000	8,100	8,760	8,490
Fundraising	3,200	3,120	3,700	4,210
Sales	20,400	27,100	27,950	29,050
Miscellaneous	2,100	1,900	1,300	1,760
Total	58,460	57,859	58,110	60,700

Figure 5.5. Collapsing the table's borders

How do I display spreadsheet data in an attractive and usable way?

Solution

The (X)HTML table is the best way to structure spreadsheet data, but it's not the most attractive. Luckily, we can style the table using CSS, which keeps markup to a minimum and allows us to control our data table's appearance from the style sheet.

The data we saw displayed as an HTML table earlier in this chapter is an example of spreadsheet data. That markup, which is shown unstyled in Figure 5.6, forms the basis for the following example.

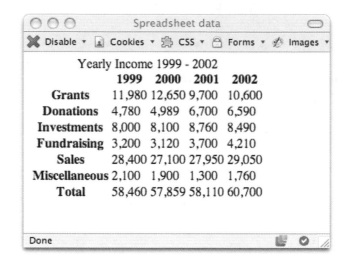

Figure 5.6. Unformatted, unattractive tabular data

Let's apply the following style sheet to that table:

```
                                                    spreadsheet.css
body {
  font: 0.8em Verdana, Geneva, Arial, Helvetica, sans-serif;
}

.datatable {
  border: 1px solid #D6DDE6;
  border-collapse: collapse;
}
.datatable td, .datatable th {
  border: 1px solid #D6DDE6;
  text-align: right;
  padding: 0.2em;
}
.datatable th {
  border: 1px solid #828282;
  background-color: #BCBCBC;
  font-weight: bold;
  text-align: left;
  padding: 0.2em;
}

.datatable caption {
```

```
  font: bold 120% "Times New Roman", Times, serif;
  background-color: #B0C4DE;
  color: #33517A;
  padding: 0.4em 0 0.3em 0;
  border: 1px solid #789AC6;
}
```

Figure 5.7 shows the result, which is quite attractive, if I do say so myself!

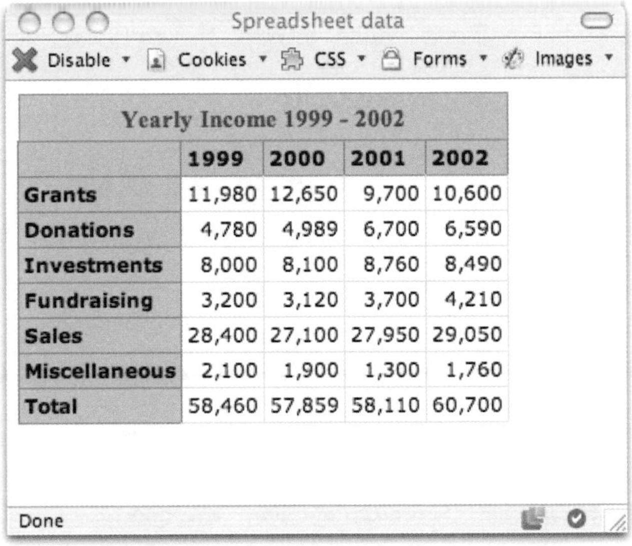

Figure 5.7. A more attractive table formatted with CSS

Discussion

In this solution, I aimed to display the table in a way that's similar to the appearance of a desktop spreadsheet. First, I provided a basic rule for the body—this is the kind of rule that would be likely to appear in the style sheet of any CSS-styled site:

spreadsheet.css (excerpt)

```
body {
  font: 0.8em Verdana, Geneva, Arial, Helvetica, sans-serif;
}
```

Next, I styled the table as a whole:

```
spreadsheet.css (excerpt)

.datatable {
  border: 1px solid #D6DDE6;
  border-collapse: collapse;
}
```

As we've already seen, `border` displays a border around the outside of the table, while `border-collapse` removes spaces between the table's cells.

Next, I turned my attention to the table cells:

```
spreadsheet.css (excerpt)

.datatable td {
  border: 1px solid #D6DDE6;
  text-align: right;
  padding: 0.2em
}
```

Here, I added a border to the table cells and used `text-align` to right-align their contents for that spreadsheety look. If you preview the document at this point, you'll see a border around each cell in the table, except the header cells, as shown in Figure 5.8.

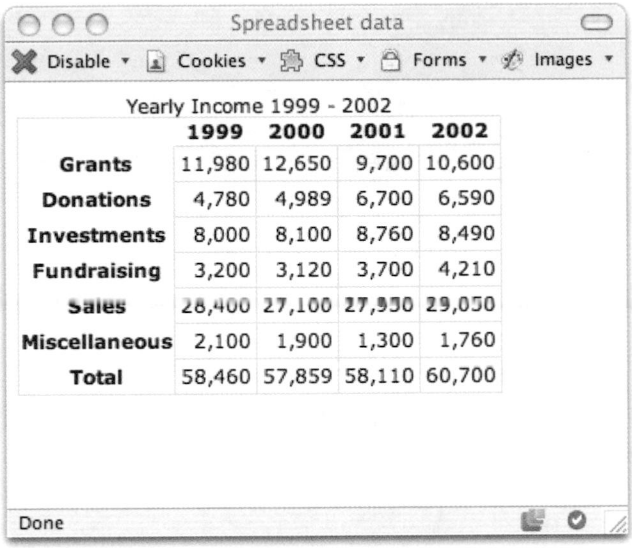

Yearly Income 1999 - 2002

	1999	2000	2001	2002
Grants	11,980	12,650	9,700	10,600
Donations	4,780	4,989	6,700	6,590
Investments	8,000	8,100	8,760	8,490
Fundraising	3,200	3,120	3,700	4,210
Sales	28,400	27,100	27,950	29,050
Miscellaneous	2,100	1,900	1,300	1,760
Total	58,460	57,859	58,110	60,700

Figure 5.8. Applying the `border` property to the `table` and `td` elements

Next, I added a border to the `th` (heading) cells. I used a darker color for this border, because I also added a background color to these cells to highlight the fact that they're headings, not regular cells:

spreadsheet.css *(excerpt)*

```
.datatable th {
  border: 1px solid #828282;
  background-color: #BCBCBC;
  font-weight: bold;
  text-align: left;
  padding: 0.2em;
}
```

To complete the table, I styled the caption to make it look like part of the table:

spreadsheet.css *(excerpt)*

```
.datatable caption {
  font: bold 0.9em "Times New Roman", Times, serif;
  background-color: #B0C4DE;
  color: #33517A;
```

```
    padding: 0.4em 0 0.3em 0;
    border: 1px solid #789AC6;
}
```

How do I display table rows in alternating colors?

Solution

It can be difficult to ensure that you remain on a particular row as your eyes work across a large table of data. Displaying table rows in alternating colors is a common way to help users identify which row they're focused on. Whether you're adding rows by hand, or you're displaying the data from a database, you can use CSS classes to create this effect.

Here's the table markup you'll need:

alternate.html *(excerpt)*

```
<table summary="List of new students 2003" class="datatable">
  <caption>Student List</caption>
  <tr>
    <th scope="col">Student Name</th>
    <th scope="col">Date of Birth</th>
    <th scope="col">Class</th>
    <th scope="col">ID</th>
  </tr>
  <tr>
    <td>Joe Bloggs</td>
    <td>27/08/1997</td>
    <td>Mrs Jones</td>
    <td>12009</td>
  </tr>
  <tr class="altrow">
    <td>William Smith</td>
    <td>20/07/1997</td>
    <td>Mrs Jones</td>
    <td>12010</td>
  </tr>
  <tr>
```

```
      <td>Jane Toad</td>
      <td>21/07/1997</td>
      <td>Mrs Jones</td>
      <td>12030</td>
    </tr>
    <tr class="altrow">
      <td>Amanda Williams</td>
      <td>19/03/1997</td>
      <td>Mrs Edwards</td>
      <td>12021</td>
    </tr>
    <tr>
      <td>Kylie Jameson</td>
      <td>18/05/1997</td>
      <td>Mrs Jones</td>
      <td>12022</td>
    </tr>
    <tr class="altrow">
      <td>Louise Smith</td>
      <td>17/07/1997</td>
      <td>Mrs Edwards</td>
      <td>12019</td>
    </tr>
    <tr>
      <td>James Jones</td>
      <td>04/04/1997</td>
      <td>Mrs Edwards</td>
      <td>12007</td>
    </tr>
</table>
```

Here's the CSS to style it:

alternate.css (excerpt)

```
body {
  font: 0.8em Arial, Helvetica, sans-serif;
}
.datatable {
  border: 1px solid #D6DDE6;
  border-collapse: collapse;
  width: 80%;
}
.datatable td {
```

```
  border: 1px solid #D6DDE6;
  padding: 0.3em;
}
.datatable th {
  border: 1px solid #828282;
  background-color: #BCBCBC;
  font-weight: bold;
  text-align: left;
  padding-left: 0.3em;
}
.datatable caption {
  font: bold 110% Arial, Helvetica, sans-serif;
  color: #33517A;
  text-align: left;
  padding: 0.4em 0 0.8em 0;
}
.datatable tr.altrow {
  background-color: #DFE7F2;
  color: #000000;
}
```

The result can be seen in Figure 5.9.

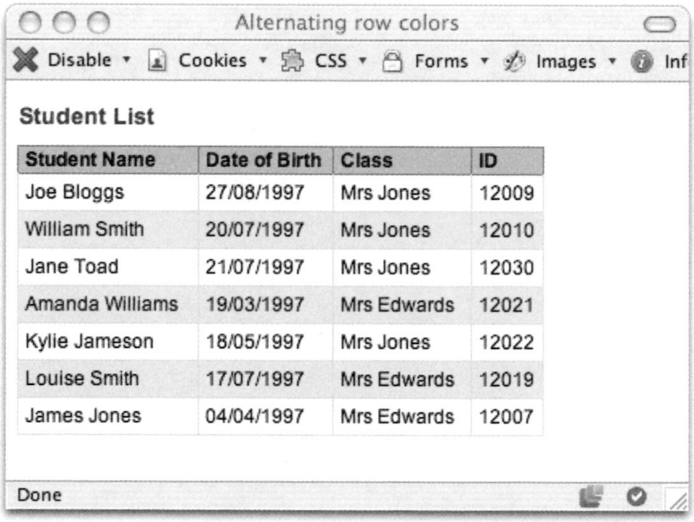

Figure 5.9. Using alternating row colors to help people use large tables of data

Discussion

I applied the `altrow` class to every second row of the HTML table above:

```
<tr class="altrow">
```

In the CSS, I styled the table using properties that will be familiar if you've looked at the previous solutions in this chapter. I also added the following class.

```
.datatable tr.altrow {
  background-color: #DFE7F2;
  color: #000000;
}
```

This class will be applied to all `tr` elements with a class of `altrow` that appear within a table that has a class of `datatable`.

If you're creating your table dynamically—for instance, using ASP, PHP, or a similar technology to pull data from a database—then, to create the alternating row effect, you must write this class out for every second row that you display.

How do I change a row's background color when the cursor hovers over it?

Solution

One way to boost the readability of tabular data is to change the color of the rows as users move the cursor over them, to highlight the row they're reading, as Figure 5.10 shows.

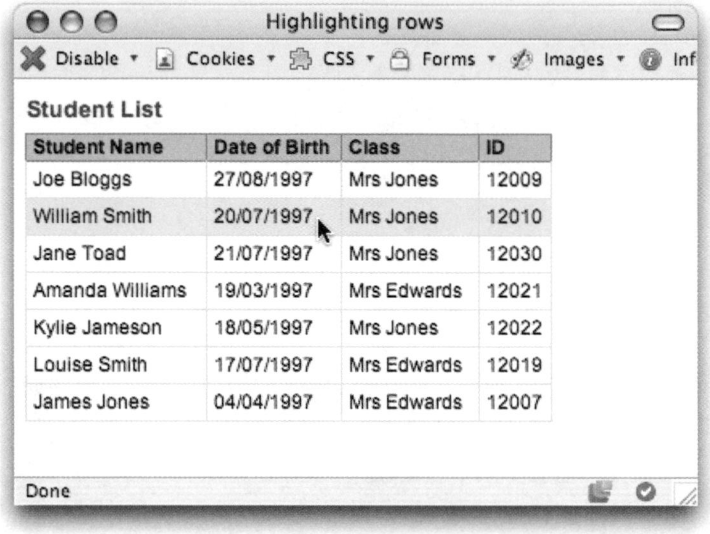

Figure 5.10. Highlighting a row on mouseover

This can be a very simple solution. In Internet Explorer 7 and Mozilla-based browsers (including Netscape, Firefox, and so on), all you need to do to create this effect is add the following rule to your CSS:

alternate.css *(excerpt)*

```
.datatable tr:hover {
  background-color: #DFE7F2;
  color: #000000;
}
```

Job done!

Discussion

This solution will work in all recent browsers—including Internet Explorer 7—but it will not work in Internet Explorer 6 or earlier. However, as long as your tables are clear without this highlighting effect in place, the highlight feature could be regarded as a "nice to have," rather than a necessary tool without which the site will be unusable.

If you *must* get this feature working for Internet Explorer 6 users, you can use some simple JavaScript to implement the effect. To change a row's background color when the cursor moves over it in Internet Explorer 6 and earlier, you must first also apply the desired style properties to a CSS class, which I've named `hilite` in this example:

hiliterow.css *(excerpt)*

```css
.datatable tr:hover, .datatable tr.hilite {
  background-color: #DFE7F2;
  color: #000000;
}
```

Then, add the following JavaScript code to your page after the table:

hiliterow.html *(excerpt)*

```html
<script type="text/javascript">
var rows = document.getElementsByTagName('tr');
for (var i = 0; i < rows.length; i++) {
  rows[i].onmouseover = function() {
    this.className += ' hilite';
  }
  rows[i].onmouseout = function() {
    this.className = this.className.replace('hilite', '');
  }
}
</script>
```

This code locates all the `<tr>` tags in the document and assigns a `mouseover` and `mouseout` event handler to each. These event handlers apply the CSS `hilite` class to the rows when the cursor is moved over them, and removes it when the cursor moves away. As you can see in Figure 5.11, this combination of CSS and HTML produces the desired effect.

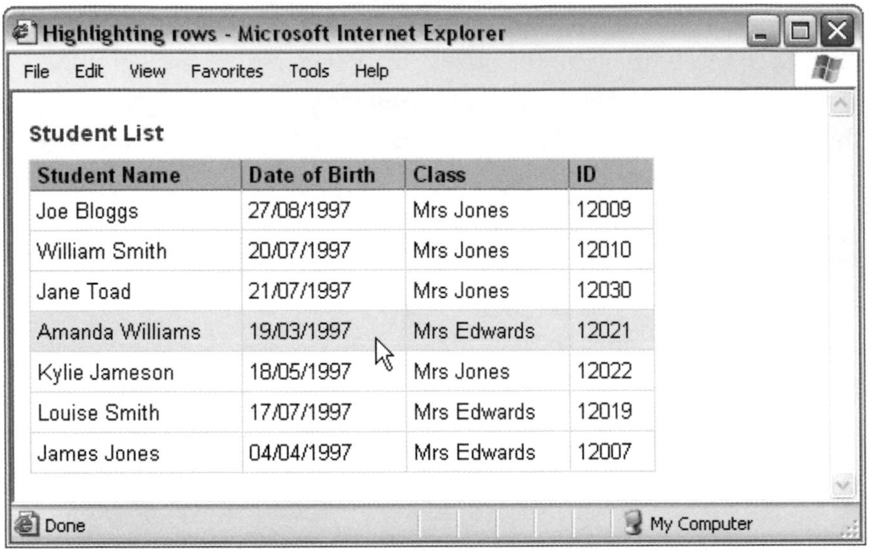

Figure 5.11. Highlighting a row in Internet Explorer 6 with the help of JavaScript

The JavaScript code works by setting a tag's CSS class dynamically. In this case, we add the `hilite` class to a `<tr>` tag when the `mouseover` event is triggered, as captured by the `onmouseover` property:

hiliterow.html (excerpt)

```
rows[i].onmouseover = function() {
  this.className += ' hilite';
}
```

We then remove the class when the `mouseout` event is fired:

hiliterow.html (excerpt)

```
rows[i].onmouseout = function() {
  this.className = this.className.replace('hilite', '');
}
```

You can create very attractive, subtle effects by changing the class of elements in response to user actions using JavaScript. Another way in which you could use this technique would be to highlight a content area by changing the class applied to a `div` when the `mouseover` event for that element is triggered.

Unobtrusive JavaScript

You might have noticed that we didn't add any JavaScript to the table itself—instead, we did our work within the `script` element only. This technique is called **unobtrusive JavaScript**—it aims to keep JavaScript separate from your document in the same way that we keep the presentation of CSS separate from the markup.

The JavaScript needs to run after the table has loaded, because until that point, there are no rows for the JavaScript to work on. Another approach would be to write a function that runs when the page has completed loading—this would mean that you could keep the JavaScript in a separate file that's linked to from your page.

How do I display table columns in alternating colors?

While alternate row colors are quite a common feature of data tables, we see alternately colored columns less frequently. However, they can be a helpful way to show groupings of data.

Solution

If we use the `col` element to describe our table's columns, we can employ CSS to add a background to those columns. You can see the `col` elements I've added—one for each column—in the table markup below. I've also added classes to them in much the same way that we added a `class` to the table's rows in "How do I display table rows in alternating colors?".

columns.html (excerpt)

```
<table class="datatable">
  <col class="odd" />
  <col class="even" />
  <col class="odd" />
  <col class="even" />

  <tr>
    <th>Pool A</th>
    <th>Pool B</th>
```

```
      <th>Pool C</th>
      <th>Pool D</th>
    </tr>
    <tr>
      <td>England</td>
      <td>Australia</td>
      <td>New Zealand</td>
      <td>France</td>
    </tr>
    <tr class="even">
      <td>South Africa</td>
      <td>Wales</td>
      <td>Scotland</td>
      <td>Ireland</td>
    </tr>
    <tr>
      <td>Samoa</td>
      <td>Fiji</td>
      <td>Italy</td>
      <td>Argentina</td>
    </tr>
    <tr class="even">
      <td>USA</td>
      <td>Canada</td>
      <td>Romania</td>
      <td>Europe 3</td>
    </tr>
    <tr>
      <td>Repechage 2</td>
      <td>Asia</td>
      <td>Repechage 1</td>
      <td>Namibia</td>
    </tr>
</table>
```

We can add style rules for the classes we applied to our `col` elements, as shown here; the result is depicted in Figure 5.12:

columns.css (excerpt)

```
body {
  font: 0.8em Arial, Helvetica, sans-serif;
}
```

```
.datatable {
  border: 1px solid #D6DDE6;
  border-collapse: collapse;
  width: 80%;
}

.datatable col.odd {
  background-color: #80C9FF;
  color: #000000;
}

.datatable col.even {
  background-color: #BFE4FF;
  color: #000000;
}

.datatable td {
  border:2px solid #ffffff;
  padding: 0.3em;
}

.datatable th {
  border:2px solid #ffffff;
  background-color: #00487D;
  color: #FFFFFF;
  font-weight: bold;
  text-align: left;
  padding: 0.3em;
}
```

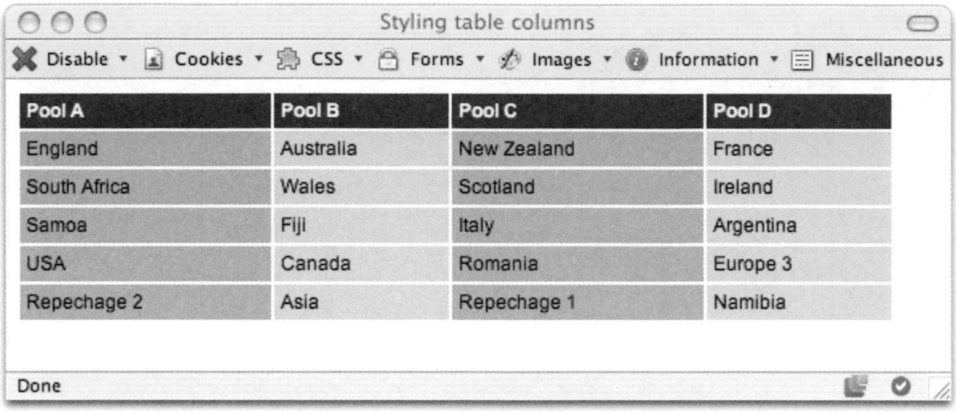

Pool A	Pool B	Pool C	Pool D
England	Australia	New Zealand	France
South Africa	Wales	Scotland	Ireland
Samoa	Fiji	Italy	Argentina
USA	Canada	Romania	Europe 3
Repechage 2	Asia	Repechage 1	Namibia

Figure 5.12. Creating alternately striped columns by styling the `col` element

Discussion

The `col` element provides us with further flexibility for styling a table's columns to ensure that they're visually distinct, thus making our table attractive and easier to understand. It's also possible to nest `col` elements within a `colgroup` element, which allows us to control the appearance of columns by applying style rules to the parent `colgroup` element. If a `colgroup` element is not present, the browser assumes that your table contains one single `colgroup` that houses all of your `col` elements.

Here's an example of nested `col` elements:

colgroups.html *(excerpt)*

```
<table class="datatable">
<colgroup class="odd">
  <col />
  <col />
</colgroup>
<colgroup class="even">
  <col />
  <col />
</colgroup>
…
```

Here are the style rules, which are applied to the `colgroup` element, rather than to `col`:

```
                                          colgroups.css (excerpt)

.datatable colgroup.odd {
  background-color: #80C9FF;
  color: #000000;
}

.datatable colgroup.even {
  background-color: #BFE4FF;
  color: #000000;
}
```

The result of this change is a table with two columns of one color, and two of another, as shown in Figure 5.13.

Figure 5.13. Styling columns using `colgroup`

How do I display a calendar using CSS?

Calendars, such as the example from a desktop application shown in Figure 5.14, also involve tabular data. The days of the week along the top of the calendar represent the headings of the columns. Therefore, a calendar's display constitutes the legitimate use of a table, but you can keep markup to a minimum by using CSS to control the look and feel.

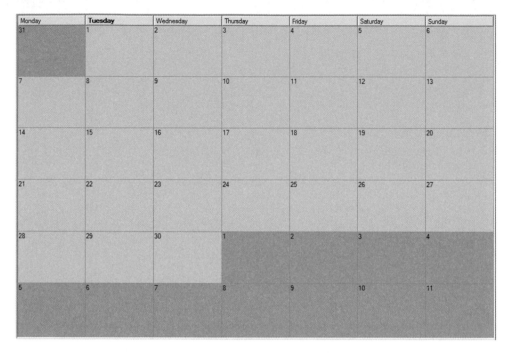

Figure 5.14. A calendar from a desktop application

Solution

Our solution uses an accessible, simple table that leverages CSS styles to create the attractive calendar shown in Figure 5.15. Given its simple structure, it's ideal for use in a database-driven application in which the table is created via server-side code:

cal.html *(excerpt)*

```
<!DOCTYPE html PUBLIC "-//W3C//DTD XHTML 1.0 Strict//EN"
    "http://www.w3.org/TR/xhtml1/DTD/xhtml1-strict.dtd">
<html xmlns="http://www.w3.org/1999/xhtml" lang="en-US">
<head>
<title>Calendar</title>
<meta http-equiv="content-type"
    content="text/html; charset=utf-8" />
<link rel="stylesheet" type="text/css" href="cal.css" />
</head>
<body>
<table class="clmonth" summary="Calendar for May 2007">
```

```
<caption>May 2007</caption>
<tr>
  <th scope="col">Monday</th>
  <th scope="col">Tuesday</th>
  <th scope="col">Wednesday</th>
  <th scope="col">Thursday</th>
  <th scope="col">Friday</th>
  <th scope="col">Saturday</th>
  <th scope="col">Sunday</th>
</tr>
<tr>
  <td class="previous">31</td>
  <td class="active">1
    <ul>
      <li>New pupils' open day</li>
      <li>Year 8 theater trip</li>
    </ul></td>
  <td>2</td>
  <td>3</td>
  <td>4</td>
  <td>5</td>
  <td>6</td>
</tr>
<tr>
  <td class="active">7
    <ul>
      <li>Year 7 English exam</li>
    </ul></td>
  <td>8</td>
  <td>9</td>
  <td>10</td>
  <td>11</td>
  <td>12</td>
  <td>13</td>
</tr>
<tr>
  <td>14</td>
  <td>15</td>
  <td>16</td>
  <td class="active">17
    <ul>
      <li>Sports Day</li>
    </ul></td>
  <td class="active">18
```

```
      <ul>
        <li>Year 7 parents' evening</li>
        <li>Prizegiving</li>
      </ul></td>
    <td>19</td>
    <td>20</td>
  </tr>
  <tr>
    <td>21</td>
    <td>22</td>
    <td>23</td>
    <td class="active">24
      <ul>
        <li>Year 8 parents' evening</li>
      </ul></td>
    <td>25</td>
    <td>26</td>
    <td>27</td>
  </tr>
  <tr>
    <td>28</td>
    <td>29</td>
    <td class="active">30
      <ul>
        <li>First night of school play</li>
      </ul></td>
    <td>31</td>
    <td class="next">1</td>
    <td class="next">2</td>
    <td class="next">3</td>
  </tr>
</table>
</body>
</html>
```

cal.css

```
body {
  background-color: #ffffff;
  color: #000000;
  font-size: 90%;
}
.clmonth {
  border-collapse: collapse;
```

```
    width: 780px;
}
.clmonth caption {
  text-align: left;
  font: bold 110% Georgia, "Times New Roman", Times, serif;
  padding-bottom: 0.4em;
}
.clmonth th {
  border: 1px solid #AAAAAA;
  border-bottom: none;
  padding: 0.2em 0.6em 0.2em 0.6em;
  background-color: #CCCCCC;
  color: #3F3F3F;
  font: 80% Verdana, Geneva, Arial, Helvetica, sans-serif;
  width: 110px;
}
.clmonth td {
  border: 1px solid #EAEAEA;
  font: 80% Verdana, Geneva, Arial, Helvetica, sans-serif;
  padding: 0.2em 0.6em 0.2em 0.6em;
  vertical-align: top;
}
.clmonth td.previous, .clmonth td.next {
  background-color: #F6F6F6;
  color: #C6C6C6;
}
.clmonth td.active {
  background-color: #B1CBE1;
  color: #2B5070;
  border: 2px solid #4682B4;
}
.clmonth ul {
  list-style-type: none;
  margin: 0;
  padding-left: 1em;
  padding-right: 0.6em;
}
.clmonth li {
  margin-bottom: 1em;
}
```

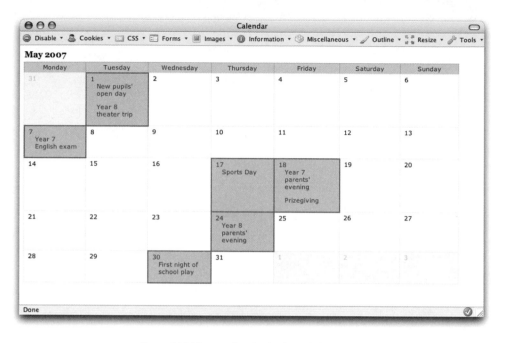

Figure 5.15. The completed calendar styled with CSS

Discussion

This example starts out as a very simple table. It has a caption, which is the month we're working with, and I've marked up the days of the week as table headers using the <th> tag:

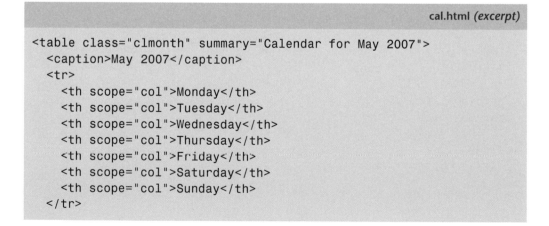

cal.html *(excerpt)*

```
<table class="clmonth" summary="Calendar for May 2007">
  <caption>May 2007</caption>
  <tr>
    <th scope="col">Monday</th>
    <th scope="col">Tuesday</th>
    <th scope="col">Wednesday</th>
    <th scope="col">Thursday</th>
    <th scope="col">Friday</th>
    <th scope="col">Saturday</th>
    <th scope="col">Sunday</th>
  </tr>
```

The table has a class of clmonth. I've used a class rather than an ID because, in some situations, you might want to display more than one month on the page. If you then found that you needed to give the table an ID—perhaps to allow you to show and hide the table using JavaScript—you could add an ID as well as the class.

The days are held within individual table cells, and the events for each day are marked up as a list within the appropriate table cell.

In the markup below, you can see that I've added classes to two of the table cells. Class previous is applied to cells containing days that fall within the preceding month (we'll use next later for days in the following month); class active is applied to cells that contain event information, in order that we may highlight them:

cal.html *(excerpt)*

```
<tr>
  <td class="previous">31</td>
  <td class="active">1
    <ul>
      <li>New pupils' open day</li>
      <li>Year 8 theater trip</li>
    </ul>
  </td>
  <td>2</td>
  <td>3</td>
  <td>4</td>
  <td>5</td>
  <td>6</td>
</tr>
```

The table, without CSS, displays as shown in Figure 5.16.

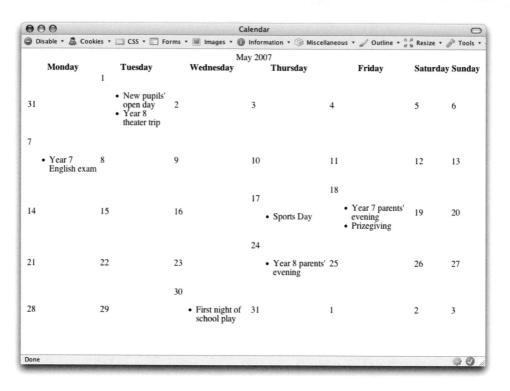

Figure 5.16. Displaying the calendar without CSS

Now that we have the structural markup in place, we can style the calendar. I set a basic style for the body, including a base font size. I then set a style for the class `clmonth` in order for the borders to collapse, leaving no space between cells, and set a width for the table:

cal.css *(excerpt)*

```css
body {
  background-color: #ffffff;
  color: #000000;
  font-size: 90%;
}
.clmonth {
  border-collapse: collapse;
  width: 780px;
}
```

I styled the `caption` within the class `clmonth`, then created styles for the table headers (`th`) and table cells (`td`):

```
                                                   cal.css (excerpt)
.clmonth caption {
  text-align: left;
  font: bold 110% Georgia, "Times New Roman", Times, serif;
  padding-bottom: 0.4em;
}
.clmonth th {
  border: 1px solid #AAAAAA;
  border-bottom: none;
  padding: 0.2em 0.6em 0.2em 0.6em;
  background-color: #CCCCCC;
  color: #3F3F3F;
  font: 80% Verdana, Geneva, Arial, Helvetica, sans-serif;
  width: 110px;
}
.clmonth td {
  border: 1px solid #EAEAEA;
  font: 80% Verdana, Geneva, Arial, Helvetica, sans-serif;
  padding: 0.2em 0.6em 0.2em 0.6em;
  vertical-align: top;
}
```

As you can see in Figure 5.17, our calendar is beginning to take shape.

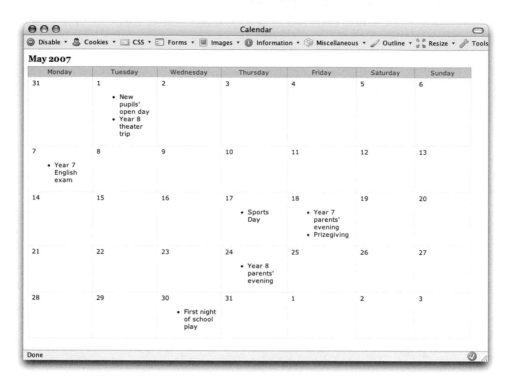

Figure 5.17. Styling the `caption`, `th`, and `td` elements to make the calendar more user friendly

We can now style the lists of events within each table cell, removing the bullet and adding space between list items:

```
                                                          cal.css (excerpt)

.clmonth ul {
  list-style-type: none;
  margin: 0;
  padding-left: 1em;
  padding-right: 0.6em;
}
.clmonth li {
  margin-bottom: 1em;
}
```

Finally, we add styles for the `previous` and `next` classes, which give the effect of graying out those days that are not part of the current month. We also style the `active` class, which highlights those days on which events will take place:

cal.css *(excerpt)*

```css
.clmonth td.previous, .clmonth td.next {
  background-color: #F6F6F6;
  color: #C6C6C6;
}
.clmonth td.active {
  background-color: #B1CBE1;
  color: #2B5070;
  border: 2px solid #4682B4;
}
```

This is just one of many ways to create a calendar. Online calendars are commonly used on blogs, where they have clickable days that visitors can use to view entries made that month. By removing the events from our HTML markup, representing the day names with single letters—M for Monday, and so on—and making a few simple changes to our CSS, we can create a simple mini-calendar that's suitable for this purpose, like the one shown in Figure 5.18.

Figure 5.18. Creating a mini-calendar

Here's the HTML and CSS you'll need for this version of the calendar:

cal_mini.html *(excerpt)*

```html
<table class="clmonth" summary="Calendar for May 2007">
  <caption>May 2007</caption>
  <tr>
```

```
      <th scope="col">M</th>
      <th scope="col">T</th>
      <th scope="col">W</th>
      <th scope="col">T</th>
      <th scope="col">F</th>
      <th scope="col">S</th>
      <th scope="col">S</th>
    </tr>
    <tr>
      <td class="previous">31</td>
      <td class="active">1</td>
      <td>2</td>
      <td>3</td>
      <td>4</td>
      <td>5</td>
      <td>6</td>
    </tr>
    <tr>
      <td class="active">7</td>
      <td>8</td>
      <td>9</td>
      <td>10</td>
      <td>11</td>
      <td>12</td>
      <td>13</td>
    </tr>
    <tr>
      <td>14</td>
      <td>15</td>
      <td>16</td>
      <td class="active">17</td>
      <td class="active">18</td>
      <td>19</td>
      <td>20</td>
    </tr>
    <tr>
      <td>21</td>
      <td>22</td>
      <td>23</td>
      <td class="active">24</td>
      <td>25</td>
      <td>26</td>
      <td>27</td>
    </tr>
```

```
  <tr>
    <td>28</td>
    <td>29</td>
    <td class="active">30</td>
    <td>31</td>
    <td class="next">1</td>
    <td class="next">2</td>
    <td class="next">3</td>
  </tr>
</table>
```

cal_mini.css

```
body {
  background-color: #ffffff;
  color: #000000;
  font-size: 90%;
}
.clmonth {
  border-collapse: collapse;
}
.clmonth caption {
  text-align: left;
  font: bold 110% Georgia, "Times New Roman", Times, serif;
  padding-bottom: 0.4em;
}
.clmonth th {
  border: 1px solid #AAAAAA;
  border-bottom: none;
  padding: 0.2em 0.4em 0.2em 0.4em;
  background-color: #CCCCCC;
  color: #3F3F3F;
  font: 80% Verdana, Geneva, Arial, Helvetica, sans-serif;
}
.clmonth td {
  border: 1px solid #EAEAEA;
  font: 80% Verdana, Geneva, Arial, Helvetica, sans-serif;
  padding: 0.2em 0.4em 0.2em 0.4em;
  vertical-align: top;
}
.clmonth td.previous, .clmonth td.next {
  background-color: #F6F6F6;
  color: #C6C6C6;
}
```

```
.clmonth td.active {
  background-color: #B1CBE1;
  color: #2B5070;
  border: 2px solid #4682B4;
}
```

Summary

In this chapter, we've discovered that tables are alive and well—when used for their original purpose of displaying tabular data, that is! CSS gives you the ability to turn data tables into really attractive interface items, without negatively impacting their accessibility. So don't be afraid to use tables to display tabular data—that's their job!

6

Forms and User Interfaces

Forms are an inescapable part of web design and development. We use them to capture personal data from our users, to post information to message boards, to add items to shopping carts, and to update our blogs—among many other things!

Despite the necessity of forms on the Web, HTML makes virtually no styling options available to the designer, so forms have traditionally been rendered in the default style of the browser. CSS has brought with it many ways to address form elements, so this chapter will consider what can be styled in a form and why you might want to do so. That said, this chapter will also cover some of the less-common HTML form tags and attributes whose application can boost the accessibility and usability of our forms, as well as providing additional elements to which we can apply CSS.

In the following pages, we'll consider forms laid out using CSS positioning as well as their table-based counterparts. Debate rages as to whether it is appropriate to lay out a form using a table; my take is that, if a form is tabular in nature—for instance, like the one in the spreadsheet example we'll encounter in this chapter—a table is the most logical way to structure the fields. Otherwise, your form is likely to be more accessible if it's laid out using CSS.

As we work with forms, it's especially important to consider the usability of the forms themselves. Forms are designed to accept user input, but they'll fail in that task if, though they look beautiful, site visitors aren't sure how to use them.

How do I style form elements using CSS?

Unstyled form elements will display according to browser and operating system defaults. However, you can use CSS to create forms that correspond to your site's visual design.

Solution

Styles can be created for form elements just as they can for any other HTML element. The form shown in Figure 6.1 is unstyled; it's displayed according to Firefox's default styles on Mac OS X, and it will look different on different browsers and operating systems.

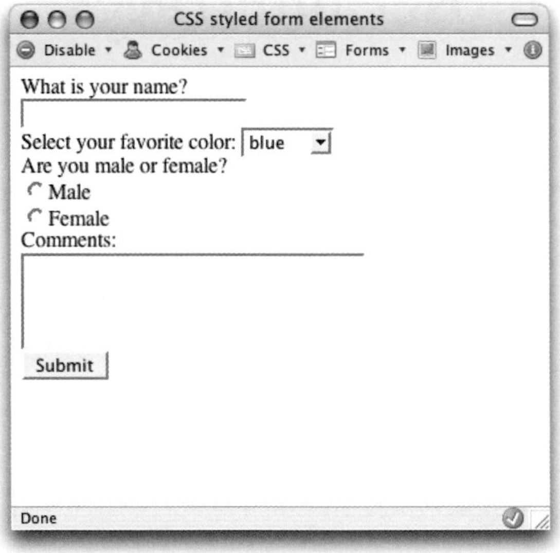

Figure 6.1. The basic appearance assumed by an unstyled form according to Firefox's default styles

Here's a typical form:

```
<!DOCTYPE html PUBLIC "-//W3C//DTD XHTML 1.0 Strict//EN"
    "http://www.w3.org/TR/xhtml1/DTD/xhtml1-strict.dtd">
<html xmlns="http://www.w3.org/1999/xhtml" lang="en-US">
<head>
  <title>CSS styled form elements</title>
  <meta http-equiv="content-type"
    content="text/html; charset=utf-8" />
  <link rel="stylesheet" type="text/css" href="elements.css" />
</head>
<body>
  <form method="post" action="example1.html" id="form1">
    <div><label for="name">What is your name?</label><br/>
    <input type="text" name="name" id="name" /></div>
    <div><label for="color">Select your favorite color:</label>
      <select name="color" id="color">
        <option value="blue">blue</option>
        <option value="red">red</option>
        <option value="green">green</option>
        <option value="yellow">yellow</option>
      </select>
    </div>
    <div><label for="sex">Are you male or female?</label><br/>
      <input type="radio" name="sex" id="male"
          value="male" />Male<br/>
      <input type="radio" name="sex" id="female"
          value="female" />Female
    </div>
    <div>
      <label for="comments">Comments:</label><br/>
      <textarea name="comments" id="comments" cols="30"
          rows="4"></textarea>
    </div>
    <div>
      <input type="submit" name="btnSubmit" id="btnSubmit"
          value="Submit" />
    </div>
  </form>
</body>
</html>
```

We can change the look of this form by creating CSS rules for the `form`, `input`, `textarea`, and `select` elements:

```
                                                              elements.css
form {
  border: 1px dotted #aaaaaa;
  padding: 0.5em;
}
input {
  color: #00008B;
  background-color: #ADD8E6;
  border: 1px solid #00008B;
}
select {
  width: 100px;
  color: #00008B;
  background-color: #ADD8E6;
  border: 1px solid #00008B;
}
textarea {
  width: 200px;
  height: 40px;
  color: #00008B;
  background-color: #ADD8E6;
  border: 1px solid #00008B;
}
```

The new look is depicted in Figure 6.2.

Discussion

As you'd expect, the definition of rules for the HTML elements `form`, `input`, `textarea`, and `select` will affect any instances of these elements in a page to which your style sheet is attached. You can use a variety of CSS properties to change the appearance of a form's fields. For example, CSS allows you to change almost every aspect of an `<input type="text">` field:

```
<input type="text" name="name" id="name" />
```

```
input {
  color: #00008B;
  background-color: #ADD8E6;
  border: 1px solid #00008B;
  font: 0.9em Arial, Helvetica, sans-serif;
  padding: 0.2em;
  width: 200px;
}
```

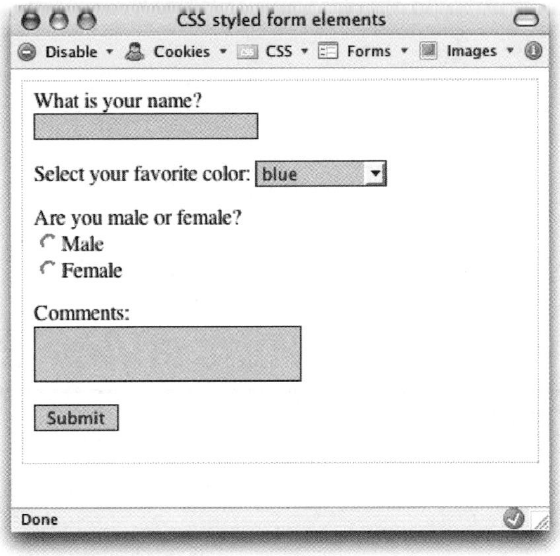

Figure 6.2. The form displaying differently following the application of CSS

Safari and Background Colors

Unfortunately, as of this writing, Safari does not support the application of background colors to all form fields (text fields and `textarea` elements work, but other controls, such as buttons and drop-down menus, do not).

For this reason, as well as the fact that not all users can distinguish colors well, you should never rely on field background colors for the usability of your site—for instance, instructions like, "The yellow fields are required" would be a big no-no.

Let's break down these styles:

`color`	changes the color of the text that's typed inside the field
`background-color`	defines the field's background
`border`	affects the border around the field; any of the other border styles here can be used
`font`	changes the font size and typeface of the text within the field
`padding`	moves the text typed within a field away from the edges of the box
`width`	allows the creation of form fields of the right width for the data you expect users to enter (You don't need a long field for a user's first initial, for example.)

How do I apply different styles to fields in a single form?

The `input` element has many different types, and the styles that you need for a text field are unlikely to be the same as those you want to use for your buttons or checkboxes. How can you create specific styles for different form fields?

Solution

You can use CSS classes to specify the exact styles that individual fields will use. The form in the following example has two `input` elements, one of which displays a text field, while the other displays a **Submit** button. Different classes are applied to each:

fields.html *(excerpt)*

```
<form method="post" action="fields.html">
<div>
  <label for="name">What is your name?</label><br />
  <input type="text" name="name" id="name" class="txt" />
</div>
<input type="submit" name="btnSubmit" id="btnSubmit"
```

```
          value="Submit" class="btn" />
</form>
```

fields.css

```
form {
  border: 1px dotted #aaaaaa;
  padding: 3px 6px 3px 6px;
}
input.txt {
  color: #00008B;
  background-color: #ADD8E6;
  border: 1px inset #00008B;
  width: 200px;
}
input.btn {
  color: #00008B;
  background-color: #ADD8E6;
  border: 1px outset #00008B;
  padding: 2px 4px 2px 4px;
}
```

Figure 6.3 shows the result.

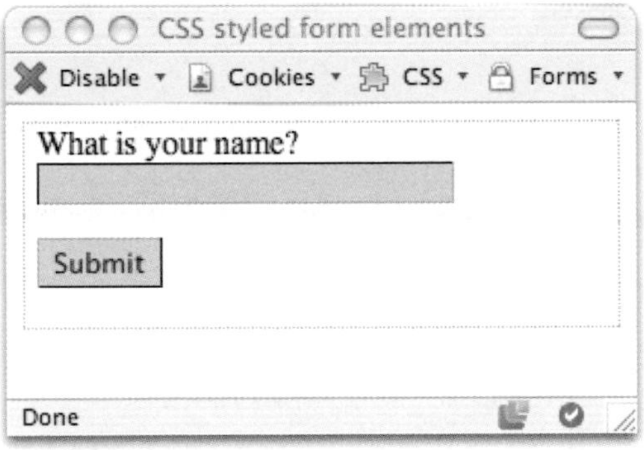

Figure 6.3. Applying different classes to each of the input fields

Discussion

As we've seen, the input element can have several different types, and these types may require different styles in order to display appropriately. In the example above, we used classes to differentiate between an `input` element with a type of `text` and an `input` element with a type of `submit`. Had we simply created one set of styles for `input`, we might have ended up with the following (having set a width and used an inset border on the text field):

```
input {
  color: #00008B;
  background-color: #ADD8E6;
  border: 1px inset #00008B;
  width: 200px;
}
```

Applied to the form above, these styles would have displayed as shown in Figure 6.4.

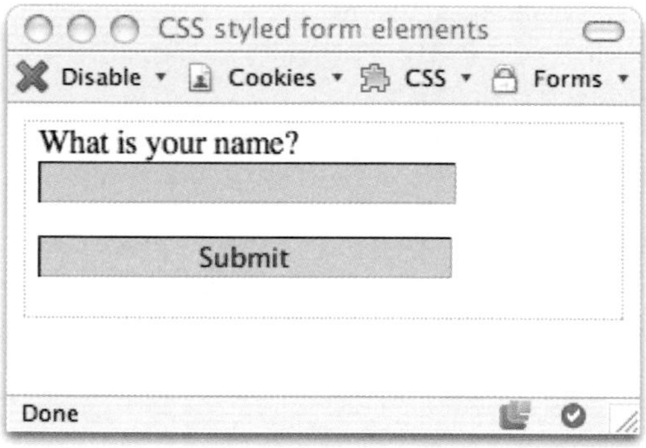

Figure 6.4. Applying the same styles to both input fields

The **Submit** button now looks rather like a text field; it certainly doesn't look like a button!

Using different classes allows us to style each element exactly as we want it to display. The forms in any application will likely need to cater for a variety of different types of data. Some text fields may only require the user to enter two characters; others may need to accept a name or other short word; others must take an entire sentence. By creating CSS classes for small, medium, and large text fields, you can choose the field that's appropriate to the data you expect the user to enter. This, in turn, helps users feel confident that they're entering the correct information.

Style Early, Style Often

When I begin work on a site that includes a lot of forms, one of my first steps is to create within the style sheet a number of classes for standard forms. It doesn't matter if the style needs to change at a later date—that just involves tweaking the style sheet values. The important thing is that classes are applied from the outset, so that any changes affect all the forms on the site.

How do I stop my form creating additional white space and line breaks?

A form is a block-level element and, like a paragraph, will display on a new line by default. This is usually the behavior you'd want to implement, but on some occasions you may wish to add a small form within the flow of a document—for instance, placing a small search box alongside other header elements.

Solution

You can use the `display` property with a value of `inline` to display a form as an inline element:

inline.html (excerpt)

```
Your email address:
<form method="post" action="inline.html">
  <div><input type="text" name="name" id="name" class="txt" />
  <input type="submit" name="btnSubmit" id="btnSubmit"
     value="Submit" class="btn" /></div>
</form>
```

inline.css

```
form {
  display: inline;
}
input.txt {
  color: #00008B;
  background-color: #E3F2F7;
  border: 1px inset #00008B;
  width: 200px;
```

```
}
input.btn {
  color: #00008B;
  background-color: #ADD8E6;
  border: 1px outset #00008B;
}
```

As you can see in Figure 6.5, this CSS causes the form to join the document flow, and sit inline with the text that surrounds it.

Figure 6.5. Displaying a form inline

How do I make a Submit button look like text?

It's generally a good idea to make buttons look like buttons if you expect people to click on them. However, on occasion, you might want to have your form's **Submit** button look more like plain text.

Solution

Take a look at this style rule:

textbutton.css *(excerpt)*

```
.btn {
  background-color: transparent;
  border: 0;
  padding: 0;
}
```

The text **Next »** that appears on the second line in Figure 6.6 is actually a button!

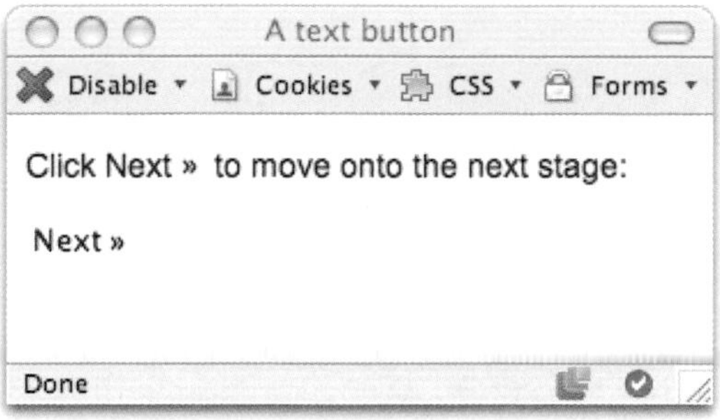

Figure 6.6. Making a button look like text

Safari Protects its Buttons

Continuing its theme of limited form styling support, Safari doesn't let you alter the look of buttons the way other browsers do, and this solution does not apply to that browser. As I mentioned above, you do need to take care when styling any element to look like something else—the usability of your application could be severely compromised if it is not immediately obvious that your button is clickable!

How do I ensure that users with text–only devices understand how to complete my form?

It's good to create an attractive and usable form for visitors who have standard web browsers, but bear in mind that many users will have a text-only view of your site. Before you use CSS to style your form, ensure that it's structured in a way that makes the form's completion easy for text-only users.

Solution

One of the most important ways to make your form more accessible is to ensure that all users understand which label belongs with each form field. If they're using text-only devices or screen readers, which will read the form aloud to visually im-paired users, visitors can find it very difficult to determine which details they're supposed to enter into each field unless your form is well planned and created.

The `label` element ties a label to a specific form field—it's the ideal solution to this particular problem. Like other elements on the page, the `label` element is easily styled with CSS rules:

```
<form method="post" action="textonly.html">
  <table>
    <tr>
      <td><label for="fullname">Name:</label></td>
      <td><input type="text" name="fullname" id="fullname"
          class="txt" /></td>
    </tr>
    <tr>
      <td><label for="email">Email Address:</label></td>
      <td><input type="text" name="email" id="email" class="txt"
          /></td>
    </tr>
    <tr>
      <td><label for="password1">Password:</label></td>
      <td><input type="password" name="password1" id="password1"
          class="txt" /></td>
    </tr>
    <tr>
      <td><label for="password2">Confirm Password:</label></td>
      <td><input type="password" name="password2" id="password2"
          class="txt" /></td>
    </tr>
    <tr>
      <td><label for="level">Membership Level:</label></td>
      <td><select name="level">
          <option value="silver">silver</option>
          <option value="gold">gold</option>
        </select></td>
    </tr>
  </table>
  <p>
    <input type="submit" name="btnSubmit" id="btnSubmit"
        value="Sign Up!" class="btn" />
  </p>
</form>
```

textonly.css

```css
h1 {
  font: 1.2em Arial, Helvetica, sans-serif;
}
input.txt {
  color: #00008B;
  background-color: #E3F2F7;
  border: 1px inset #00008B;
  width: 200px;
}
input.btn {
  color: #00008B;
  background-color: #ADD8E6;
  border: 1px outset #00008B;
}
label {
  font : bold 0.9em  Arial, Helvetica, sans-serif;
}
```

The results of these styles can be seen in Figure 6.7—though the benefits of these styles for visually impaired users are obviously not going to be apparent in a printed book! That said, as well as improving the form's usability for text-only browsers and screen readers, these styles will cause visual browsers to place the cursor in the corresponding field when the user clicks on one of the labels. When you add a label, everybody wins!

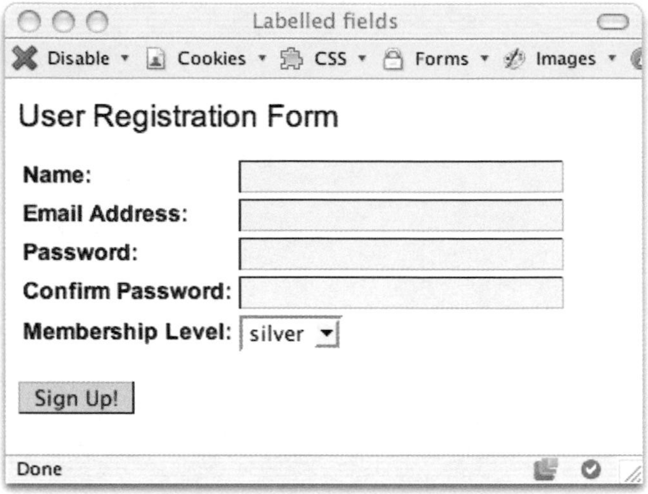

Figure 6.7. Displaying the form in the browser

Discussion

The `label` element makes it possible to indicate clearly what information users need to enter into a field. As we've discussed, forms that may be read out to users by their screen readers need to make the purpose of each field immediately obvious. With a layout such as the one provided in this example, which uses a table to display the label in one cell and the field in another, it's especially important that we include a `label` element. (In the solution that follows, I'll demonstrate how to achieve the same form layout without using a table.)

You can use the `label` element in two ways. If your form field is right next to the label text, you can simply wrap both the label text and the field with the element's start and end tags:

```
<label>Name: <input type="text" name="fullname" id="fullname"
    class="txt" /></label>
```

If, as in our example above, you cannot wrap the label and field, as they're not siblings in the document structure, you can use the `<label>` tag's `for` attribute instead. In this case, you must insert as a value the ID of the field that the label describes:

textonly.html *(excerpt)*

```
<tr>
  <td><label for="fullname">Name:</label></td>
  <td><input type="text" name="fullname" id="fullname"
        class="txt" /></td>
</tr>
```

Once you have your `label` element in place, you'll have made an important step towards ensuring that those using screen readers will understand how to complete your form. Keep in mind that you can also use CSS to style the `label` element itself:

textonly.css *(excerpt)*

```
label {
  font: bold 0.9em  Arial, Helvetica, sans-serif;
}
```

How do I lay out a two-column form using CSS instead of a table?

Forms can be tricky to lay out without tables, but the task isn't impossible. Figure 6.8 shows a form layout that looks remarkably table-like, but if you examine the HTML code that follows, you'll find there's not a table in sight!

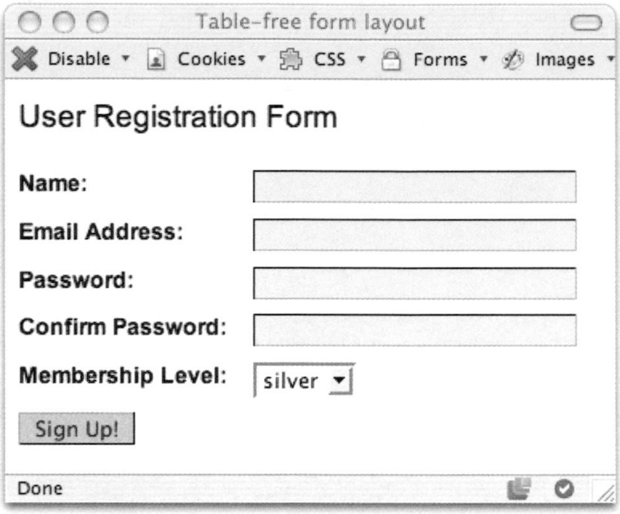

Figure 6.8. A two-column form laid out using CSS

```
                                                    tablefree.html

<!DOCTYPE html PUBLIC "-//W3C//DTD XHTML 1.0 Strict//EN"
    "http://www.w3.org/TR/xhtml1/DTD/xhtml1-strict.dtd">
<html xmlns="http://www.w3.org/1999/xhtml" lang="en-US">
<head>
<title>Table-free form layout</title>
<meta http-equiv="content-type"
    content="text/html; charset=utf-8" />
<link rel="stylesheet" type="text/css" href="tablefree.css" />
</head>
<body>
<h1>User Registration Form</h1>
<form method="post" action="tablefree.html">
  <div>
    <label for="fullname">Name:</label>
    <input type="text" name="fullname" id="fullname"
        class="txt" />
  </div>
  <div>
    <label for="email">Email Address:</label>
    <input type="text" name="email" id="email" class="txt" />
  </div>
  <div>
    <label for="password1">Password:</label>
```

```
      <input type="password" name="password1" id="password1"
          class="txt" />
    </div>
    <div>
      <label for="password2">Confirm Password:</label>
      <input type="password" name="password2" id="password2"
          class="txt" />
    </div>
    <div>
      <label for="level">Membership Level:</label>
      <select name="level">
        <option value="silver">silver</option>
        <option value="gold">gold</option>
      </select>
    </div>
    <div>
      <input type="submit" name="btnSubmit" id="btnSubmit"
          value="Sign Up!" class="btn" />
    </div>
  </form>
</body>
</html>
```

tablefree.css

```
h1 {
  font: 1.2em Arial, Helvetica, sans-serif;
}
input.txt {
  color: #00008B;
  background-color: #E3F2F7;
  border: 1px inset #00008B;
  width: 200px;
}
input.btn {
  color: #00008B;
  background-color: #ADD8E6;
  border: 1px outset #00008B;
}
form div {
  clear: left;
  margin: 0;
  padding: 0;
  padding-top: 0.6em;
```

```
}
form div label {
  float: left;
  width: 40%;
  font: bold 0.9em Arial, Helvetica, sans-serif;
}
```

Discussion

The example above creates a common form layout. As we saw earlier in this chapter, this layout's often achieved using a two-column table in which the label is placed in one cell, the field in another:

textonly.html *(excerpt)*

```
<form method="post" action="textonly.html">
  <table>
    <tr>
      <td><label for="fullname">Name:</label></td>
      <td><input type="text" name="fullname" id="fullname"
          class="txt" /></td>
    </tr>
    <tr>
      <td><label for="email">Email Address:</label></td>
      <td><input type="text" name="email" id="email" class="txt"
          /></td>
    </tr>
    <tr>
      <td><label for="password1">Password:</label></td>
      <td><input type="password" name="password1" id="password1"
          class="txt" /></td>
    </tr>
    <tr>
      <td><label for="password2">Confirm Password:</label></td>
      <td><input type="password" name="password2" id="password2"
          class="txt" /></td>
    </tr>
    <tr>
      <td><label for="level">Membership Level:</label></td>
      <td><select name="level">
          <option value="silver">silver</option>
          <option value="gold">gold</option>
        </select></td>
```

```
      </tr>
    </table>
    <p>
      <input type="submit" name="btnSubmit" id="btnSubmit"
          value="Sign Up!" class="btn" />
    </p>
</form>
```

This form has been laid out using a table to ensure that all the fields line up neatly. Without the table, the fields appear immediately after the labels, as Figure 6.9 shows.

Figure 6.9. A form laid out without a table

In the markup that's used to create the form shown in Figure 6.9, each form row is located within a div element, causing the field to appear immediately after the label:

tablefree.html *(excerpt)*

```
<form method="post" action="tablefree.html">
  <div>
    <label for="fullname">Name:</label>
    <input type="text" name="fullname" id="fullname" class="txt"
        />
  </div>
  <div>
```

```
    <label for="email">Email Address:</label>
    <input type="text" name="email" id="email" class="txt" />
  </div>
  …
```

To recreate the effect of the table-based layout using only CSS, we don't have to make any changes to our markup. All we need is some simple CSS:

tablefree.css

```
form div {
  clear: left;
  margin: 0;
  padding: 0;
  padding-top: 0.6em;
}
form div label {
  float: left;
  width: 40%;
  font: bold 0.9em Arial, Helvetica, sans-serif;
}
```

What we're doing here is addressing our `label` element directly in the style sheet. We float it to the left, give it a `width` value and modify its font settings.

As the `float` property takes an element out of the document flow, we need to give our `div`s a `clear` property with the value `left`, to ensure that each `div` starts below the `label` in the preceding `div`. We also give our `div`s a `padding-top` value, in order to space out the rows, and that's it!

How do I group related fields?

Large web forms can be made much more usable if the visitor can ascertain which questions are related. We need a way to show the relationships between information—a way that helps users with standard browsers as well as those using text-only devices and screen readers.

Solution

We can group related fields using the `fieldset` and `legend` elements:

```html
<form method="post" action="fieldset.html">
  <fieldset>
    <legend>Personal Information</legend>
    <div>
      <label for="fullname">Name:</label>
      <input type="text" name="fullname" id="fullname"
        class="txt" />
    </div>
    <div>
      <label for="email">Email Address:</label>
      <input type="text" name="email" id="cmail" class="txt" />
    </div>
    <div>
      <label for="password1">Password:</label>
      <input type="password" name="password1" id="password1"
        class="txt" />
    </div>
    <div>
      <label for="password2">Confirm Password:</label>
      <input type="password" name="password2" id="password2"
        class="txt" />
    </div>
  </fieldset>
  <fieldset>
    <legend>Address Details</legend>
    <div>
      <label for="address1">Address line one:</label>
      <input type="text" name="address1" id="address1"
        class="txt" />
    </div>
    <div>
      <label for="address2">Address line two:</label>
      <input type="text" name="address2" id="address2"
        class="txt" />
    </div>
    <div>
      <label for="city">Town / City:</label>
      <input type="text" name="city" id="city" class="txt" />
    </div>
    <div>
      <label for="zip">Zip / Post code:</label>
      <input type="text" name="zip" id="zip" class="txt" />
```

```
      </div>
    </fieldset>
    <div>
      <input type="submit" name="btnSubmit" id="btnSubmit"
        value="Sign Up!" class="btn" />
    </div>
  </form>
```

fieldset.css

```
h1 {
  font: 1.2em Arial, Helvetica, sans-serif;
}
input.txt {
  color: #00008B;
  background-color: #E3F2F7;
  border: 1px inset #00008B;
  width: 200px;
}
input.btn {
  color: #00008B;
  background-color: #ADD8E6;
  border: 1px outset #00008B;
}
form div {
  clear: left;
  margin: 0;
  padding: 0;
  padding-top: 5px;
}
form div label {
  float: left;
  width: 40%;
  font: bold 0.9em Arial, Helvetica, sans-serif;
}
fieldset {
  border: 1px dotted #61B5CF;
  margin-top: 1.4em;
  padding: 0.6em;
}
legend {
  font: bold 0.8em Arial, Helvetica, sans-serif;
  color: #00008B;
```

```
   background-color: #FFFFFF;
}
```

Figure 6.10 shows how the groupings are displayed by the browser.

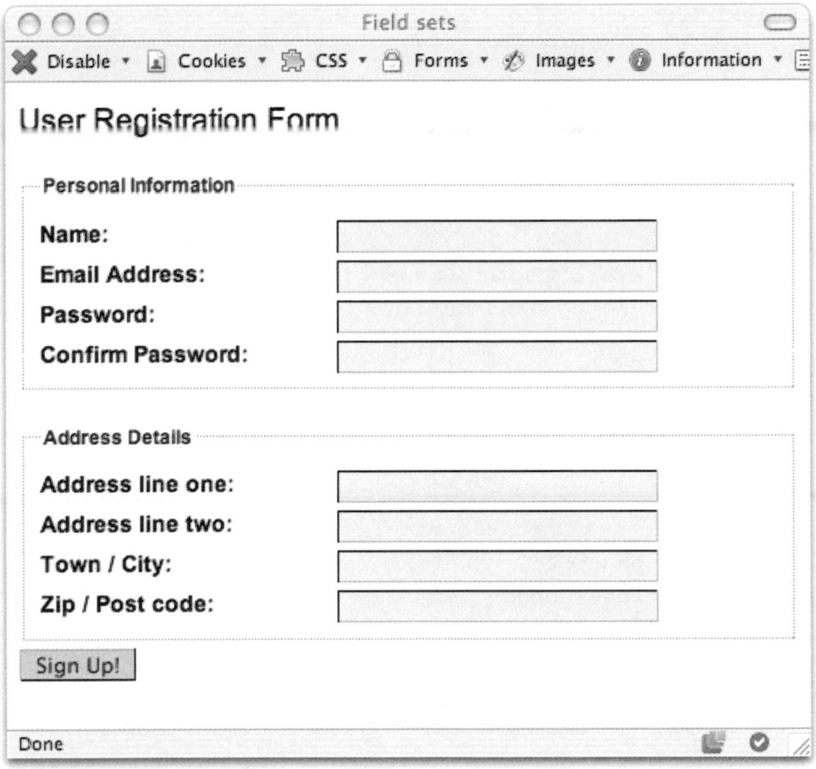

Figure 6.10. Creating two sections in a form using the `<fieldset>` tag

Discussion

The `<fieldset>` and `<legend>` tags are a great way to group related information in a form. These tags provide an easy means to group items visually, and are understood by screen readers and text-only devices, which can perceive that the tagged items are logically grouped together. This wouldn't be the case if you simply wrapped the related items in a styled `div` users of a standard browser would understand the relationship, but those who couldn't see the results of our CSS would not.

To group form fields, simply wrap the related fields with a `<fieldset>` tag and, immediately after your opening `<fieldset>` tag, add a `<legend>` tag that contains a title for the group:

fieldset.html *(excerpt)*

```
<fieldset>
  <legend>Personal Information</legend>
  <div>
    <label for="fullname">Name:</label>
    <input type="text" name="fullname" id="fullname" class="txt"
        />
  </div>
  <div>
    <label for="email">Email Address:</label>
    <input type="text" name="email" id="email" class="txt" />
  </div>
  <div>
    <label for="password1">Password:</label>
    <input type="password" name="password1" id="password1"
        class="txt" />
  </div>
  <div>
    <label for="password2">Confirm Password:</label>
    <input type="password" name="password2" id="password2"
        class="txt" />
  </div>
</fieldset>
```

Like other HTML tags, `<fieldset>` and `<legend>` are displayed with a default style by browsers. The default style surrounds the grouped elements with a box, and the `<legend>` tag appears in the top-left corner of that box. Figure 6.11 shows the `<fieldset>` and `<legend>` tags as they display by default in Firefox on Mac OS X.

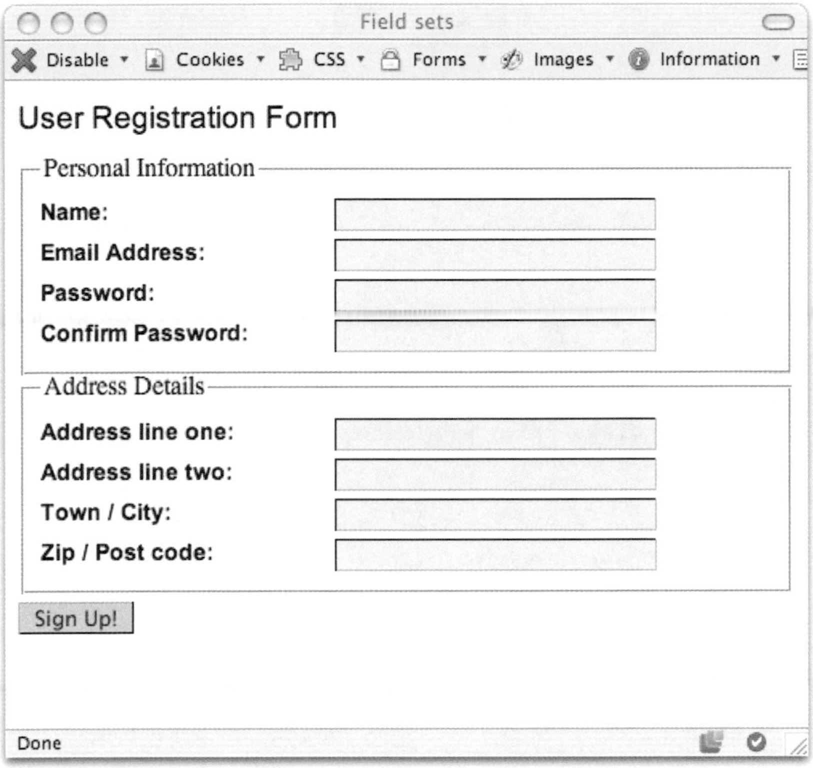

Figure 6.11. Viewing unstyled `<fieldset>` and `<legend>` tags

How do I style **accesskey** hints?

Access keys allow users to jump quickly to a certain place in a document or follow a link—all they need to do is press a combination of **Alt** (or equivalent) and another, specific key. You have to let users know what that other key is, of course!

Solution

The convention that's followed by many computer operating systems is to indicate which letter of a key word is its access key by underlining that letter. For example, on a Windows machine, **Alt-F** opens the **File** drop-down menu. This functionality is indicated by the underlining of the letter "F" in **File**, as shown in Figure 6.12.

Figure 6.12. The underline beneath the letter "F" in the word **File**

You can use a similar technique on your site, underlining the appropriate letters to identify your access keys.

```
                                                    accesskeys.html (excerpt)
<fieldset>
  <legend><span class="akey">P</span>ersonal
    Information</legend>
  <div>
    <label for="fullname">Name:</label>
    <input type="text" name="fullname" id="fullname" class="txt"
        accesskey="p" />
  </div>
```

```
                                                      accesskeys.css (excerpt)
.akey {
  text-decoration: underline;
}
```

As you can see in Figure 6.13, the access key for each field set is underlined.

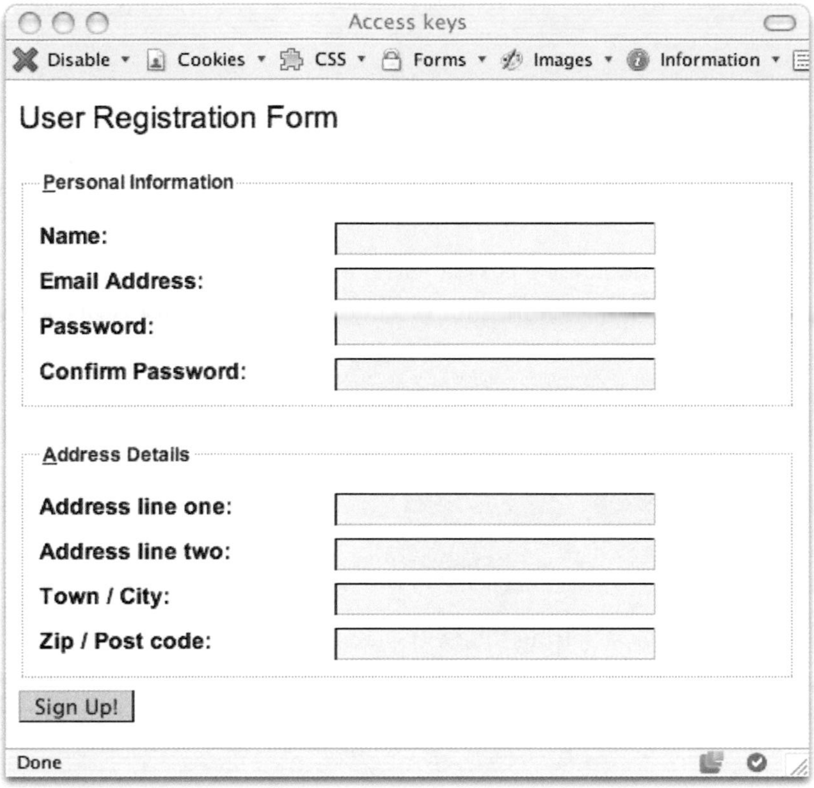

Figure 6.13. Indicating access keys with lines under the "P" in **Personal** and "A" in **Address**

Discussion

Access keys can be very helpful to site users who have mobility problems and can't use a mouse, as well as to users who simply prefer using the keyboard to navigate, rather than the mouse. You could, for example, provide an access key that allowed these visitors to jump straight to the form by pressing one key, or to go to the search box by pressing another. The convention of underlining the letter that corresponds to the access key will be familiar to visitors who use this functionality, even if other users don't know what it means.

To add access key functionality to a form field, you simply need to add the attribute `accesskey="x"` to that field, where x is the character you've chosen for the access key:

accesskeys.html *(excerpt)*

```
<div>
  <label for="fullname">Name:</label>
  <input type="text" name="fullname" id="fullname" class="txt"
    accesskey="p" />
</div>
```

In our example, I've added an access key to the first form element of each group. When a user presses the access key, focus will move to that first form field so that users can begin to complete the form. To highlight the access key, I've taken the first letter of the field set `<legend>` (for example, the "P" in "Personal Details") and wrapped it in a span with a class of `akey`:

accesskeys.html *(excerpt)*

```
<legend><span class="akey">P</span>ersonal Information</legend>
```

I've styled the `akey` class, setting the `text-decoration` property to `underline`:

accesskeys.css *(excerpt)*

```
.akey {
  text-decoration: underline;
}
```

Not all browsers implement access keys in the same way. For example, Internet Explorer and Firefox 1.5 use the **Alt** key, but Firefox 2 uses **Alt-Shift** (at the time of writing, however, this only works for alphabetical access keys, not numeric ones). Safari uses **Ctrl**, and Opera uses **Shift-Esc** but allows users to configure their own key combinations.

Access Keys May be Less Accessible than they Appear

When creating access keys, take care not to override default browser keyboard shortcuts!

How do I use different colored highlights in a `select` menu?

Earlier, we learned how to color the background of a `select` menu in a form. But is it possible to include several colors in the menu to highlight different options?

Solution

You can assign classes to menu options to apply multiple background colors within the drop-down menu. `color` and `background-color` are the only properties you can set for a menu item.

 Safari has no Stripes

Remember, Safari doesn't yet support background colors on form elements, so this solution will not work in that browser.

Here's the code you'll need:

select.html (excerpt)

```
<form method="post" action="example8.html">
  <div>
    <label for="color">Select your favorite color:</label>
    <select name="color" id="color">
      <option value="">Select One</option>
      <option value="blue" class="blue">blue</option>
      <option value="red" class="red">red</option>
      <option value="green" class="green">green</option>
      <option value="yellow" class="yellow">yellow</option>
    </select>
  </div>
  <div>
    <input type="submit" name="btnSubmit" id="btnSubmit"
        value="Send!" class="btn" />
  </div>
</form>
```

```
                                                  select.css (excerpt)
.blue {
  background-color: #ADD8E6;
  color: #000000;
}
.red {
  background-color: #E20A0A;
  color: #ffffff;
}
.green {
  background-color: #3CB371;
  color: #ffffff;
}
.yellow {
  background-color: #FFF280;
  color: #000000;
}
```

Thanks to this code, the drop-down menu in Figure 6.14 looks very colorful indeed. Note, however, that we wouldn't normally want to use such presentational class names in our CSS. For example, giving a heading a class name of blue would be a poor decision, as you might decide later to change the color of all headings to green—you'd then either be left with a bunch of headings that had a class of blue but in fact displayed as green, or you'd have to change all of your markup. However, in the case of a color selection form, like in this example, common sense prevails!

Figure 6.14. Options displaying within a selectmenu to which classes are applied

Style with Substance

Use different background colors on sets of related options, or apply alternating row colors in your `select` menu.

I have a form that allows users to enter data as if into a spreadsheet. How do I style it with CSS?

While laying out forms using CSS is possible—and recommended in most cases—there are some cases in which data is more easily entered into a form within a table. One obvious example is a spreadsheet-like web application.

Users may already be accustomed to entering data into a spreadsheet using Microsoft Excel or another package. Keep this in mind as you design your application interface—mimicking familiar interfaces often helps users to feel comfortable with your application. Making your form look like a spreadsheet by laying it out in a table, and using CSS to format it, may be the way to go. Let's take a look at the code:

spreadsheet.html (excerpt)

```
<form method="post" action="spreadsheet.html">
<table class="formdata" summary="This table contains a form to
    input the yearly income for years 1999 through 2002">
  <caption>Complete the Yearly Income 1999 - 2002</caption>
  <tr>
    <th></th>
    <th scope="col">1999</th>
    <th scope="col">2000</th>
    <th scope="col">2001</th>
    <th scope="col">2002</th>
  </tr>
  <tr>
    <th scope="row">Grants</th>
    <td><input type="text" name="grants1999" id="grants1999" />
    </td>
    <td><input type="text" name="grants2000" id="grants2000" />
    </td>
    <td><input type="text" name="grants2001" id="grants2001" />
```

```
      </td>
      <td><input type="text" name="grants2002" id="grants2002" />
      </td>
    </tr>
    <tr>
      <th scope="row">Donations</th>
      <td><input type="text" name="donations1999" id="donations1999"
        /></td>
      <td><input type="text" name="donations2000" id="donations2000"
        /></td>
      <td><input type="text" name="donations2001" id="donations2001"
        /></td>
      <td><input type="text" name="donations2002" id="donations2002"
        /></td>
    </tr>
    <tr>
      <th scope="row">Investments</th>
      <td><input type="text" name="investments1999"
        id="investments1999" /></td>
      <td><input type="text" name="investments2000"
        id="investments2000" /></td>
      <td><input type="text" name="investments2001"
        id="investments2001" /></td>
      <td><input type="text" name="investments2002"
        id="investments2002" /></td>
    </tr>
    <tr>
      <th scope="row">Fundraising</th>
      <td><input type="text" name="fundraising1999"
        id="fundraising1999" /></td>
      <td><input type="text" name="fundraising2000"
        id="fundraising2000" /></td>
      <td><input type="text" name="fundraising2001"
        id="fundraising2001" /></td>
      <td><input type="text" name="fundraising2002"
        id="fundraising2002" /></td>
    </tr>
    <tr>
      <th scope="row">Sales</th>
      <td><input type="text" name="sales1999" id="sales1999" /></td>
      <td><input type="text" name="sales2000" id="sales2000" /></td>
      <td><input type="text" name="sales2001" id="sales2001" /></td>
      <td><input type="text" name="sales2002" id="sales2002" /></td>
    </tr>
```

```
  <tr>
    <th scope="row">Miscellaneous</th>
    <td><input type="text" name="misc1999" id="misc1999" /></td>
    <td><input type="text" name="misc2000" id="misc2000" /></td>
    <td><input type="text" name="misc2001" id="misc2001" /></td>
    <td><input type="text" name="misc2002" id="misc2002" /></td>
  </tr>
  <tr>
    <th scope="row">Total</th>
    <td><input type="text" name="total1999" id="total1999" /></td>
    <td><input type="text" name="total2000" id="total2000" /></td>
    <td><input type="text" name="total2001" id="total2001" /></td>
    <td><input type="text" name="total2002" id="total2002" /></td>
  </tr>
</table>
<div><input type="submit" name="btnSubmit" id="btnSubmit"
      value="Add Data" /></div>
</form>
```

spreadsheet.css

```
table.formdata {
  border: 1px solid #5F6F7E;
  border-collapse: collapse;
  margin: 1em 0 2em 0;
}
table.formdata th {
  border: 1px solid #5F6F7E;
  background-color: #E2E2E2;
  color: #000000;
  text-align: left;
  font-weight: normal;
  padding: 0.2em 0.4em 0.2em 0.4em;
  margin: 0;
}
table.formdata td {
  margin: 0;
  padding: 0;
  border: 1px solid #E2E2E2;
}
table.formdata input {
  width: 80px;
  padding: 0.2em 0.4em 0.2em 0.4em;
  margin: 0;
```

```
    border: none;
}
```

The styled form, which looks very spreadsheet-like, is shown in Figure 6.15.

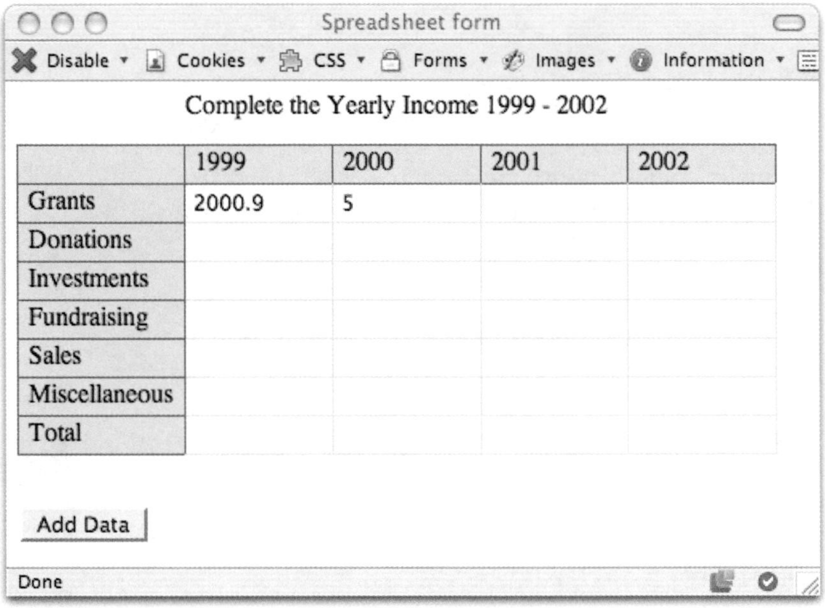

Figure 6.15. A form styled to resemble a spreadsheet

Discussion

The aim here is to create a form that looks similar to a spreadsheet, such as the Excel spreadsheet shown in Figure 6.16. Recently, I created forms similar to this for a web application that had many tables of data. The client wanted the table to turn into an editable table when it was selected for editing—while it retained the appearance of the original data table, the contents could be edited by the user.

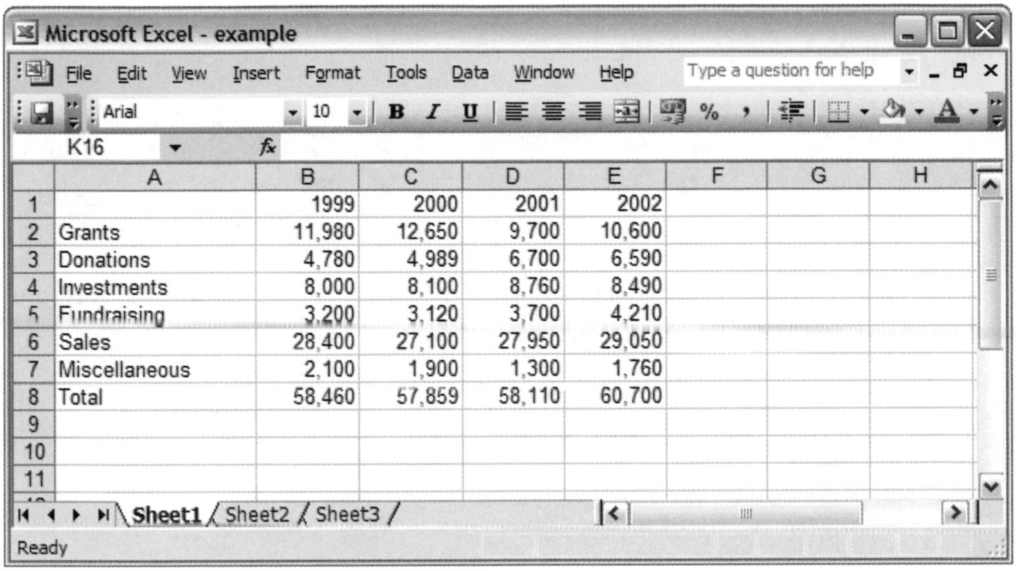

Figure 6.16. A spreadsheet displaying in Excel

The first step to achieve this effect is to lay out the form within a structured table, using table headings (th elements) where appropriate, and adding a caption and summary for accessibility purposes. The complete code for this form is provided in the solution above. Before we add any CSS, the form should display as shown in Figure 6.17.

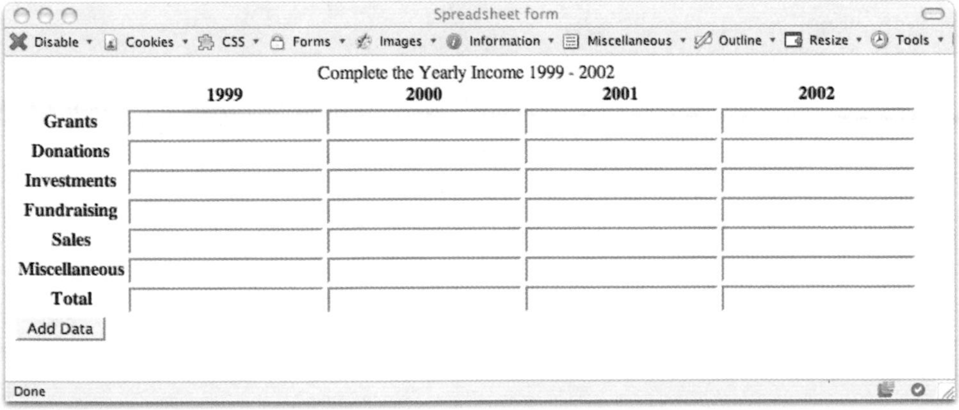

Figure 6.17. The unstyled form, ready for CSS formatting

To create the style rules for this form, we must establish for the table a `class` that contains all the spreadsheet fields. I've given the table a class name of `formdata`:

spreadsheet.html *(excerpt)*

```
<table class="formdata" summary="This table contains a form to
    input the yearly income for years 1999 through 2002">
```

In the style sheet, class `formdata` has a single-pixel border in a dark, slate gray, and the `border-collapse` property is set to `collapse`:

spreadsheet.css *(excerpt)*

```
table.formdata {
  border: 1px solid #5F6F7E;
  border-collapse: collapse;
}
```

Next, we can style the table headings. I've used the `<th>` tag for the top and left-hand column headings, so to style these, all I need to do is address the `<th>` tags within a table of class `formdata`:

spreadsheet.css *(excerpt)*

```
table.formdata th {
  border: 1px solid #5F6F7E;
  background-color: #E2E2E2;
  color: #000000;
  text-align: left;
  font-weight: normal;
  padding: 0.2em 0.4em 0.2em 0.4em;
  margin: 0;
}
```

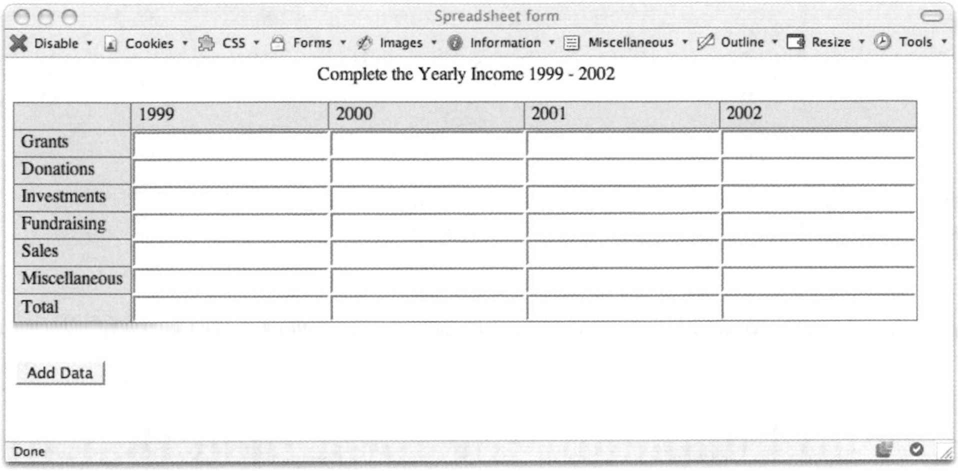

Figure 6.18. The form display after the `table` and `th` elements are styled

To produce an editable table, we need to hide the borders of the form fields and add borders to the table cells. As the only `input` elements within the table are the text fields that we want to style, we can simply address all `input` elements in the table with a class of `formdata`; this saves us having to add classes to all our fields.

We add a border to the `td` element, and set the borders on the `input` element to `0`. We specify a width for the `input` element, as we know that the type of data that will be added won't need a large field. We then add some padding so that text that's typed into the form field doesn't bump up against the border:

spreadsheet.css (excerpt)

```
table.formdata td {
  margin: 0;
  padding: 0;
  border: 1px solid #E2E2E2;
}
table.formdata input {
  width: 80px;
  padding: 0.2em 0.4em 0.2em 0.4em;
  margin: 0;
  border-width: 0;
  border-style: none;
}
```

That's all there is to it! If you use this technique, make sure that your users understand that the table is editable. Removing borders from form fields isn't going to help users if it means they can't work out how to complete the form—or don't even realize that the form exists!

Some Browsers Still Display Input Element Borders

Certain browsers—most notably Safari on Mac OS X—will display the input element borders, so while the effect won't be quite as neat, it will still be completely usable.

How do I highlight the form field that the user clicks into?

Applications such as Excel highlight the focused form field when the user clicks on it or tabs to it. Is it possible to create this effect in our web form?

Solution

We can create this effect using pure CSS, thanks to the :focus pseudo-class. While this solution works in Internet Explorer 7, unfortunately it doesn't work in the more commonly used Internet Explorer 6:

spreadsheet2.css *(excerpt)*

```
table.formdata input {
  width: 80px;
  padding: 0.2em 0.4em 0.2em 0.4em;
  margin: 0;
  border: 2px solid #ffffff;
}
.formdata input:focus {
  border: 2px solid #000000;
}
```

Figure 6.19 shows how this code displays.

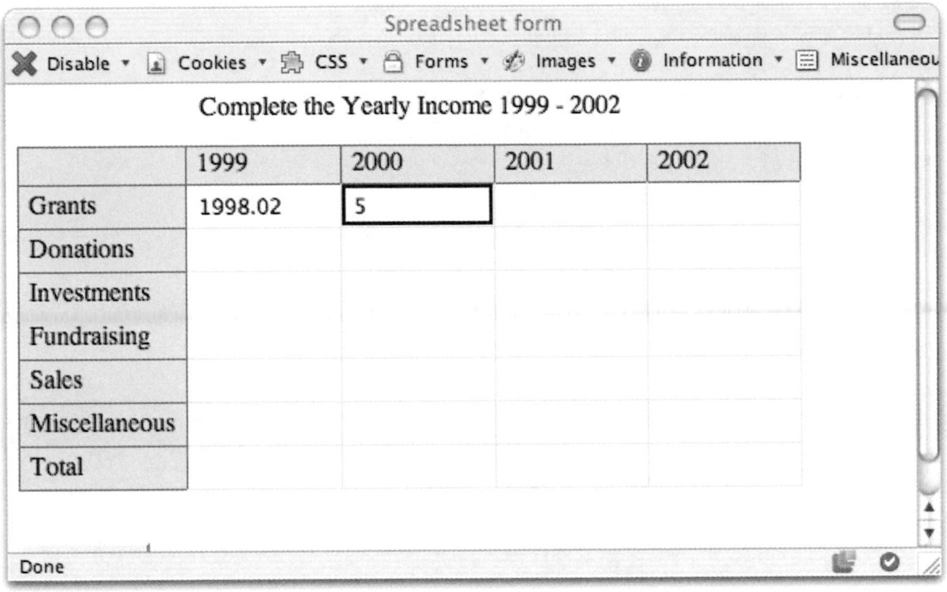

Figure 6.19. Highlighting the form field in focus in Firefox

Discussion

This solution for adding a border (or changing the background color) of the form field when it receives focus is a simple one. In fact, it's as simple as adding the pseudo-class selector `:focus` to your style sheet to display a different style for the `input` element when the user clicks into it.

Unfortunately, as I've already mentioned, Internet Explorer 6 does not support the `:focus` pseudo-class, so this effect will not display for a large number of your application's users.

There is a way around this problem that, unfortunately, requires a little JavaScript. Add the following JavaScript after the table in your document:

spreadsheet2.html *(excerpt)*

```
<script type="text/javascript">
var editcells =
  document.getElementById('form1').getElementsByTagName('input');
for (var i = 0; i < editcells.length; i++) {
```

```
    editcells[i].onfocus = function() {
      this.className += ' hilite';
    }
    editcells[i].onblur = function() {
      this.className = this.className.replace('hilite', '');
    }
  }
</script>
```

Once you've added this code, you'll need to add the class `hilite` to your CSS file, using the same rules we used for the `:focus` pseudo-class:

spreadsheet2.css (excerpt)

```
.formdata input:focus, .formdata input.hilite {
  border: 2px solid #000000;
}
```

Your field highlighting will now work in Internet Explorer 6 as well as those browsers that support the `:focus` pseudo-class.

Summary

In this chapter, we've looked at a variety of ways to style forms using CSS, from simply changing the look of form elements, to using CSS to lay forms out. We've seen how CSS can greatly enhance the appearance and usability of forms. We've also touched on the accessibility of forms for users of alternative devices, and we've seen how, by being careful when marking forms up, you can make it easier for all visitors to use your site or web application.

Cross-browser Techniques

This chapter contains solutions for making your sites work well in many browsers. It's unlikely that every visitor to your site is using the most up-to-date version of Internet Explorer, Firefox, or Safari, so you'll want to take the time to ensure that users with older or less common browsers enjoy their experience of your site.

As we've seen, you can use CSS to separate the structure and content of your documents from the presentation of your site. If you take this approach, visitors who use devices that can't render your design—either because they're limited from a technical standpoint, such as some PDA or phone browsers, or as a result of their own functional advantages, such as screen readers that speak your pages' text for the benefit of visually impaired users—will still be able to access the content. CSS gives you the freedom to meet the needs of these users *and* to create beautiful designs for the majority of users, whose browsers do support CSS.

As well as discussing the nuances of different browsers and devices, this chapter will provide you with techniques to troubleshoot CSS bugs in browsers that support CSS. Keep in mind that this chapter couldn't possibly cover every known CSS bug—even if it tried, it would likely be out of date before it was printed, as new bugs, and new bug fixes, appear all the time. What I've tried to do here is explain some of the main culprits that cause browser-related problems with CSS. I've explained how those problems might be solved, where you can go to get up-to-date bug-squashing advice, and how to step through a problem, isolate its cause, and ask for help in a way that's likely to get you a useful answer.

In which browsers should I test my site?

Once upon a time, web designers only worried whether or not their sites looked good in Internet Explorer and Netscape Navigator; those days are now long gone. While Internet Explorer currently has the largest share of the browser market, several other important desktop—and other—browsers are in use, including screen readers, and browsers on PDAs and web phones.

Solution

The answer to this question is to test your sites in as many browsers as you can. The types of browsers that you're able to install will depend on the operating systems to which you have access. Table 7.1 lists the major browsers that can be installed on Windows, Mac OS X, and Linux. At the very least, you're likely to want to test in Internet Explorer 6 and 7, a Mozilla-based browser, Opera, and if your operating system allows it, a KHTML-based browser such as Konqueror or Safari.

 Tracking Down Obscure and Obsolete Browsers

Older and more unusual browsers can be downloaded from http://browsers.evolt.org/.

I only have access to one operating system. How can I test in more of these browsers?

Unless you have an entire test suite in your office, you'll probably find that you're unable to install certain browsers because they're operating-system specific. For a list of the most popular browsers, see Table 7.1.

Table 7.1. Popular browsers

Browser (Engine)	Win	Mac	Linux	Download From
Internet Explorer 6 and older	✓			http://browsers.evolt.org/?ie/32bit/standalone
Internet Explorer 7	✓			http://www.microsoft.com/ie/
Firefox (Gecko)	✓	✓	✓	http://www.mozilla.com/
Camino (Gecko)		✓		http://www.caminobrowser.org/
Opera	✓	✓	✓	http://www.opera.com/
Safari (WebCore)	✓	✓		http://www.apple.com/safari/

Solution

There are a variety of solutions that will let you run an additional operating system on your computer, thereby giving you the ability to install and use the browsers developed for that operating system.

Windows Users

Windows users are in a good position to test on a wide variety of browsers. Internet Explorer, in its various incarnations, accounts for roughly 70–80% of the general browsing public, and most of the other major browsers offer Windows versions. Unfortunately, when it comes to testing on Mac-only browsers such as Safari, the options available in Windows are limited.

Testing on Mac Browsers

Mac OS X is the most difficult platform to emulate at present. Having a Mac around is therefore almost essential for any serious web designer—though your Mac doesn't need to be particularly fast or have an enormous amount of memory if all you use it for is testing sites in Safari.

It's possible to emulate the Mac OS X operating system on a Windows XP machine to some extent, using an open source emulator called PearPC.[1] However, at the time

---

[1] http://pearpc.sourceforge.net/

of writing, the emulator was slow, buggy, and incomplete. Future releases of PearPC may deliver a viable option for running Safari under Windows, but at the time of writing it was more useful for geeks who enjoy tinkering with emulators than for web designers seeking a robust testing platform.

In mid-2007, Apple surprised the web community by releasing a version of its Safari browser for Windows. Unfortunately, Safari for Windows could never be relied upon to render a page that's identical to its older (and more popular) Mac-based cousin. It can, however, be useful as an indication of where possible rendering problems may lie.

Testing on Linux Browsers

While there's currently no way to emulate a Mac on a Windows computer, various options are available to those who would like to be able to view sites in Linux-specific browsers.

Linux Live CDs

Live CDs are versions of Linux that run completely from a CD, and can be run as a testing environment on your computer without you needing to actually install Linux onto your hard disk. One of the most well known of the Live CDs is Knoppix, which can be downloaded from The Knoppix web site.[2] Knoppix comes with the KDE desktop environment, which includes Konqueror. A comprehensive list of other Live CDs—such as the Ubuntu Live CD, which has the Gnome desktop as standard—is available at FrozenTech.[3]

Dual Booting with Linux

Another option, if you want to run another operating system, is to dual boot your computer. You can install Windows and Linux, then select the platform you want to boot into when you start up your machine. A good walkthrough of the process you'll need to use to get your dual-boot system up and running can be found at the About Debian Linux site.[4]

---

[2] http://www.knoppix.net/
[3] http://www.frozentech.com/content/livecd.php
[4] http://www.aboutdebian.com/dualboot.htm

Mac Users

Mac users who have newer Intel Macs can feel smug—your environment can easily be used to test sites in all three operating systems. Even if you have a PowerPC Mac, you can still test both Windows and Mac browsers, albeit more slowly than is possible with an Intel Mac.

Testing on Windows Browsers

Mac users who want to test sites on Windows browsers have three options.

Parallels

Since Apple launched its new Intel-based machines, customers have been able to run virtual machines as VMWare does: via the third party application Parallels, pictured in Figure 7.1.[5] You can run both Windows and Linux in Parallels. You can even run multiple versions of Windows, so you can test Internet Explorer 6 and 7 on the same computer!

Boot Camp

Another option for Mac users wishing to install Windows is the Boot Camp software, which enables you to dual boot your Intel Mac with Windows.[6] Unlike Parallels or other virtual machine software, Boot Camp will require you to reboot into Windows—it won't allow you to run Windows inside a window on your desktop—but it does offer another way in which to test your work.

If you are a designer who wants to be able to work on only one machine, the Intel Macs are well worth investigating, and I say that as a Linux desktop user!

---

[5] http://www.parallels.com/
[6] http://www.apple.com/macosx/bootcamp/

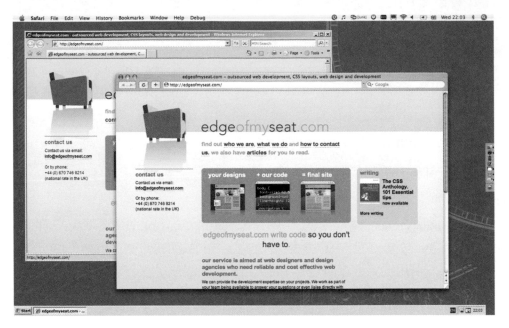

Figure 7.1. Internet Explorer 7 and Safari on an Intel Mac using Parallels

Virtual PC for Mac

Microsoft Virtual PC for Mac enables Mac users who aren't lucky enough to be using an Intel Mac to install and run Windows applications. Find out more at Microsoft's Mactopia.[7]

Linux Users

Linux users are in much the same boat as Windows users when it comes to testing on Mac-only browsers. On the bright side, Wine and VMWare offer convenient ways for Linux users to run various versions of Internet Explorer without needing to reboot their machines.

Testing on Mac Browsers

The only option for running Safari on a Linux machine is to use an open source emulator called PearPC.[8] However, at the time of writing, the emulator was slow, buggy, and incomplete, and could not be relied upon as a robust testing platform.

---

[7] http://www.microsoft.com/mac/products/virtualpc/virtualpc.aspx
[8] http://pearpc.sourceforge.net/

However, since Safari is based on the KHTML rendering engine, which is also used by (and was originally developed by) the KDE browser Konqueror, Konqueror tends to render things in a similar way to Safari. This is certainly no substitute for having a Mac on hand to use for testing, but it can provide a rough indication of how your pages will render in Safari.

Testing on Windows Browsers

As with Windows, the easiest option for Linux users who want to test sites on Windows browsers is usually to dual boot their machines, but a number of tools that facilitate side-by-side testing with Windows browsers on Linux are available.

VMWare

A version of VMWare is available for Linux; it allows users to run a Linux host system and create VMWare virtual machines on which they can install other operating systems, such as Windows.

Wine

Wine is an open source implementation of the Windows API, which runs on top of Linux. Installing Wine will enable you to run some Windows programs in Linux—with varying success! You can find out more about Wine at Wine HQ.[9] The Internet Explorer packages created especially to run under Wine make the install process far simpler. They're available from IEs 4 Linux.[10]

Far easier to install and configure than Wine itself is Crossover Office.[11] This commercial product, which incorporates Wine, allows customers to install Windows applications on Linux; Internet Explorer 6 is currently supported.

Dual Booting

Linux users also have the option of dual booting their system as a way to install a version of Windows—as much as it may pain them to do so!

---

[9] http://www.winehq.com/
[10] http://www.tatanka.com.br/ies4linux/
[11] http://www.codeweavers.com/

Is there a service that can show me how my site looks in various browsers?

Being able to test your site in a variety of browsers is the best way to check that it works well in all of them; however, unless you can set up a test suite in your office, it's likely that there'll be some browsers to which you won't have access.

Solution

You can check how your site displays and functions in multiple browsers on multiple operating systems at BrowserCam.[12]

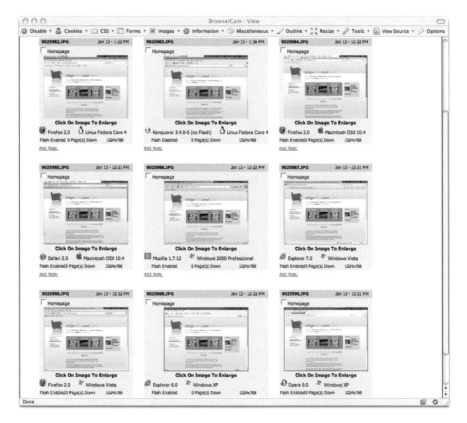

Figure 7.2. Using BrowserCam to test a site

---

[12] http://www.browsercam.com/

You'll have to pay for this service, but if you only have access to one operating system, BrowserCam can be a great way to get a feel for your site's behavior in browsers that you couldn't otherwise access. A sample of the results BrowserCam displays can be seen in Figure 7.2.

Discussion

In addition to the screenshot service depicted in Figure 7.2, BrowserCam offers a service called Remote Access through which you can log into one of its machines directly to test your site on an alternative platform. This service is particularly helpful if you've used JavaScript, and need to interact with your page to see how things look. In addition to BrowserCam, free services, such as iCapture,[13] which takes screenshots of sites in Safari on OS X, and SiteVista,[14] are also available.

BrowserCam Group Purchases

While a full subscription to BrowserCam might seem expensive, a low-cost way to gain access to the service is to join up as part of a group. A group annual subscription allows up to 25 people to access the service concurrently. If you don't have 25 friends who are willing to chip in, check out sites like Fundable,[15] whose users often organize group purchases—just perform a site search for BrowserCam. Or you could get a bunch of people together through a web design-related mailing list of which you are a member.

Another way to check that your site works in browsers to which you don't have access is to request a site check on a mailing list. Most web design and development mailing lists and forums, including the SitePoint Forums,[16] are quite used to having users ask for people to check their sites, and you can return the favor by viewing other people's sites in the browsers that you use.

---

[13] http://www.danvine.com/icapture/
[14] http://www.sitevista.com/
[15] http://fundable.org/
[16] http://www.sitepoint.com/forums/

Can I install multiple versions of Internet Explorer on Windows?

There are major differences between Internet Explorer 7 and Internet Explorer 6 in terms of the ways they render CSS, but Windows normally allows only one version of Internet Explorer to be installed at a time. How can we test sites in older, but still used, versions of Internet Explorer?

Solution

Microsoft's Virtual PC 2007 software enables us to test both Internet Explorer 6 and 7 on one computer, and is available as a free download. You'll need to take a few steps to get your Windows machine running Internet Explorer 7 as the main browser, and a virtual machine running Internet Explorer 6, but this is a great way to test your work.

1. Upgrade to Internet Explorer 7 if you haven't done so already.

2. Download and install Virtual PC 2007 from Microsoft's Virtual PC site.[17]

3. Download a time-limited Virtual PC virtual machine image from Microsoft's Download Center.[18] This image comes with Microsoft Windows XP SP2 and Internet Explorer 6 pre-installed. The beauty of using this image is that you don't need to pay for an additional Windows license to run it. You can get additional information on this issue from the official Internet Explorer blog.[19]

4. To use the virtual machine image, extract the archive and start up Virtual PC. Browse for the image files, and your separate version of Windows will start up in a window on your desktop.

At the time of writing, Microsoft doesn't offer virtual machine images for earlier versions of Internet Explorer; however, some standalone versions are available to help you spot CSS rendering issues. You can download an installer of multiple

---

[17] http://www.microsoft.com/windows/virtualpc/default.mspx
[18] http://go.microsoft.com/fwlink/?LinkId=70868
[19] http://blogs.msdn.com/ie/archive/2006/11/30/ie6-and-ie7-running-on-a-single-machine.aspx

standalone versions of Internet Explorer at Tredosoft.[20] These browsers can be temperamental and prone to crashing. These versions are also not reliable for testing JavaScript, since they use the currently installed JScript engine, not the older versions of JScript that would normally be installed with these versions of Internet Explorer. However, these browsers are reliable enough for CSS developers who want to test their work.

In Figure 7.3, the three browsers running on my Windows XP machine (which has Internet Explorer 6 installed by default) display the same page: an example of a bug, documented on Position is Everything.[21] The browser at top left is Internet Explorer 5, which displays the content using its particular implementation of the box model. The top-right browser is Internet Explorer 5.5; it displays the "phantom boxes" that the demo is presenting. At the bottom is Internet Explorer 6, which renders the site correctly.

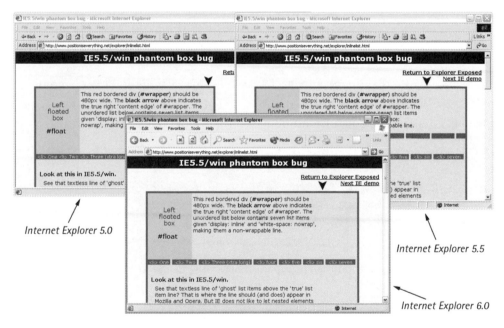

Figure 7.3. Three versions of Internet Explorer running on one computer

[20] http://tredosoft.com/Multiple_IE
[21] http://www.positioniseverything.net/explorer/inlinelist.html

How do I display a basic style sheet for really old browsers?

CSS is now used so extensively on the Web that users of really old browsers, such as Netscape 4, are destined to have fairly poor online experiences, regardless of which sites they visit. However, we can still be kind to users of these old browsers by at least making sure that our advanced use of CSS doesn't crash the browser, or cause the content to be completely unreadable. To do this, we serve a very simple style sheet to these browsers, and attach our real style sheet using a technique that older browsers don't understand.

Solution

Netscape 4 and other old browsers don't understand the import method of linking to a style sheet. We can use this fact to our advantage, serving one set of styles to these browsers, and leaving newer browsers, which understand import, to read the full style sheet.

In the head of your document, attach a basic style sheet using the link element—this can be read by all browsers that support CSS. Then, attach your full style sheet (or style sheets) using the import method, which will not be read by the old browsers:

basicstyles.html

```
<!DOCTYPE html PUBLIC "-//W3C//DTD XHTML 1.0 Strict//EN"
    "http://www.w3.org/TR/xhtml1/DTD/xhtml1-strict.dtd">
<html xmlns="http://www.w3.org/1999/xhtml"
    xml:lang="en" lang="en">
<head>
  <meta http-equiv="content-type" content="text/html;
      charset=utf-8" />
  <title>Serving a basic style sheet</title>
  <link rel="stylesheet" href="basic_basic.css" type="text/css"
      media="screen"  />
  <style type="text/css" media="screen">@import
      "basic_default.css";</style>
</head>
<body>
  <div class="content">
  <h1>Serving a basic style sheet to old browsers</h1>
```

```
<p>CSS is now used so extensively on the web that users of really
    old browsers such as Netscape 4 are going to have a pretty
    poor experience all in all. However, we can still be kind to
    users of really old browsers by at least making sure our
    advanced use of CSS doesn't crash their browser or cause the
    content to be completely unreadable. The way we do this is to
    serve a very simple style sheet to these browsers and attach
    our real style sheet using a manner that they do not
    understand.</p>
  </div>
</body>
</html>
```

The basic style sheet shown below—**basic_basic.css**—defines some simple styles to boost the page's readability. You could make this style sheet slightly more advanced if you wish, assuming you have a copy of Netscape 4 to test on, and can check that anything you add is safe for that browser. However, at the current time, very few people use these old browsers. Presenting them with a basic document should be fine—it will at least ensure that the site is readable for them, in contrast to much of the rest of the Web.

basic_basic.css

```
body {
  background-color: #fff;
  color: #000;
  margin: 0;
  padding: 5%;
}

body, h1, h2, h3, h4, h5, h6, ol, ul, li, p {
  font-family: verdana, arial, helvetica, sans-serif;
  color: #000;
}
```

Keep in mind that the newer browsers will read both the linked and imported style sheets, so within your site's main style sheet, you'll need to override any of the basic styles that you don't want to appear in newer browsers, as well as applying the styles you want users of newer browsers to see.

In the code below, I've added a few rules to demonstrate the effects of this approach, which can be seen in Figure 7.4 and Figure 7.5.

```css
h1 {
  color: #cc0022;
  margin: 0;
}

.content {
  background-color: #ececec;
  padding: 0.6em;
}
```
basic_default.css

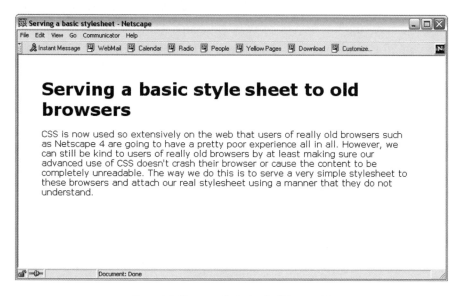

Figure 7.4. The page displaying in Netscape 4.8

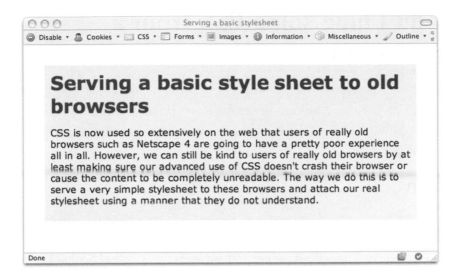

Figure 7.5. The same page displaying in Firefox 2

Discussion

Browsers that offer very minimal CSS support are problematic because they understand just enough CSS to attempt to render your styles, but not enough to be able to do so properly! The advanced CSS in use on an average site today is likely to display poorly or even crash a very old browser, so hiding these styles with the help of `import` prevents this. You don't even need to add a basic style sheet—if you simply use `import` on its own, those old browsers will display the document using the browser's internal styles.

However, the use of the basic linked style sheet offers an additional benefit: it lets us avoid the Flash of Unstyled Content phenomenon.[22] This annoying bug causes Internet Explorer users to see the site with the default Internet Explorer styles momentarily before the styles from your style sheet load in. Adding a link before the import—as we do in this solution—also solves that problem. So we're able to be kind to a couple of generations of crumbly browsers with one trick!

---

[22] http://www.bluerobot.com/web/css/fouc.asp/

How do I hide some CSS from a particular browser?

You might have discovered that certain CSS rules, or sets of rules, simply break in newer browsers as a result of bugs in the browsers themselves. How can we hide certain parts of our CSS in order to cope with bugs in browsers that, otherwise, display our CSS well?

Solution

As no browser has a perfect implementation of CSS, we can make use of bugs and features that are not supported in particular browsers to hide certain properties from those browsers. These kinds of techniques are referred to as **CSS hacks** or **filters**.

The solution below illustrates a commonly used hack that helps us cope with the rendering differences between Internet Explorer 5.x, and later versions of the browser. For information about other hacks that are available, refer to the discussion below.

The Box Model Hack

Internet Explorer 5 and 5.5 interpret the CSS box model incorrectly. A correct implementation of the CSS box model will add to the specified width of a given block any padding and borders that have been applied to that block, to calculate the actual visible width of the block. So a `div` that's 200 pixels wide, and has 20 pixels of padding on both the right and left, and a five-pixel border, will have a total width of 250 pixels. In the world of Internet Explorer 5, however, the width of this `div` will total 200 pixels *including* the borders and padding. As you can imagine, this rendering issue will make a mess of any CSS layout that relies on the precise widths of page elements.

The problem can be seen clearly in Figure 7.6. The browser pictured at the top is Internet Explorer 5, which, with its incorrect implementation of the box model, displays the `div` 50 pixels narrower than does Internet Explorer 6. The latter browser uses a correct implementation of the box model.

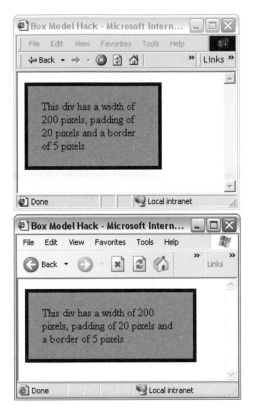

Figure 7.6. Internet Explorer 5 and 6 displaying different implementations of the box model

Here's the code that's being displayed in Figure 7.6:

box-model-hack.html (excerpt)

```
<!DOCTYPE html PUBLIC "-//W3C//DTD XHTML 1.0 Strict//EN"
    "http://www.w3.org/TR/xhtml1/DTD/xhtml1-strict.dtd">
<html xmlns="http://www.w3.org/1999/xhtml" lang="en-US">
<head>
<title>Box Model Hack</title>
<meta http-equiv="content-type"
    content="text/html; charset=utf-8" />
<link rel="stylesheet" type="text/css" href="box-model-hack.css"
    />
</head>
<body>
<div id="mybox">
<p>This div has a width of 200 pixels, padding of 20 pixels and a
```

```
      border of 5 pixels.</p>
</div>
</body>
</html>
```

box-model-hack.css

```
#mybox {
  padding: 20px;
  border: 5px solid #000000;
  background-color: #00BFFF;
  width: 200px;
}
```

To make Internet Explorer 5 display the box at the same width as newer browsers that accurately comply with box model implementation, we need to specify a width of 250 pixels for the box in Internet Explorer 5 and 5.5 *only*.

To achieve this, we can take advantage of a bug in the Internet Explorer 5/5.5 CSS parser, using a method developed by Tantek Çelik:[23]

box-model-hack2.css

```
#mybox {
  padding: 20px;
  border: 5px solid #000000;
  background-color: #00BFFF;
}
#mybox {
  width: 250px;
  voice-family: "\"}\"";
  voice-family: inherit;
  width: 200px;
}
html > body #mybox {
  width: 200px;
}
```

With this style sheet, the two browsers agree on the width of the box, as Figure 7.7 illustrates.

---

[23] http://tantek.com/CSS/Examples/boxmodelhack.html

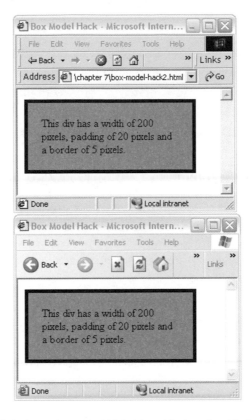

Figure 7.7. The box displaying at the same width in Internet Explorer 5 and 6 after we apply the filter

This trick works because, with the hack in place, Internet Explorer 5/5.5 does not see the second or third occurrences of the width property, and therefore renders the box at the first specified width (250 pixels). Standards-compliant browsers render the box at the second, correct width (200 pixels). The final declaration addresses browsers that have the same parsing bug as Internet Explorer 5/5.5, but implement a correct box model, ensuring that they display the correct width. This has become known as the "be nice to Opera 5" rule, as it's one of the browsers affected.

There are other versions of this hack, but when people refer to using "the box model hack," they're generally talking about this or a very similar variation.

Discussion

The box model hack is frequently seen on web sites and within example style sheets that are made available for download, so you may well come across it in your work, but this solution also serves as an explanation of how to use CSS hacks and filters. A whole range of hacks and filters is available to help you address specific browsers, and the nature of some bugs will likely see you resort to using them.

Avoid Hacks if Possible!

Using a hack should be a last resort after you have tried to get your page to render consistently using regular CSS techniques. Before you use a CSS hack, make sure that it really is the only way you can achieve the effect you want. Sometimes, you can work around a bug by changing your approach slightly; at other times, the difference doesn't really matter and the site still looks reasonably good in the buggy browsers.

CSS hacks make your code less readable, and can damage the forwards-compatibility of your site. CSS hacks depend on two bugs: the layout problem you're attempting to work around, and the bug that allows you to target or filter the browser. Since it's impossible to predict which bugs will be fixed first, avoid CSS hacks if you can.

Choosing a Hack

If you do decide that you really must use a hack, try to find something that works due to a *lack* of support in the browser from which you want to hide the CSS, rather than an incorrect implementation of the CSS specification. That way, you're unlikely to have any problems when a newer browser is released.

The available information on hacks changes all the time as new browser versions are released, and new hacks discovered, so it's worth bookmarking a site that has an up-to-date hacks list, and checking it for new information if you experience problems with a specific browser.

My favorite sites for this type of information are:

■ CSS Filters from the now-defunct dithered.com, at Communis (http://www.communis.co.uk/dithered/css_filters/index.html)

- the CSS Hack category on the CSS-Discuss Wiki
  (http://css-discuss.incutio.com/?page=CssHack)
- the articles on Position Is Everything
  (http://positioniseverything.net/articles.html)

Commenting Hacks

Once your hack is in place, be sure to comment it properly. When you come back to the site at a later date, you may not remember why you implemented the hack, and anyone who takes over from you or works on your team may become confused by the less common hacks if they can't see at a glance what's going on. Here's an example of appropriate hack commenting:

box-model-hack2.css *(excerpt)*

```css
/* box model hack -
   see http://tantek.com/CSS/Examples/boxmodelhack.html */
#mybox {
  width: 250px;
  voice-family: "\"}\"";
  voice-family: inherit;
  width: 200px;
}
html > body #mybox {
  width: 200px;
}
```

How can I send different styles to a particular browser?

At the time of writing, the biggest problem for CSS developers is the large number of people still using Internet Explorer 6—a browser that provides poor, buggy support for much of the CSS spec. While Microsoft fixed most of the well-known bugs and added support for much more of the CSS 2.1 spec in Internet Explorer 7, we've been left with a group of users who cannot or will not upgrade beyond Internet Explorer 6.

Solution

There are two methods by which you can target Internet Explorer 6 and serve it specific rules. Some filters exist for targeting other browsers; see "How do I hide some CSS from a particular browser?" for details.

CSS Hacks or Filters

The first option is to use a CSS hack within your style sheet to show specific information to the browser. For example, the **star html hack** is a common hack that uses a bug in Internet Explorer 6 and 5.5 to render rules placed after * html. This hack is commonly used to get around the lack of min-height in Internet Explorer 6:

```
/* rules for standards-savvy browsers, including IE7 */
.box {
  min-height: 100px;
}
/* for IE6 and below */
* html .box {
  height: 100px;
}
```

Internet Explorer 6 does not support min-height (the minimum height an element should take), but it incorrectly interprets height as min-height. So, though height is used to specify a fixed height in other browsers, Internet Explorer 6 takes it to mean the minimum height, so the box will expand taller than 100 pixels if need be. Of course, if we were to serve more compliant browsers height when we meant min-height, they would chop off the bottom of our content in cases where it became taller than 100 pixels!

To work around this issue, we first use min-height correctly for all of the other browsers; then, we use the star html hack before the selector that only Internet Explorer 5.5 and Internet Explorer 6 will take note of. More compliant browsers will ignore this hack.

Conditional Comments

The second method we can use to target our rules to specific browsers is conditional comments. We use these to link to our page a style sheet that's read only by the version of Internet Explorer that's targeted by the comments. This approach is very useful if you have a lot of rules that are specific to a particular version of Internet Explorer. The conditional comments need to go into the `head` of your document—you'd usually include them as the last style sheet in the `head`, as it's likely that you'll override rules that apply to other browsers with your Internet Explorer tweaks.

First, create your style sheet containing the Internet Explorer fixes—you don't need to duplicate your entire style sheet, just override or add the rules necessary to help Internet Explorer behave. Then, include the link to the style sheet within a conditional comment in the `head` of your document, like this:

```
<!--[if IE 6]>
<link rel="stylesheet" type="text/css" href="ie6.css" />
<![endif]-->
```

Discussion

Choosing whether to use a filter or conditional comments will depend on the amount of edits you need to make to your style sheet to have Internet Explorer 6 render your page appropriately.

If you have just a couple of `min-height` fixes to add, it may make more sense to use the star html hack and be able to keep that Internet Explorer 6 information in the same place as the real style rules (commented, of course!). But if you have a lot of changes to make, another style sheet will keep them tidily out of the way. In the solutions that follow, we'll look at the use of conditional comments to serve Internet Explorer 6 an additional style sheet as well as a JavaScript file.

How do I achieve alpha transparency in Internet Explorer 6?

One of the exciting additions to Internet Explorer 7 was support of PNG transparency. As I showed in Chapter 3 when we discussed background images, alpha transparency can give you true transparency, allowing overlaid images to display across different background colors without showing a pixelated halo, and allowing designers to create effects using opaque background layers. However, if you simply go ahead and use transparent PNGs, users of Internet Explorer 6 will see solid images like those shown in Figure 7.8. Is there anything that can be done to get transparent PNGs to play nicely with Internet Explorer 6?

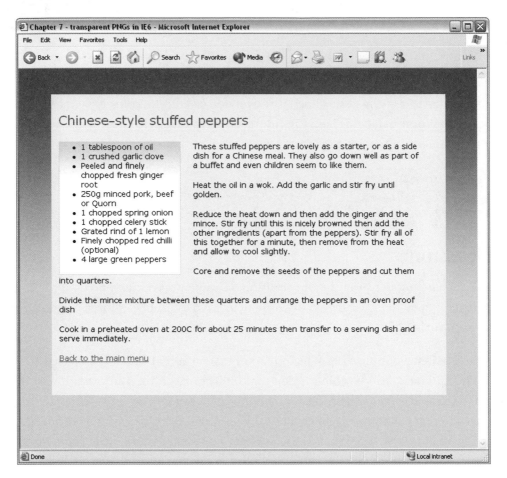

Figure 7.8. Internet Explorer 6 displaying the transparent PNG images as solid images

Solution

There is a way to get transparent PNGs to appear to work in Internet Explorer 6, but it involves the use of JavaScript. The solution was originally devised by Aaron Boodman[24] and edited by Drew McLellan in order to support background images.[25]

First, create a 1×1px transparent GIF, and save it as **x.gif**.

---

[24] http://webapp.youngpup.net/?request=/snippets/sleight.xml

[25] http://allinthehead.com/retro/289/sleight-update-alpha-png-backgrounds-in-ie

Now, create a new JavaScript file (which we'll include only for Internet Explorer 6), and add the following JavaScript:

bgsleight.js

```javascript
function addLoadEvent(func) {
  var oldonload = window.onload;
  if (typeof window.onload != 'function') {
    window.onload = func;
  } else {
    window.onload = function() {
      if (oldonload) {
        oldonload();
      }
      func();
    }
  }
}


var bgsleight = function() {

function fnLoadPngs() {
var rslt = navigator.appVersion.match(/MSIE (\d+\.\d+)/, '');
var itsAllGood = (rslt != null && Number(rslt[1]) >= 5.5);
for (var i = document.all.length - 1, obj = null; (obj =
    document.all[i]); i--) {
  if (itsAllGood &&
      obj.currentStyle.backgroundImage.match(/\.png/i) != null) {
    fnFixPng(obj);
    obj.attachEvent("onpropertychange", fnPropertyChanged);
  }
  if ((obj.tagName=='A' || obj.tagName=='INPUT') &&
      obj.style.position == ''){
  obj.style.position = 'relative';
  }
 }
}

function fnPropertyChanged() {
 if (window.event.propertyName == "style.backgroundImage") {
  var el = window.event.srcElement;
   if (!el.currentStyle.backgroundImage.match(/x\.gif/i)) {
    var bg = el.currentStyle.backgroundImage;
```

```
    var src = bg.substring(5,bg.length-2);
    el.filters.item(0).src = src;
    el.style.backgroundImage = "url(/img/shim.gif)";
   }
  }
 }

 function fnFixPng(obj) {
  var mode = 'scale';
  var bg = obj.currentStyle.backgroundImage;
  var src = bg.substring(5,bg.length-2);
  if (obj.currentStyle.backgroundRepeat == 'no-repeat') mode =
      'crop';
   obj.style.filter =
       "progid:DXImageTransform.Microsoft.AlphaImageLoader(src='"
       + src + "', sizingMethod='" + mode + "')";
   obj.style.backgroundImage = "url(/img/shim.gif)";
  }

  return {
  init: function() {
   if (navigator.platform == "Win32" && navigator.appName ==
       "Microsoft Internet Explorer" && window.attachEvent) {
   addLoadEvent(fnLoadPngs);
   }
  }
 }
}();

bgsleight.init();
```

Use a conditional comment to include the new JavaScript file so that it's used only by Internet Explorer:

bgsleight.html *(excerpt)*

```
<!--[if IE 6]>
<script type="text/javascript" src="bgsleight.js"></script>
<![endif]-->
```

If you save your page and view it in Internet Explorer at this point, you'll see that the background attached to the div element with ID content has disappeared. To make it display again, we'll need to give it a height. A height of just 1% will do—Internet Explorer will treat that as `min-height`, and will expand the `div` to contain all of its contents. As we want only Internet Explorer to see this `height` value, we can either put it in a `style` element in the document's `head`, or add it to a separate Internet Explorer 6-only style sheet that's linked to from within the conditional comments:

bgsleight.html *(excerpt)*

```
<!--[if IE 6]>
<style type="text/css">
#content {
  height: 1%;
}
</style>
<script type="text/javascript" src="bgsleight.js"></script>
<![endif]-->
```

Refresh your page in Internet Explorer, and the opaque background will display over the background color, as shown in Figure 7.9.

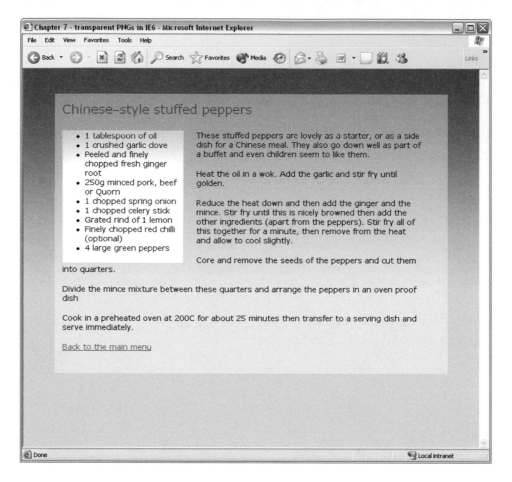

Figure 7.9. Internet Explorer 6 displaying the transparent PNG images

Discussion

This hack can be somewhat problematic. You may find that areas of the page appear as if covered by the background image, which makes links unclickable and text input fields unable to take focus. If that happens, you'll usually find that adding `position: relative` to the element fixes the problem, but it will also add a layer of complication to your work. That said, this option does enable the design flexibility that results from the use of proper transparency, and with a bit of care you can get it to work well.

Avoiding the Hack

Another way to deal with the issue would be to create different images for Internet Explorer 6, and add an Internet Explorer 6 style sheet that used non-transparent images to override the PNGs used for other browsers. The site would look different in Internet Explorer 6, but as that browser's usage declines, this may become an acceptable solution.

What is DOCTYPE switching and how do I use it?

You're developing a site using XHTML and CSS, testing in Internet Explorer 6 and 7, and it all seems to be going well … Then you look at the layout with Mozilla and realize it's displaying very differently to the way it's rendering in Internet Explorer. What's going on?

Solution

Internet Explorer bugs aside, the most likely issue is that Internet Explorer is rendering your document in **Quirks Mode**. Many modern browsers have two rendering modes. Quirks Mode renders documents according to the buggy implementations of older browsers such as Netscape 4 and Internet Explorer 4 and 5. Standards or **Compliance Mode** renders documents as per the W3C specifications.

- Documents that use older DOCTYPEs, are poorly formed, or have no DOCTYPE at all, display using Quirks Mode.
- Documents that are using strict HTML or XHTML DOCTYPEs render using Compliance Mode.

Unfortunately, it's not quite as simple as that where Internet Explorer 6 is concerned. For example, if you include anything at all above the DOCTYPE statement—including the XML declaration—Internet Explorer 6 will render in Quirks Mode.

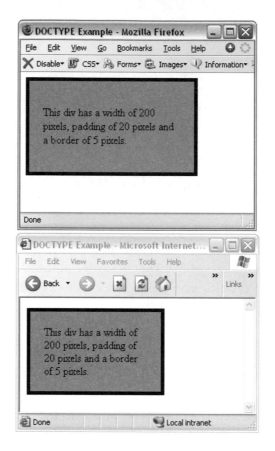

Figure 7.10. Internet Explorer in Quirks Mode rendering the same document differently than Firefox in Compliance Mode

Figure 7.10 shows the following document rendered in both Mozilla Firefox (at the top) and Internet Explorer 6 (at the bottom).

doctype-quirks.html

```
<?xml version="1.0" encoding="utf-8"?>
<!DOCTYPE html PUBLIC "-//W3C//DTD XHTML 1.0 Strict//EN"
    "http://www.w3.org/TR/xhtml1/DTD/xhtml1-strict.dtd">
<html xmlns="http://www.w3.org/1999/xhtml" lang="en-US">
<head>
<title>DOCTYPE Example</title>
<meta http-equiv="content-type"
    content="text/html; charset=utf-8" />
<link rel="stylesheet" type="text/css" href="box-model-hack.css"
    />
```

```
</head>
<body>
<div id="mybox">
  <p>This div has a width of 200 pixels, padding of 20 pixels and
    a border of 5 pixels.</p>
</div>
</body>
</html>
```

If you read about the box model hack in "How do I hide some CSS from a particular browser?", you might realize that, in Figure 7.10, Internet Explorer 6 renders the page with the broken CSS Box Model implementation used by Internet Explorer 5 and 5.5. It does so because we included the xml declaration above the DOCTYPE. If you delete this from the document, so that the DOCTYPE declaration is the first thing on the page, as shown in the code below, Internet Explorer will render in Compliance Mode, as Figure 7.11 illustrates. Internet Explorer 7 will not switch into Quirks Mode when it encounters an XML prologue, however, so it behaves much like the other newer browsers in that respect.

doctype-compliance.html

```
<!DOCTYPE html PUBLIC "-//W3C//DTD XHTML 1.0 Strict//EN"
    "http://www.w3.org/TR/xhtml1/DTD/xhtml1-strict.dtd">
<html xmlns="http://www.w3.org/1999/xhtml" lang="en-US">
<head>
<title>DOCTYPE Example</title>
<meta http-equiv="content-type"
    content="text/html; charset=utf-8" />
<link rel="stylesheet" type="text/css" href="box-model-hack.css"
    />
</head>
<body>
<div id="mybox">
  <p>This div has a width of 200 pixels, padding of 20 pixels and
    a border of 5 pixels.</p>
</div>
</body>
</html>
```

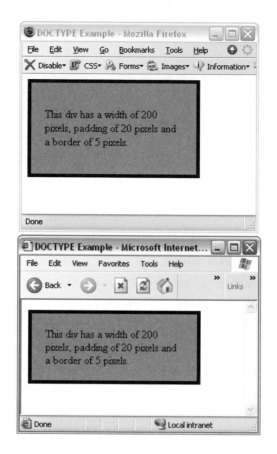

Figure 7.11. Internet Explorer and Firefox rendering the page in Compliance Mode

Discussion

If you're building a new site, I recommend that you aim to meet the requirements of Compliance Mode, whichever DTD you're working to. New browsers will be likely to support the W3C standards and will render pages using those standards whether or not they support any DOCTYPE switching.

If you continue to design for older browsers, and rely on Quirks Mode in their newer counterparts, you may find that your site doesn't work in a browser that doesn't have a Quirks Mode. It's better to work in Compliance Mode in new browsers, and deal with the older browsers using the fixes we've already discussed, as these are a known entity—the latest version of Mozilla is not!

The following DOCTYPEs should force the browsers that support DOCTYPE switching—Internet Explorer 6, Mozilla, Internet Explorer 5 Mac, and Opera 7—into Compliance Mode. Remember that even a comment above the DOCTYPE statement will switch Internet Explorer 6 back into Quirks Mode.[26]

HTML 4.01 Transitional

```
<!DOCTYPE HTML PUBLIC "-//W3C//DTD HTML 4.01 Transitional//EN"
    "http://www.w3.org/TR/html4/loose.dtd">
```

HTML 4.01 Frameset

```
<!DOCTYPE HTML PUBLIC "-//W3C//DTD HTML 4.01 Frameset//EN"
    "http://www.w3.org/TR/html4/frameset.dtd">
```

HTML 4.01 Strict

```
<!DOCTYPE HTML PUBLIC "-//W3C//DTD HTML 4.01//EN"
    "http://www.w3.org/TR/html4/strict.dtd">
```

XHTML 1.0 Transitional

```
<!DOCTYPE html PUBLIC "-//W3C//DTD XHTML 1.0 Transitional//EN"
    "http://www.w3.org/TR/xhtml1/DTD/xhtml1-transitional.dtd">
```

XHTML 1.0 Frameset

```
<!DOCTYPE html PUBLIC "-//W3C//DTD XHTML 1.0 Frameset//EN"
    "http://www.w3.org/TR/xhtml1/DTD/xhtml1-frameset.dtd">
```

XHTML 1.0 Strict

```
<!DOCTYPE html PUBLIC "-//W3C//DTD XHTML 1.0 Strict//EN"
    "http://www.w3.org/TR/xhtml1/DTD/xhtml1-strict.dtd">
```

---

[26] A full list of DOCTYPEs, and their effects on various browsers, is available at http://gutfeldt.ch/matthias/articles/doctypeswitch/table.html.

XHTML 1.1

```
<!DOCTYPE html PUBLIC "-//W3C//DTD XHTML 1.1//EN"
    "http://www.w3.org/TR/xhtml11/DTD/xhtml11.dtd">
```

I think I've found a CSS bug! What do I do?

We all find ourselves in situations in which our CSS just will not work! Though you've tried every solution you can think of, some random bit of text continues to appear and disappear in Internet Explorer 6, or part of your layout spreads across half the content in Safari. Before the bug drives you mad, take a deep breath and relax. There is a solution!

Solution

This is a solution that helps you find the solution!

1.   **Take a break.**

     Once we designers have gotten frustrated battling a problem, to apply any kind of rational process for finding a solution is difficult at best. So take a break. Go for a walk, tidy your desk, or do some housework. If you're at work with your boss looking over your shoulder so that you can't even get to the coffee machine in peace, work on something else—answer some mail, tidy up some content. Do anything to take your mind off the problem for a while.

2.   **Validate your style sheet and document.**

     If you haven't already done so, your next step should be to validate the CSS and the (X)HTML document. Errors in your CSS or markup may well cause problems and, even if they're not the actual cause of your bug, they often make it more difficult to find a solution.

3.   **Isolate the problem.**

     Can you get your bug to occur in isolation from the rest of your document? CSS bugs often display only when a certain group of conditions is met, so trying to find out exactly where the problem occurs may help you work out how it can be fixed. Try and reproduce the problem in a document that doesn't contain the rest of your layout.

4. **Search the Web.**

If what you have is a browser bug, it's likely that someone else has seen it before. There are plenty of great sites that detail browser bugs and explain how to get around them. I always check the following sites when I'm up against a problem:

- CSS Pointers Group, at http://css.nu/pointers/bugs.html

- Position is Everything, at http://www.positioniseverything.net/

- The Browser Bug Category on the css-d wiki, at http://css-discuss.incutio.com/?page=CategoryBrowserBug

Also, search the css-discuss archives,[27] and don't forget Google!

5. **Ask for help.**

If you haven't managed to find a solution as you've moved through the above steps, ask for help. Even the most experienced developers hit problems that they just can't see past. Sometimes, just talking through the issue with a bunch of people who haven't been staring at it all week can help you resolve the problem, or come up with new ideas to test—even if no one has an immediate solution.

When you post to a forum or mailing list, remember these rules of thumb:

- If the list or forum has archives, search them first, just in case you're about to ask one of those questions that's asked at least once a day.

- Make sure that your CSS and HTML validates; otherwise, the answer you'll get is most likely to be, "go and validate your document and see if that helps."

- Upload an example to a location to which you can link from your forum post. If you manage to reproduce the problem outside a complex layout, so

---

[27] http://www.css-discuss.org/

much the better—this will make it easier for others to work out what's going on.

■ Explain the solutions you've tried so far. This saves the recipients of your message from pursuing those same dead-ends, and shows that you've attempted to fix the problem yourself before asking for help.

■ Give your message a descriptive subject line. People are more likely to read a post entitled, "Duplicate boxes appearing in IE5" than one that screams, "HELP!" Good titles also make the list archives more useful, as people can see at a glance the titles of posts in a thread.

■ Be polite and to the point.

■ Be patient while you wait for answers. If you don't receive a reply after a day or so, and it's a busy list, it is usually acceptable to post again with the word "REPOST" in the subject line. Posts can be overlooked in particularly large boards, and this is a polite way to remind users that you have not received any assistance with your problem.

■ When you receive answers, try implementing the poster's suggestions. Don't get upset or angry if the recommendations don't work, or you feel that the poster is asking you to try very basic things. I've seen threads go on for many posts as different posters weigh in to help someone solve a problem, and continue the discussion until a solution is found. Give people a chance to help!

■ If you find a solution—or you don't, and decide instead to change your design to avoid the problem—post to the thread to explain what worked and what didn't. This shows good manners towards those who helped you, but will also help anyone who searches the archive for information on the same problem. It's very frustrating to search an archive and find several possible solutions to a problem, but to not know which (if any) was successful!

Many web design and development mailing lists are used by people who are very knowledgeable about CSS. In my opinion, the best CSS-specific list is css-discuss.[28] It's a high-traffic list, but the people on it are very helpful, and you can pick up a lot just by reading the posts and browsing the archives. SitePoint also has a great, active CSS forum full of helpful and experienced people.[29]

See the next solution for a real-world walkthrough of a common bug, and the process you might take to find a solution and fix it.

Some of my content is appearing and disappearing in Internet Explorer 6! What should I do?

In one incarnation of my business site, I added some images to the site and all seemed well in my default browser—Mozilla Firefox—as Figure 7.12 shows. Then, I checked it in Internet Explorer 6. What I saw was the page displayed in Figure 7.13—two paragraphs of text were missing in action! If I refreshed the page, or scrolled, the text reappeared. Something very odd was going on!

Solution

In this solution, I'll step you through the process I used to resolve this bug, in order to show you the tactics you might use when you're up against a problem of this type.

First, I checked my document at the W3C markup validator,[30] and my CSS at the W3C CSS Validator.[31] I wanted to make sure that there was no problem within my document, or the CSS, that would cause Internet Explorer 6 to behave strangely. Both the document and the CSS were valid, so I knew the problem wasn't related to this.

[28] http://www.css-discuss.org/
[29] http://www.sitepoint.com/launch/cssforum/
[30] http://validator.w3.org
[31] http://jigsaw.w3.org/css-validator/

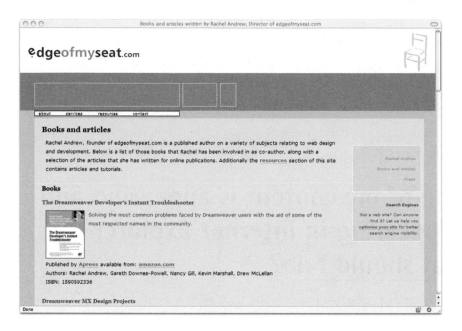

Figure 7.12. The document displaying as expected in Firefox

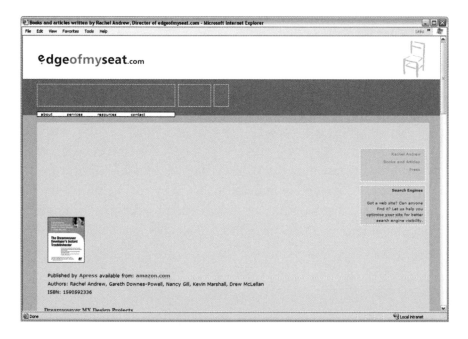

Figure 7.13. The document rendering poorly in Internet Explorer 6

Isolating the Problem

It was time to isolate the problem, which meant looking closely at the code. In this particular design, each book is described within a div container with a class of cBlock. Within cBlock, I have a paragraph with a class of booktext, an image, and a normal paragraph. The style sheet sets up various margins and padding, floats the image to the left, and makes sure that the normal paragraph is clear of the floated image:

```
<h1>Books and articles</h1>
<p>Rachel Andrew, founder of edgeofmyseat.com…</p>
<h2>Books</h2>
<h3>The Dreamweaver Developer's Instant Troubleshooter</h3>
<div class="cBlock">
  <p class="booktext">
    <img src="img/instant_troubleshooter.jpg" width="100"
        height="124" alt="Cover" />
    Solving the most common problems faced by Dreamweaver users
    with the aid of some of the most respected names in the
    community.
  </p>
  <p>
    Published by <a href="http://www.apress.com">Apress</a>
    available from: <a href="http://www.amazon.com/exec/obidos/ASI
N/1590592336/edgeofmyseat-20">amazon.com</a><br />
    Authors: Rachel Andrew, Gareth Downes-Powell, Nancy Gill,
    Kevin Marshall, Drew McLellan<br />
    ISBN: 1590592336
  </p>
</div>
```

```
.cBlock {
  margin-top: 10px;
}
.cBlock p.booktext {
  padding-left: 30px;
  padding-right: 20px;
  padding-top: 10px;
  color: #4E475F;
  background-color: transparent;
  clear: none;
}
```

```
.cBlock img {
  float: left;
  margin: 0 10px 4px 0;
  border: 1px solid #4E475F;
}
.cBlock p {
  clear: both;
}
```

By toying with the document and CSS, I discovered that if I removed the `float` property from the image, the problem disappeared, so I was fairly sure that was the source of the problem. However, I wanted to keep the floated image as it was—without it, the text would not display to the right of the image, as Figure 7.14 shows.

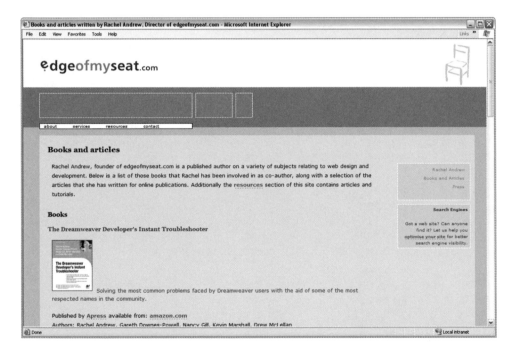

Figure 7.14. Fixing the disappearing text problem by removing the float property

Searching the Web

I now knew what caused the problem, so I decided to see whether I could find any details on this bug, or a method to fix it. My layout wasn't very complicated, so I figured that if I was seeing this problem, other people would have seen it, too.

On the Position is Everything web site, I found details of the Internet Explorer 6 Peekaboo Bug:[32]

> A liquid box has a float inside, and content that appears alongside that float. All is well, until it's viewed in IE 6. "Wah? Where's my content?!" You reload the page, and nothing. When you scroll down, or perhaps switch to another window, upon returning to the 'scene of the crime' there it all is, fat 'n sassy!

That sounded just like my bug! Better still, the page gave me some information on how to get rid of it. I decided to try out the newest method presented there: "The Holly Hack." This seemed to be the one that would have the least impact on my layout, which worked in other browsers.

This method utilizes a CSS hack that was developed to cure another Internet Explorer 6-specific problem.[33] Looking down the page, I found the CSS that seemed as if it should fix the problem, so I added it to my style sheet:

```
.cBlock {
  margin-top: 10px;
}
.cBlock p.booktext {
  padding-left: 30px;
  padding-right: 20px;
  padding-top: 10px;
  color: #4E475F;
  background-color: transparent;
  clear: none;
}
.cBlock img {
  float: left;
  margin: 0 10px 4px 0;
```

[32] http://www.positioniseverything.net/explorer/peekaboo.html
[33] http://www.positioniseverything.net/explorer/threepxtest.html

```
    border: 1px solid #4E475F;
}

/* Hide from IE5-mac. Only IE-win sees this.
The Holly Hack -
http://www.positioniseverything.net/explorer/threepxtest.html
Used to combat the IE6 Peekaboo Bug
\*/
* html .cBlock img {
  margin-right: 10px;
}
* html p {
  height: 1%;
  margin-left: 0;
}
/* End hide from IE5/mac
End Holly Hack*/

.cBlock p {
  clear: both;
}
```

Upon testing the page again in Internet Explorer 6, I saw that the problem had indeed vanished. I then checked the site in other browsers, just to be sure that it didn't cause any unwanted side-effects. It's always a good idea to test your site again in all browsers after you implement a hack. Even though sites that demonstrate these hacks tend to be kept up to date, and users will let the owners know if a solution is found to cause issues in any browser, there may be problems that haven't been uncovered yet—or, you may have made a mistake as you implemented the hack.

What do the error and warning messages in the W3C Validator mean?

Validating your documents and CSS is an important step in ensuring that your site renders correctly in standards-complaint browsers. Sometimes, however, the error and warning messages can be very confusing.

Solution

You can validate your (X)HTML documents online at the W3C Validator;[34] CSS documents can be validated at the W3C CSS Validator.[35] Many authoring tools, such as Dreamweaver, have inbuilt validators, and plugins are available for browsers such as Firefox to help you to validate your pages.[36]

With both CSS and (X)HTML documents, start validating at the top. Sometimes, you'll run a document through the validator and receive a huge list of errors. However, when you fix the first error that the validator has encountered, many of the subsequent errors often disappear. This is especially likely to occur in an (X)HTML document. If you have forgotten to close a tag correctly, the validator believes that the tag is still open, and it will give you a whole list of errors to tell you that element X is not allowed within element Y. Close the offending tag and those errors will instantly be resolved.

A related problem is found in documents with an HTML DTD, where the developer has closed a tag using XML syntax, like this:

```
<link rel="stylesheet" href="stylesheet.css" type="text/css" />
```

If you've done this in a document that doesn't have an XHTML DOCTYPE, you'll receive errors indicating that there is a closing HEAD element in the wrong place. To make the document obey the HTML standard, simply remove the slash from the tag:

```
<link rel="stylesheet" href="stylesheet.css" type="text/css">
```

Errors and Warnings

A CSS document is not valid CSS if it contains errors such as invalid syntax, missing semicolons, and so on. You will need to fix these errors to have the document validate, and to ensure that your style sheet behaves as expected.

---

[34] http://validator.w3.org/

[35] http://jigsaw.w3.org/css-validator/

[36] http://users.skynet.be/mgueury/mozilla/

If your style sheet is error-free, it will validate. A valid document, however, may still contain warnings when you run it through the validator. Whether you take notice of these warnings or not is entirely up to you. The most common warning states that you have failed to specify an acceptable background color for a specific element. This could indicate a problem with your design—for example, your design could result in part of the text on your page being rendered unreadable—or it could simply indicate an aspect of your design that has the potential to cause problems, even if you've intentionally designed it that way (for instance, you're expecting the background of an element beneath the element in question to show through). Warnings should act as a reminder to check you haven't forgotten anything, but remember that a style sheet that validates with warnings is still perfectly valid!

Summary

This chapter has covered a wide range of solutions to problems that you may not have experienced so far. This will almost certainly be the case if you have not yet designed sites that use CSS, rather than tables, for positioning. It's at that point that the more interesting browser bugs start to rear their ugly heads, and testing in a wide range of browsers, and browser versions, becomes very important indeed.

What I hope to have shown you in this chapter is how I go about testing sites, finding bugs, and getting help. I've also aimed to broaden your options in terms of displaying your pages appropriately for different users. If you're reading through this book chapter by chapter, you might find that much of this information makes more sense in light of Chapter 9, which deals with the use of CSS for layout.

Chapter  8

Accessibility and Alternative Devices

CSS allows us to separate the structure and content of our documents from the presentation of the site. This means that visitors using devices that can't render the site's design—either because they're limited from a technical standpoint, such as some PDA or phone browsers, or as a result of their own functional advantages, such as screen readers that speak a page's text for the benefit of visually impaired users—will still be able to access the content. However, we're still free to create beautiful designs for the majority of users who do have browsers that support CSS.

While separating content and structure from presentation, and considering how best to structure the underlying document, will mean that users of screen readers and browsers that don't support CSS can easily understand your site, you still need to be aware of other users who, though they can see the design of the site, have particular accessibility-related needs. Simply using CSS for layout purposes does not make your site accessible to everyone. For example, many people who suffer some kind of vision loss can read text that's clearly laid out and can be enlarged. This chapter also covers the use of alternative style sheets (also called alternate style sheets), style sheets for different media (such as print style sheets), and browser-based style sheet switching with the aid of JavaScript.

How do I test my site in a text-only browser?

Checking your site using a text-only browser is an excellent way to find out how accessible it really is. If you find it easy to navigate your site using a text-only browser, it's likely that visitors using screen readers will also be able to do so.

Solution

You can view pages from your site using Lynx, a text-only browser, through the online Lynx Viewer.[1] While this is a useful test, Lynx is free to download and install, so why not install a copy on your system? This option provides the added advantage that you'll be able to test pages before you upload them to the Web.

Linux/Unix Users

You may find that Lynx is already installed on your system; if not, you should be able to obtain a copy easily via your package management system. Alternatively, you can download the source from the Lynx software distribution site.[2]

Windows Users

Installing Lynx on Windows used to be a tricky process, but now an installer is available from csant.info.[3] Download and run the installer, which will also make Lynx available from your **Start** menu.

Mac OS X Users

Lynx for Mac OS X is available from the Apple web site.[4]

Discussion

Lynx behaves consistently across all platforms, but you'll need to learn a few simple commands in order to use it for web browsing. Figure 8.1 shows a typical site displayed in Lynx.

---

[1] http://www.delorie.com/web/lynxview.html

[2] http://lynx.isc.org/release/

[3] http://www.csant.info/lynx.htm

[4] http://www.apple.com/downloads/macosx/unix_open_source/lynxtextwebbrowser.html

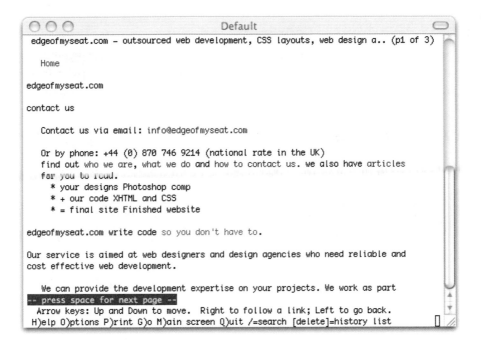

Figure 8.1. Viewing a site in Lynx

To open a web page, hit **G** and enter the URL. Press **Enter**, and Lynx will load that URL. If the site that you're trying to visit uses any form of cookies, Lynx will ask you if you wish to accept them. Type **Y** for yes, **N** for no, **A** to accept cookies from that site always, or **V** to ensure that you never accept cookies from that site.

Use the arrow keys to navigate using Lynx. The up and down arrow keys will let you jump from link to link. The right arrow key will follow the link that you're currently on, while the left arrow key will take you back to the previous page.

To complete a form, navigate to each form field using the down arrow key and, once you're there, type normally into the field.

You can use Lynx to view local files, which is useful during development. If you're running a local web server, such as Apache or IIS, you can just point Lynx to localhost URLs. Note, though, that the browser will also read an HTML file directly if you provide it with the path and filename.

For more information on how to use Lynx, hit **H** to display the help system, which you can navigate as you would any site.

> ### See Accessibility in Action
>
> Spend some time visiting your favorite sites in a text-only browser—you'll soon start to appreciate how important it is to ensure that you have `alt` text on images, and a well-structured document!

How do I test my site in a screen reader?

The best way to understand the experience had by a user visiting your site with a screen reader is to try it out for yourself; however, the most popular and well-known screen reader in use today, JAWS, is expensive (although there is a demonstration version available that will run for 40 minutes) and entails a steep learning curve. What other options do web developers have to test their sites in a screen reader?

Solution

The free Firefox extension, Fire Vox, can give you an excellent impression of the way a site sounds when it's read through a screen reader, and is available as a download for those running Firefox on Windows, Mac OS X, or Linux. Download Fire Vox from the author, Charles L. Chen's web site,[5] and follow the installation instructions for your operating system. The brief tutorial offered on the site will help you get started using Fire Vox.

Discussion

While trying out a screen reader is a great way to get a feel for the experience a visually impaired user has online, it's impossible for those of us who have good vision to really understand the experience, or even, with the limited use of screen readers in site testing, to become as adept with the software as do those who rely on it to use the Web. So unless you have time to learn to use the software properly, testing sites with a screen reader should be seen as an activity that will help you to gain insight into these users' experiences, rather than as a true test of your site's screen reader compatibility.

---

[5] http://www.firevox.clcworld.net/downloads.html

How do I create style sheets for specific devices, such as screen readers or WebTV?

It's possible to show different CSS to different browsers, but what about other devices?

Solution

The CSS specification includes a specification for **media types**, which allow web page authors to restrict a style sheet, or section of a style sheet, to a given medium.

You can tag a style sheet with any of these media types. For example, the following markup tags the linked style sheet for use by aural browsers:

```
<link rel="stylesheet" type=text/css" href="aural.css"
    media="aural" />
```

In-page style sheets can also be tagged this way:

```
<style type="text/css" media="all">
...
</style>
```

In both these examples, the `media` attribute has a value of the media type for which the style sheet has been created. This style sheet will only be used by devices that support the specified media type.

Discussion

The following list of media types is taken from the CSS2.1 specification.[6]

all   suitable for all devices

braille   intended for tactile feedback devices, such as braille browsers

embossed   intended for paged braille printers

---

[6] http://www.w3.org/TR/CSS21/media.html#media-types

handheld	intended for handheld devices (typically small screen, limited-bandwidth devices)
print	intended for paged material and for documents viewed on screen in Print Preview mode
projection	intended for projected presentations
screen	intended primarily for color computer screens
speech	intended for speech synthesizers (Note that CSS2 had a similar media type called `aural` for this purpose.)
tty	intended for media using a fixed-pitch character grid (such as teletypes, terminals, or portable devices with limited display capabilities); authors should not use pixel units with the `tty` media type
tv	intended for television-type devices (low resolution, color, limited-scrollability screens with sound available)

In addition to the `media` attribute described above, we can address multiple media types in one style sheet using the **media at-rule**.

Here's an example of this approach in action. The style sheet below dictates that printed documents will print with a font size of ten points, while on the screen, the font will display at a size of 12 pixels. Both print and screen devices will display the text in black:

```
@media print {
  body {
    font-size: 10pt;
  }
}
@media screen {
  body {
    font-size: 12px;
  }
}
@media screen, print {
  body {
    color: #000000;
  }
```

```
    }
}
```

Currently, there are very few devices that fully support the media types you would expect them to. At the time of this writing, Emacspeak[7] with the Emacs/w3[8] browser is the only known screen reader/browser combination that supports `speech` or `aural` CSS media types.

Most mobile browsers have either very minimal or no CSS support. Those that do support CSS tend to honor `screen` styles, while support for the `handheld` media attribute remains buggy. The standout exceptions are Opera Mini and Opera Mobile, which honor `handheld` styles while ignoring `screen` styles, in accordance with the standards.

The media type that's most usefully supported by modern browsers is the `print` media type. The next solution discusses how you can use this media type to create print versions of your pages.

Don't Start from Scratch

If you're creating a style sheet for a new media type, the easiest way to get started is to save a copy of your existing style sheet under a new name. That way, you already have all your selectors at hand, and can simply change the styles that you've created for each.

How do I create a print style sheet?

Web pages rarely print well, as techniques that are designed to make a page look good on a screen are usually different from those used to create a document that prints well. However, it's possible to use the CSS media types to provide a style sheet that's applied when the document is printed.

Solution

We can create a special print style sheet for our visitors like so:

---

[7] http://emacspeak.sourceforge.net/
[8] http://www.gnu.org/software/w3/

print-stylesheet.html

```
<!DOCTYPE html PUBLIC "-//W3C//DTD XHTML 1.0 Strict//EN"
    "http://www.w3.org/TR/xhtml1/DTD/xhtml1-strict.dtd">
<html xmlns="http://www.w3.org/1999/xhtml" lang="en-US">
<head>
<title>Print Style Sheet</title>
<meta http-equiv="content-type"
    content="text/html; charset=utf-8" />
<link rel="stylesheet" type="text/css" href="main.css"
    title="default" />
<link rel="stylesheet" type="text/css" href="print.css"
    media="print" />
</head>
<body>
<div id="banner"></div>
<div id="content">
  <h1>Chinese-style stuffed peppers</h1>
  <p>These stuffed peppers are lovely as a starter, or as a side
    dish for a Chinese meal. They also go down well as part of a
    buffet and even children seem to like them.</p>
  <h2>Ingredients</h2>
  …
</div>
<div id="navigation">
  <ul id="mainnav">
    <li><a href="#">Recipes</a></li>
    <li><a href="#">Contact Us</a></li>
    <li><a href="#">Articles</a></li>
    <li><a href="#">Buy Online</a></li>
  </ul>
</div>
</body>
</html>
```

main.css

```
body, html {
  margin: 0;
  padding: 0;
}
#navigation {
  width: 200px;
  font: 90% Arial, Helvetica, sans-serif;
```

```
  position: absolute;
  top: 41px;
  left: 0;
}
#navigation ul {
  list-style: none;
  margin: 0;
  padding: 0;
  border: none;
}
#navigation li {
  border-bottom: 1px solid #ED9F9F;
  margin: 0;
}
#navigation li a:link, #navigation li a:visited {
  display: block;
  padding: 5px 5px 5px 0.5em;
  border-left: 12px solid #711515;
  border-right: 1px solid #711515;
  color: #ffffff;
  background-color: #b51032;
  text-decoration: none;
}
#navigation li a:hover {
  color: #ffffff;
  background-color: #711515;
}
#content {
  margin-left: 260px;
  margin-right: 60px;
}
#banner {
  height: 40px;
  background-color: #711515;
  border-bottom: 1px solid #ED9F9F;
  text-align: right;
  padding-right: 20px;
  margin-top: 0;
}
#banner ul {
  margin: 0;
  padding: 0;
}
#banner li {
```

```
    display: inline;
}
#banner a:link, #banner a:visited {
  font: 80% Arial, Helvetica, sans-serif;
  color: #ffffff;
  background-color: transparent;
}
#content p, #content li {
  font: 80%/1.6em Arial, Helvetica, sans-serif;
}
#content p {
  margin-left: 1.5em;
}
#content h1, #content h2 {
  font: 140% Georgia, "Times New Roman", Times, serif;
  color: #B51032;
  background-color: transparent;
}
#content h2 {
  font: 120% Georgia, "Times New Roman", Times, serif;
  padding-bottom: 3px;
  border-bottom: 1px dotted #ED9F9F;
}
```

print.css

```
body, html {
  margin: 0;
  padding: 0;
}
#navigation {
  display: none;
}
#content {
  margin-left: 20pt;
  margin-right: 30pt;
}
#banner {
  display: none;
}
#content p, #content li {
  font: 12pt/20pt "Times New Roman", Times, serif;
}
#content p {
```

```
    margin-left: 20pt;
}
#content h1, #content h2 {
  font: 16pt Georgia, "Times New Roman", Times, serif;
  color: #4b4b4b;
  background-color: transparent;
}
#content h2 {
  font: 14pt Georgia, "Times New Roman", Times, serif;
  padding-bottom: 2pt;
  border-bottom: 1pt dotted #cccccc;
}
```

Discussion

Creating a print style sheet can be very helpful to your visitors, particularly if your page has many graphics. Printing pages from a site that has many graphics can be costly in terms of printer ink, and slow on older printers. And some sites really don't print well at all because of the color combinations or layouts used. For example, Figure 8.2 shows a page that has a simple two-column CSS layout, with navigation in the sidebar, and a main content area that contains a recipe.

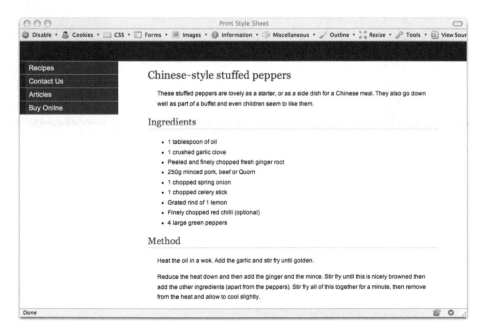

Figure 8.2. Displaying a two-column layout in the browser

Figure 8.3 shows this layout in Print Preview, which reflects the way it would appear when printed.

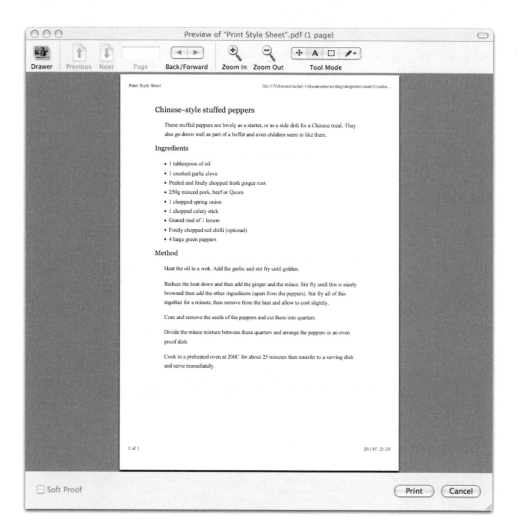

Figure 8.3. The layout appears in Print Preview

Those images really give us a clear idea of the practical differences between the on-screen and print displays. A standard letter or A4 sheet of paper is reasonably narrow, so by the time the print display has accounted for the menu, only half of the page width is left for the display of the recipe text. This may mean that long recipes need to be printed on two pages, rather than one.

Traditionally, sites offer print versions of documents that they expect users to print. However, this approach requires the maintenance of more than one version of the document—and users have to be savvy enough to find and click the **Print** button on the page, rather than simply printing the page using the browser's **Print** button. With the CSS method, the print style sheet will automatically come into play when visitors use their browser's print functionality.

Let's step through the process of developing the print style sheet, and linking it to your pages.

Linking a Print Style Sheet

Open your existing main style sheet and save it as **print.css** so that it becomes your print style sheet. Link this style sheet to your document with the `print` media type, like so:

```
<link rel="stylesheet" type="text/css" href="print.css"
    media="print" />
```

Creating the Print Styles

If you've saved your existing style sheet as **print.css**, you can use it to decide what needs to be changed in order to create the print style sheet.

In my layout, the navigation is contained within a `div`; the section in the style sheet for that element looks like this:

main.css (excerpt)

```
#navigation {
  width: 200px;
  font: 90% Arial, Helvetica, sans-serif;
  position: absolute;
  top: 41px;
  left: 0;
}
```

The first thing we want to do is hide the navigation, as it's useless in the print version of the document. To do this, we replace the properties in the above section of the style sheet with `display: none`:

print.css *(excerpt)*

```
#navigation {
  display: none;
}
```

We can now remove any navigation rules that apply to elements within the `navig`-`ation` element.

We can also make the content area wider, so that it takes up all the available space on the page. Find the section for the `content` element in your style sheet:

main.css *(excerpt)*

```
#content {
  margin-left: 260px;
  margin-right: 60px;
}
```

We can change the left margin to a smaller value, as we no longer need to leave space for the navigation. It's also a good idea to switch from pixel measurements (a screen unit) to points (a print unit), as we discussed in "Should I use pixels, points, ems, or something else to set font sizes?" in Chapter 2:

print.css *(excerpt)*

```
#content {
  margin-left: 20pt;
  margin-right: 30pt;
}
```

If we check the document in Print Preview, as shown in Figure 8.4, or print it via the browser, we'll find that the navigation has disappeared, and the content now fills the space much more effectively.

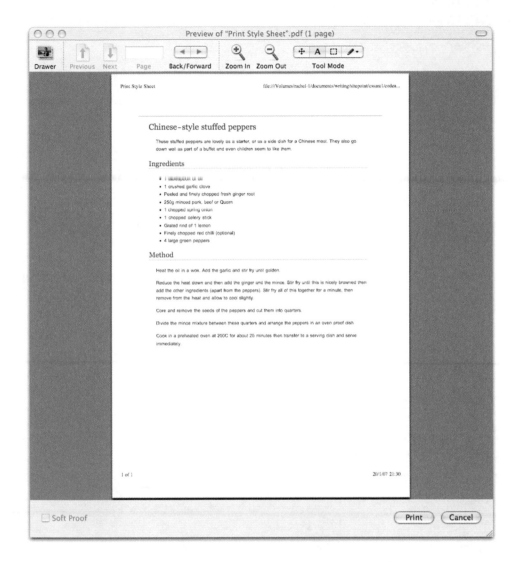

Figure 8.4. The page printing more cleanly after we remove the navigation

The line at the top of Figure 8.4 is the banner's bottom border. We can hide the banner just as we hid the navigation. First, we must find the section for banner in the style sheet:

```
                                                    main.css (excerpt)

#banner {
  height: 40px;
```

```
  background-color: #711515;
  border-bottom: 1px solid #ED9F9F;
}
```

Once again, we set the banner to `display: none` and delete the remaining rules associated with this ID:

print.css *(excerpt)*

```
#banner {
  display: none;
}
```

Finally, we can format the text. For print purposes, I normally make any colored text grayscale, unless it's important that the text stays colored. Let's use print-friendly points to size the text, so that our print style sheet renders font sizes reliably across different systems.

Additionally, you might like to consider using a serif font for your printed text, as serif fonts are generally considered easier to read on paper. Here are those changes:

print.css *(excerpt)*

```
#content p, #content li {
  font: 12pt/20pt "Times New Roman", Times, serif;
}
#content p {
  margin-left: 20pt;
}
#content h1, #content h2 {
  font: 16pt Georgia, "Times New Roman", Times, serif;
  color: #4b4b4b;
  background-color: transparent;
}
#content h2 {
  font: 14pt Georgia, "Times New Roman", Times, serif;
  padding-bottom: 2pt;
  border-bottom: 1pt dotted #cccccc;
}
```

The much plainer, but more readable print layout is shown in its final form in Figure 8.5.

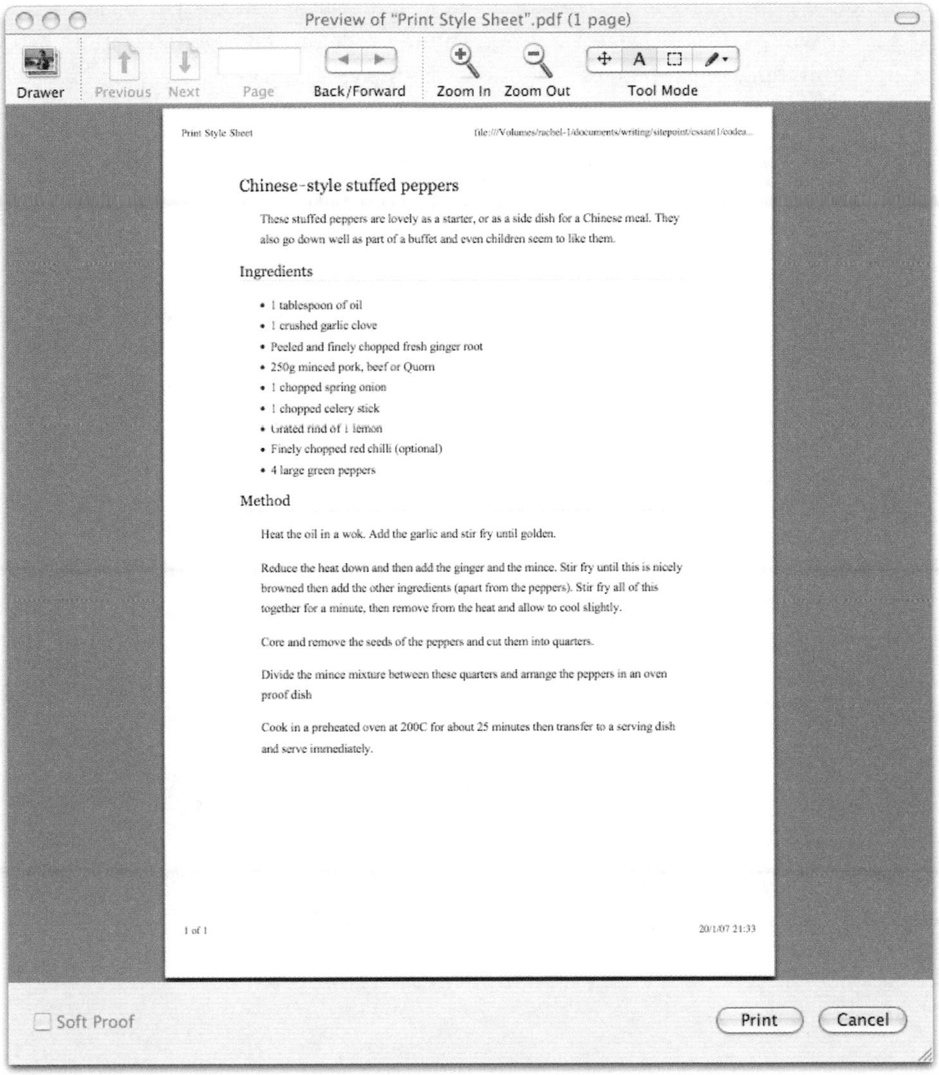

Figure 8.5. Using **Print Preview** to view the page affected by the completed style sheet

> ### Print Style Sheets and Table Layouts
>
> Print style sheets are easy to implement on CSS layouts, but you can also create effective print style sheets for table-based layouts, particularly if you use CSS to set the widths of table cells. You can then hide cells that contain navigation just as we hid the navigation `div` in the above CSS layout.

How do I add alternative style sheets to my site?

Some modern browsers allow the user to view a list of the style sheets attached to a document, and select the one they want to use to view the site. This facility can be very helpful to people who struggle to read text if its contrast with the page is low, or need a very large text size, for example.

Solution

Link your alternative style sheet with `rel="alternative stylesheet"`, and give it a descriptive title. The title will display in the browser's menu, so using a title that's descriptive, such as "high contrast" or "large text," is most helpful for users. You should also give your default style sheet a title to differentiate it from the alternative style sheet:

alternative-stylesheets.html (excerpt)

```
<link rel="stylesheet" type="text/css" href="main.css"
    title="default" />
<link rel="stylesheet" type="text/css" href="print.css"
    media="print" />
<link rel="alternative stylesheet" type="text/css"
    href="largetext.css" title="large text" />
```

largetext.css

```
body, html {
  margin: 0;
  padding: 0;
  font-size: 140%;
}
```

```
#navigation {
  width: 280px;
  font: 90% Arial, Helvetica, sans-serif;
  position: absolute;
  top: 41px;
  left: 0;
}
#navigation ul {
  list-style: none;
  margin: 0;
  padding: 0;
  border: none;
}
#navigation li {
  border-bottom: 1px solid #ED9F9F;
  margin: 0;
}
#navigation li a:link, #navigation li a:visited {
  display: block;
  padding: 5px 5px 5px 0.5em;
  border-left: 12px solid #711515;
  border-right: 1px solid #711515;
  color: #ffffff;
  background-color: #b51032;
  text-decoration: none;
}
#navigation li a:hover {
  color: #ffffff;
  background-color: #711515;
}
#content {
  margin-left: 320px;
  margin-right: 60px;
}
#banner {
  height: 40px;
  background-color: #711515;
  border-bottom: 1px solid #ED9F9F;
  text-align: right;
  padding-right: 20px;
  margin-top: 0;
}
#banner ul {
  margin: 0;
```

```
    padding: 0;
}
#banner li {
  display: inline;
}
#banner a:link, #banner a:visited {
  font: 80% Arial, Helvetica, sans-serif;
  color: #ffffff;
  background-color: transparent;
}
#content p, #content li {
  font: 80%/1.6em Arial, Helvetica, sans-serif;
}
#content p {
  margin-left: 1.5em;
}
#content h1, #content h2 {
  font: 140% Georgia, "Times New Roman", Times, serif;
  color: #B51032;
  background-color: transparent;
}
#content h2 {
  font: 120% Georgia, "Times New Roman", Times, serif;
  padding-bottom: 3px;
  border-bottom: 1px dotted #ED9F9F;
}
```

In Figure 8.6, you can see how the page displays when the user selects the alternative style sheet from Firefox's **View** menu.

Figure 8.6. Switching to the **large text** style sheet in Firefox

Discussion

Utilizing this browser functionality is easy, and allows you to add valuable features for users with a minimum of effort. Typically, it takes very little time to create a style sheet that displays large fonts or has a high-contrast color scheme. Simply save your existing style sheet and tweak the fonts, colors, and layout as required.

Unfortunately, browser support for this feature is still limited—it isn't provided at all in Internet Explorer. However, users who find this functionality beneficial may choose a browser specifically because it gives them access to these features. In the next solution, we'll look at a way to mimic this functionality in browsers that don't offer it as standard.

> **Look How Thoughtful I Am!**
>
> As very few sites utilize this feature at present, it would be a good idea to let your users know that you offer alternative style sheets. Perhaps include the information on a separate page that explains how to use the site, and is linked clearly from the homepage.

Zoom Layouts

A step on from simply creating a large-print style sheet is the concept of the **zoom layout**. Popularized by Joe Clark, the zoom layout uses CSS to refactor the page into a single-column layout with high-contrast colors.[9] This is most useful for visitors who use the browser's zoom feature in Opera or Internet Explorer, or use software that magnifies the screen to make reading easier. When a design is magnified in this way, the sidebars often move off the side of the viewport, resulting in a page that contains only essential content.

Zoom layouts can make things easier for visually impaired users by enlarging the font size and displaying the text in a light color on a dark background—a combination that's easier for many users to read. A style sheet that created a zoom layout for the design we've been working on throughout this chapter might contain the following rules, and display in the browser as shown in Figure 8.7:

```
zoom.css

body, html {
  margin: 1em 2em 2em 2em;
  padding: 0;
  font-size: 140%;
  background-color: #333;
  color: #fff;
}

#navigation ul {
  list-style: none;
  margin: 0;
  padding: 0;
  border: none;
```

---

[9] http://joeclark.org/access/webaccess/zoom/

```
}

#navigation li {
  float: left;
  width: 20%;
}

#navigation li a:link, #navigation li a:visited {
  color: #ff0;
}

#navigation li a:hover {
  text-decoration: none;
}

#content {
  padding: 1em 0 0 0;
  clear: left;
}

#content p, #content li {
  line-height: 1.6em;
}

#content h1, #content h2 {
  font: 140% Georgia, "Times New Roman", Times, serif;
  color: #fff;
  background-color: transparent;
}

#content h2 {
  font: 120% Georgia, "Times New Roman", Times, serif;
}
```

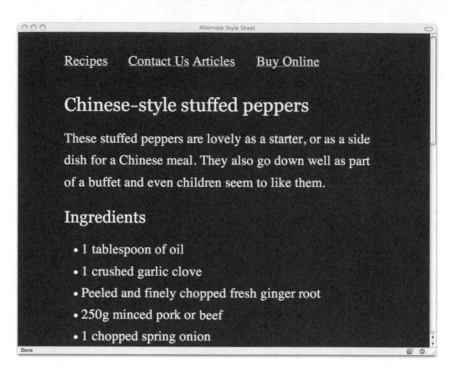

Figure 8.7. A zoom layout style sheet

How do I make a style sheet switcher?

The above solution for alternative style sheets is all very well for those who use a browser that supports the functionality, but what about everyone else? Internet Explorer has the largest user base and it doesn't support alternative style sheets at all! How can we empower users of this and other browsers to select the style sheet that's most appropriate to their needs?

Solution

Add a JavaScript style switcher to your page to enable users to select their preferred style sheet:

alternative-stylesheets-js.html *(excerpt)*

```
<link rel="stylesheet" type="text/css" href="main.css"
    title="default" />
<link rel="stylesheet" type="text/css" href="print.css"
```

```
      media="print" />
<link rel="alternative stylesheet" type="text/css"
    href="largetext.css" title="large text" />
<script language="javascript" type="text/javascript"
    src="switcher.js"></script>
</head>
<body>
<div id="banner">
  <ul id="styleswitch">
    <li><a href="javascript:;"
         onclick="setActiveStyleSheet('default'); return false;"
      >Default Style</a></li>
    <li><a href="javascript:;"
        onclick="setActiveStyleSheet('large text'); return false;"
      >Large Text</a></li>
  </ul>
</div>
```

switcher.js

```
/*
Paul Sowden's JavaScript switcher as detailed on:
http://www.alistapart.com/articles/alternate/
*/

function setActiveStyleSheet(title) {
  var i, a, main;
  for(i=0; (a = document.getElementsByTagName("link")[i]); i++) {
    if(a.getAttribute("rel").indexOf("style") != -1 &&
        a.getAttribute("title")) {
      a.disabled = true;
      if(a.getAttribute("title") == title) a.disabled = false;
    }
  }
}

function getActiveStyleSheet() {
  var i, a;
  for(i=0; (a = document.getElementsByTagName("link")[i]); i++) {
    if(a.getAttribute("rel").indexOf("style") != -1 &&
        a.getAttribute("title") && !a.disabled)
      return a.getAttribute("title");
  }
  return null;
```

```
}

function getPreferredStyleSheet() {
  var i, a;
  for(i=0; (a = document.getElementsByTagName("link")[i]); i++) {
    if(a.getAttribute("rel").indexOf("style") != -1
        && a.getAttribute("rel").indexOf("alt") == -1
        && a.getAttribute("title")
        ) return a.getAttribute("title");
  }
  return null;
}

function createCookie(name,value,days) {
  if (days) {
    var date = new Date();
    date.setTime(date.getTime()+(days*24*60*60*1000));
    var expires = "; expires="+date.toGMTString();
  }
  else expires = "";
  document.cookie = name+"="+value+expires+"; path=/";
}

function readCookie(name) {
  var nameEQ = name + "=";
  var ca = document.cookie.split(';');
  for(var i=0;i < ca.length;i++) {
    var c = ca[i];
    while (c.charAt(0)==' ') c = c.substring(1,c.length);
    if (c.indexOf(nameEQ) == 0)
      return c.substring(nameEQ.length,c.length);
  }
  return null;
}

window.onload = function(e) {
  var cookie = readCookie("style");
  var title = cookie ? cookie : getPreferredStyleSheet();
  setActiveStyleSheet(title);
}

window.onunload = function(e) {
  var title = getActiveStyleSheet();
  createCookie("style", title, 365);
```

```
}

var cookie = readCookie("style");
var title = cookie ? cookie : getPreferredStyleSheet();
setActiveStyleSheet(title);
```

The new style selection links appear in the top right-hand corner in Figure 8.8.

Figure 8.8. Changing the style sheet with JavaScript

Discussion

Adding a JavaScript style switcher to your site gives all users with JavaScript support the ability to choose the style sheet that best suits their needs.

This solution makes use of JavaScript functions from an A List Apart article entitled, "Alternative Style: Working With Alternate Style Sheets."[10] After you save the

---

[10] http://www.alistapart.com/articles/alternate/

functions to your site as **switcher.js**, all you need to do is link in the file, and add links or buttons to call the JavaScript:

alternative-stylesheets-js.html (excerpt)

```
<script language="javascript" type="text/javascript"
    src="switcher.js"></script>
```

alternative-stylesheets-js.html (excerpt)

```
<ul id="styleswitch">
  <li><a href="javascript:;"
        onclick="setActiveStyleSheet('default'); return false;"
    >Default Style</a></li>
  <li><a href="javascript:;"
        onclick="setActiveStyleSheet('large text'); return false;"
    >Large Text</a></li>
</ul>
```

The `setActiveStyleSheet` function selects the style sheet to be applied. By calling it with the title of the desired style sheet, we can allow users to select style sheets from within the browser. As such, this technique can be used in conjunction with that described in "How do I add alternative style sheets to my site?". Visitors who are able to change style sheets using their browser can still do so; others can use the JavaScript style switcher.

You can also use this technique to change a site's color scheme, and even its layout, provided you used CSS to position the page elements.

Server-side Solutions

It's also possible to allow users to change your site's style sheet by writing out the link to the selected style sheet using server-side code, such as PHP. Examples of the methods you can use to achieve this are linked to from the css-discuss Wiki.[11]

---

[11] http://css-discuss.incutio.com/?page=StyleSwitching

How do I use alternative style sheets without duplicating code?

In the examples we've seen so far in this chapter, we created our alternative style sheet by changing very few properties within the main style sheet. Do we actually need to create a whole new version of the style sheet as an alternative, or is it possible to alter only those styles that *need* to be changed?

Solution

The answer to this question is to create multiple style sheets: a base style sheet for the properties that never change, a default style sheet that contains the properties that will change, and a style sheet that includes the alternative versions of those properties:

alternative-stylesheets-js2.html *(excerpt)*

```
<link rel="stylesheet" type="text/css" href="main2.css" />
<link rel="stylesheet" type="text/css" href="defaulttext.css"
    title="default" />
<link rel="stylesheet" type="text/css" href="print.css"
    media="print" />
<link rel="alternative stylesheet" type="text/css"
    href="largetext2.css" title="large text" />
```

main2.css

```
body, html {
  margin: 0;
  padding: 0;
}
#navigation {
  font: 90% Arial, Helvetica, sans-serif;
  position: absolute;
  left: 0;
  top: 41px;
}
#navigation ul {
  list-style: none;
  margin: 0;
  padding: 0;
```

```
    border: none;
}
#navigation li {
    border-bottom: 1px solid #ED9F9F;
    margin: 0;
}
#navigation li a:link, #navigation li a:visited {
    display: block;
    padding: 5px 5px 5px 0.5em;
    border-left: 12px solid #711515;
    border-right: 1px solid #711515;
    background-color: #B51032;
    color: #FFFFFF;
    text-decoration: none;
}
#navigation li a:hover {
    background-color: #711515;
    color: #FFFFFF;
}
#banner {
    background-color: #711515;
    border-bottom: 1px solid #ED9F9F;
    text-align: right;
    padding-right: 20px;
    margin-top: 0;
}
#banner ul {
    margin: 0;
}
#banner li {
    display: inline;
}
#banner a:link, #banner a:visited {
    font: 80% Arial, Helvetica, sans-serif;
    color: #ffffff;
    background-color: transparent;
}
#content p, #content li {
    font: 80%/1.6em Arial, Helvetica, sans-serif;
}
#content p {
    margin-left: 1.5em;
}
#content h1, #content h2 {
```

```
  font: 140% Georgia, "Times New Roman", Times, serif;
  color: #B51032;
  background-color: transparent;
}
#content h2 {
  font: 120% Georgia, "Times New Roman", Times, serif;
  padding-bottom: 3px;
  border-bottom: 1px dotted #ED9F9F;
}
```

defaulttext.css

```
#navigation {
  width: 200px;
}
#content {
  margin-left: 260px;
  margin-right: 60px;
}
#banner {
  height: 40px;
}
```

largetext2.css

```
body, html {
  font-size: 1.4em;
}
#navigation {
  width: 280px;
}
#content {
  margin-left: 320px;
  margin-right: 60px;
}
#banner {
  height: 60px;
}
```

Discussion

To create the **largefonts.css** file that I used in "How do I add alternative style sheets to my site?" and "How do I make a style sheet switcher?", I changed very few of the properties that were in the original style sheet. I changed the base font size:

main.css (excerpt)

```
body, html {
  margin: 0;
  padding: 0;
}
```

largetext.css (excerpt)

```
body, html {
  margin: 0;
  padding: 0;
  font-size: 1.4em;
}
```

I also tweaked the layout slightly to make room for much larger text. In particular, I altered the `banner`, `content`, and `navigation` elements:

main.css (excerpt)

```
#navigation {
  width: 200px;
  font: 90% Arial, Helvetica, sans-serif;
  position: absolute;
  top: 41px;
  left: 0;
}
#content {
  margin-left: 260px;
  margin-right: 60px;
}

#banner {
  height: 40px;
  background-color: #711515;
  border-bottom: 1px solid #ED9F9F;
  text-align: right;
```

```
    padding-right: 20px;
    margin-top: 0;
}
```

largetext.css *(excerpt)*

```
#navigation {
  width: 280px;
  font: 90% Arial, Helvetica, sans-serif;
  position: absolute;
  top: 61px;
  left: 0;
}
#content {
  margin-left: 320px;
  margin-right: 60px;
}
#banner {
  height: 60px;
  background-color: #711515;
  border-bottom: 1px solid #ED9F9F;
  text-align: right;
  padding-right: 20px;
}
```

To avoid making a copy of the entire style sheet in order to create the **largetext.css** file, we can remove from the main style sheet those properties that we know we'll need to swap. We'll place them in a new style sheet that determines the default font size; our large-text style sheet need contain only the altered version of those properties.

Similarly, if you're using this method to change your site's color scheme, you can put all the properties that relate to color into separate style sheets, and swap only those. This way, you avoid having to maintain several different versions of what is, essentially, the same style sheet.

Flexible Layouts Mean Simpler Style Sheets

If your layout is a flexible one in which you've avoided setting elements in pixel widths, you may be able to get away with simply altering the base font size to effect a change in text size. The example above addresses a design that does have some fixed-width elements, however, as most designers are likely to have to deal with containers of a fixed width at some stage in their careers.

Summary

In this chapter, we've covered some of the ways in which the use of style sheets can make your site more accessible to a wider range of users. By starting out with an accessible document structure we're already assisting those who need to use a screen reader to read out the content of the site, and by providing alternative style sheets we can help users with other accessibility needs to customize their experience, which makes the site easier to use.

CSS Positioning and Layout

Tables or CSS? Few questions generate more heated debate within the web design and development community. But, whether you believe that the use of tables for layout will immediately send you to web design hell to be beaten forever with a red-hot (standards-compliant) poker, or you hold the more flexible view that, sometimes, the minimal use of tables for layout can be the best way to accomplish particular tasks, CSS positioning skills are a necessity for every web designer who wants to stay up to date.

This chapter will introduce the basics of CSS layout, and explore useful tricks and techniques that you can use to create unique and beautiful sites. These are the essential building blocks—starting points for your creativity. If you work through the chapter from beginning to end, you'll start by gaining a grasp of some of the fundamentals that you'll need to know to be able to create workable CSS layouts. The chapter then progresses to more detailed layout examples, so if you're already comfortable with the basics, simply dip into these solutions to find the specific technique you need.

How do I decide when to use a class and when to use an ID?

At first glance, classes and IDs seem to be used in much the same way: you can assign CSS properties to both classes and IDs, and apply them to change the way (X)HTML elements look. But, in which circumstances are classes best applied? And what about IDs?

Solution

The most important rule, where classes and IDs are concerned, is that an ID must be only used *once* in a document, as it uniquely identifies the element to which it is applied. Once you have assigned an ID to an element, you cannot use that ID again within that document.

Classes, on the other hand, may be used as many times as you like within the same document. Therefore, if you have on a page a feature that you wish to repeat, a class is the ideal choice.

You can apply both a class and an ID to any given element. For example, you might apply a class to all text input fields on a page; if you want to be able to address those fields using JavaScript, each field will need a separate ID, too. However, no styles need be assigned to that ID.

I tend to use IDs for the main, structural, positioned elements of the page, so I often end up with IDs such as `header`, `content`, `nav`, and `footer`. Here's an example:

```
<!DOCTYPE html PUBLIC "-//W3C//DTD XHTML 1.0 Strict//EN"
"http://www.w3.org/TR/xhtml1/DTD/xhtml1-strict.dtd">
<html xmlns="http://www.w3.org/1999/xhtml" lang="en-US">
<head>
<title>Absolute positioning</title>
<meta http-equiv="content-type"
    content="text/html; charset=utf-8" />
<link rel="stylesheet" type="text/css" href="position2.css" />
</head>
<body>
    <div id="header">
    </div>
```

```
<div id="content">
    <p>Main page content here</p>
</div>

<div id="nav">

</div>

</body>
</html>
```

Can I make an inline element display as if it were block-level, and vice-versa?

Sometimes, we need to cause the browser to treat HTML elements differently than it would treat them by default.

Solution

In Figure 9.1, you can see that we've forced a div element to display as an inline element, and a link to display as a block.

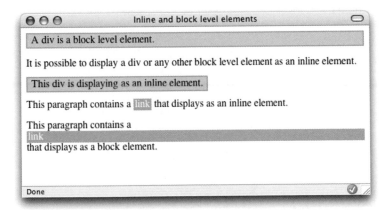

Figure 9.1. Displaying the block-level element inline, while the inline element displays as a block

Here's the markup that achieves this effect:

inline-block.html

```
<!DOCTYPE html PUBLIC "-//W3C//DTD XHTML 1.0 Strict//EN"
  "http://www.w3.org/TR/xhtml1/DTD/xhtml1-strict.dtd">
<html xmlns="http://www.w3.org/1999/xhtml" lang="en-US">
<head>
<title>Inline and block level elements</title>
<meta http-equiv="content-type"
    content="text/html; charset=utf-8" />
<style type="text/css">
#one {
 background-color: #CCCCCC;
 color: #000000;
 border: 2px solid #AAAAAA;
 padding: 2px 6px 2px 6px;
}
#two {
 background-color: #CCCCCC;
 color: #000000;
 border: 2px solid #AAAAAA;
 padding: 2px 6px 2px 6px;
 display: inline;
}
a {
 background-color: #ACACAC;
 color: #FFFFFF;
 text-decoration: none;
 padding: 1px 2px 1px 2px;

}
a.block {
 display: block;
}
</style>
</head>
<body>
<div id="one">A div is a block level element.</div>
<p>It is possible to display a div or any other block level
  element as an inline element.</p>
<div id="two">This div is displaying as an inline element.</div>
<p>This paragraph contains a <a href="http://www.sitepoint.com/"
    >link</a> that displays as an inline element.</p>
```

```
<p>This paragraph contains a <a class="block"
   href="http://www.sitepoint.com/">link</a> that displays as a
   block element.</p>
</body>
</html>
```

Discussion

Block-level elements are distinguished from inline elements in that they may contain inline elements as well as other block-level elements. They're also formatted differently than inline elements—block-level elements occupy a rectangular area of the page, spanning the entire width of the page by default, whereas inline elements flow along lines of text, and wrap to fit inside the blocks that contain them. HTML elements that are treated as block-level by default include headings (h1, h2, h3, ...), paragraphs (p), lists (ul, ol), and various containers (div, blockquote).

In the example above, we see a div that displays as normal. As it's a block-level element, it takes up the full width of the parent element, which, in this case, is the body. If it were contained within another div, or a table cell, it would stretch only to the width of that element.

If we don't want the div to behave in this way, we can set it to display inline by applying this CSS property:

```
display: inline;
```

We can cause an inline element to display as if it were a block-level element in the same way. In the above example, note that the a element displays as an inline element by default. We often want it to display as a block—for example, when we're creating a navigation barusing CSS. To achieve this, we set the display property of the element to block. In the example above, this causes the gray box that contains the linked text to expand to the full width of the screen.

How do margins and padding work in CSS?

What's the difference between the margin and padding properties, and how do they affect elements?

Solution

The margin properties add space to the *outside* of an element. You can set margins individually:

```
margin-top: 1em;
margin-right: 2em;
margin-bottom: 0.5em;
margin-left: 3em;
```

You can also set margins using a shorthand property:

```
margin: 1em 2em 0.5em 3em;
```

If all the margins are to be equal, simply use a rule like this:

```
margin: 1em;
```

This rule applies a 1em margin to all sides of the element.

Figure 9.2 shows what a block-level element looks like when we add margins to it. The code for this page is as follows:

margin.html

```
<!DOCTYPE html PUBLIC "-//W3C//DTD XHTML 1.0 Strict//EN"
    "http://www.w3.org/TR/xhtml1/DTD/xhtml1-strict.dtd">
<html xmlns="http://www.w3.org/1999/xhtml" lang="en-US">
<head>
<title>Margins</title>
<meta http-equiv="content-type"
    content="text/html; charset=utf-8" />
<style type="text/css">
p {
  border: 2px solid #AAAAAA;
```

```
  background-color: #EEEEEE;
}
p.margintest {
  margin: 40px;
}
</style>
</head>
<body>
<p>This paragraph should be displayed in the default style of…</p>
<p>This is another paragraph that has the default browser…</p>
<p class="margintest">This paragraph has a 40-pixel
margin…</p>
</body>
</html>
```

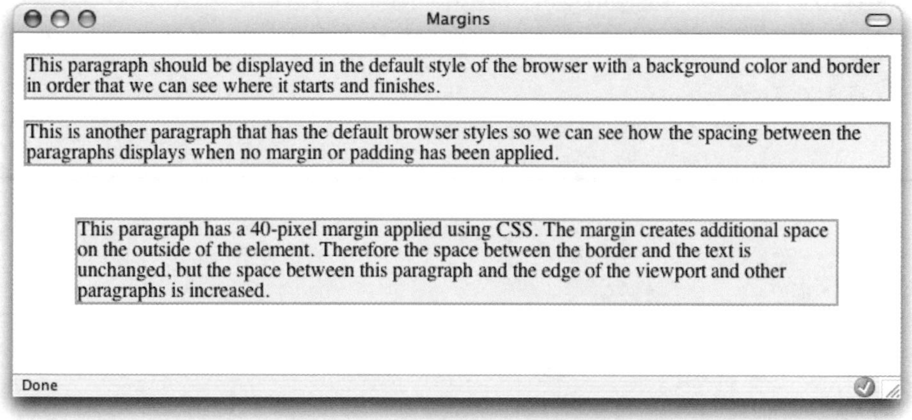

Figure 9.2. Applying margins to an element with CSS

The padding properties add space *inside* the element—between its borders and its content. You can set padding individually for the top, right, bottom, and left sides of an element:

```
padding-top: 1em;
padding-right: 1.5em;
padding-bottom: 0.5em;
padding-left: 2em;
```

You can also apply padding using this shorthand property:

```
padding: 1em 1.5em 0.5em 2em;
```

As with margins, if the padding is to be equal all the way around an element, you can simply use a rule like this:

```
padding: 1em;
```

Figure 9.3, which results from the following code, shows what a block looks like with padding applied. Compare it to Figure 9.2 to see the differences between margins and padding.

padding.html

```
<!DOCTYPE html PUBLIC "-//W3C//DTD XHTML 1.0 Strict//EN"
    "http://www.w3.org/TR/xhtml1/DTD/xhtml1-strict.dtd">
<html xmlns="http://www.w3.org/1999/xhtml" lang="en-US">
<head>
<title>Padding</title>
<meta http-equiv="content-type"
    content="text/html; charset=utf-8" />
<style type="text/css">
p {
  border: 2px solid #AAAAAA;
  background-color: #EEEEEE;
}
p.paddingtest {
  padding: 40px;
}
</style>
</head>
<body>
<p>This paragraph should be displayed in the default style …</p>
<p>This is another paragraph that has the default browser …</p>
<p class="paddingtest">This paragraph has 40 pixels of …</p>
</body>
</html>
```

Discussion

The above solution demonstrates the basics of margins and padding. As we've seen, the margin properties create space between the element to which they are applied and the surrounding elements, while padding creates space inside the element to which it is applied. Figure 9.4 illustrates this point.

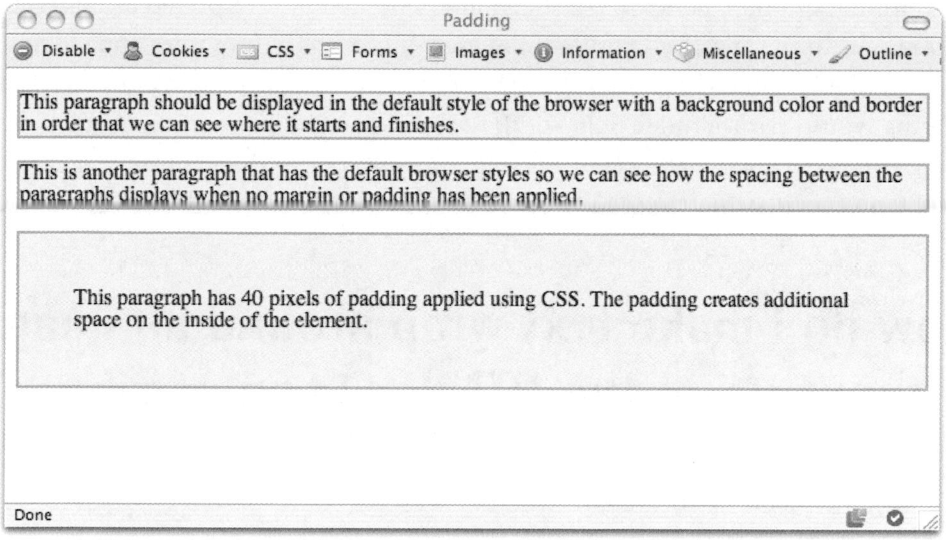

Figure 9.3. Applying padding to an element in CSS

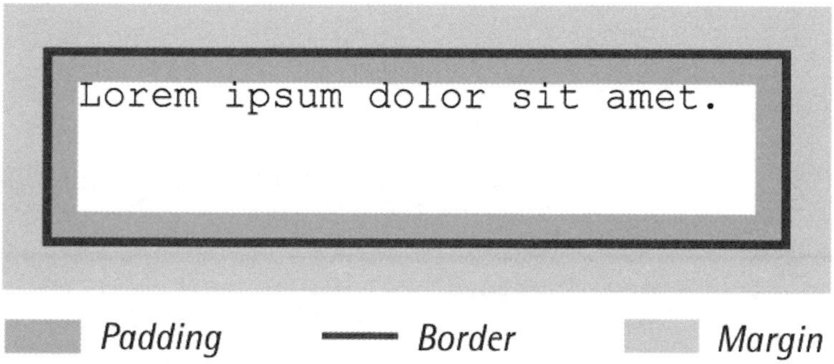

Figure 9.4. Applying margins, padding, and borders

If you're applying margins and padding to a fixed-width element, they will be added to the specified width to produce the total width for that element. So, if your element has a width of 400 pixels, and you add 40 pixels' worth of padding on all sides, you'll make the element 480 pixels wide. Add 20 pixels of margins to that, and the element will occupy a width of 520 pixels (a visible width of 480 pixels with 20 pixels of spacing on either side). If you have a very precise layout, remember to calculate your element sizes carefully, including any added margins and padding.

In Internet Explorer 5 and 5.5, padding (and borders) are interpreted as being included within the specified width of the element; in these browsers, the element just described would remain 400 pixels in width with the padding included; adding margins would reduce the visible width of the element. One workaround for this peculiarity is to apply padding to a parent element, rather than adding a margin to the element in question. Alternatively, you could use the box model hack described in Chapter 7.

How do I make text wrap around an image without using the HTML `align` attribute?

With HTML, it's possible to wrap text around an image using the `align` attribute. This attribute is now deprecated, but there is a CSS equivalent!

Solution

Use the CSS `float` property to float an image to the left or right, as shown in Figure 9.5.

Here's the code for this page:

float.html

```
<!DOCTYPE html PUBLIC "-//W3C//DTD XHTML 1.0 Strict//EN"
    "http://www.w3.org/TR/xhtml1/DTD/xhtml1-strict.dtd">
<html xmlns="http://www.w3.org/1999/xhtml" lang="en-US">
<head>
<title>Float</title>
<meta http-equiv="content-type"
    content="text/html; charset=utf-8" />
<style type="text/css">
.featureimage {
  float: left;
  width: 319px;
}
</style>
</head>
```

```
<body>
<h1>Chinese-style stuffed peppers</h1>
<img src="peppers1.jpg" width="319" height="255" alt="peppers"
    class="featureimage" />
<p>These stuffed peppers are lovely as a starter…</p>
</body>
</html>
```

Figure 9.5. Floating an image to the left using the float property

Discussion

The float property takes the element out of the document flow and "floats" it against the edge of the block-level element that contains it. Other block-level elements will then ignore the floated element and render as if it isn't there. Inline elements such as content, however, will make space for the floated element, which is why we can use float to cause our text to wrap around an image.

As we can see clearly in Figure 9.5, the text bumps right up against the side of the image. Figure 9.6 shows that, if we add a border to that image, the text bumps right up against the side of the border.

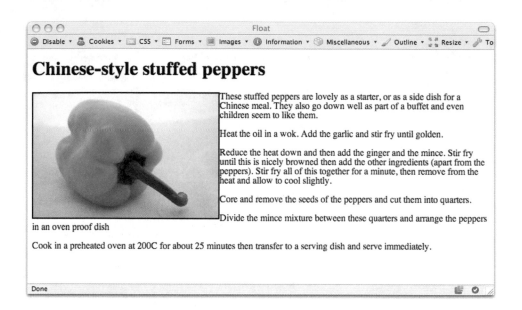

Figure 9.6. Text rendering against an image to which borders are applied

To create space between our image and the text, we need to add a margin to the image. Since the image is aligned against the left-hand margin, we'll probably only want to add right and bottom margins to move the text away from the image slightly:

float2.html *(excerpt)*

```
.featureimage {
  float: left;
  width: 319px;
  border: 2px solid #000000;
  margin-right: 20px;
  margin-bottom: 6px;
}
```

Figure 9.7 shows the resulting display, with extra space around the floated image.

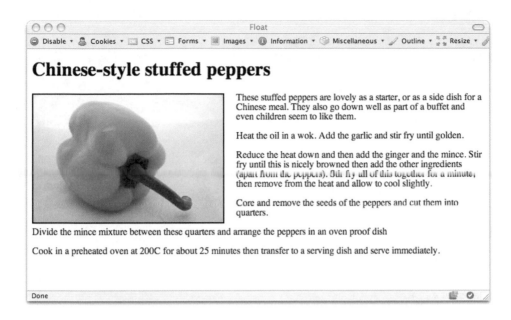

Figure 9.7. Adding right and bottom margins to an image to improve the display

How do I stop the next element moving up when I use float?

Floating an image or other element causes it to be ignored by block-level elements, although the text and inline images contained in those elements will appear to wrap around the floated element. How can you force elements on your page to display below the floated element?

Solution

The CSS property `clear` allows you to make a given element display beneath any floated elements as if they had not been floated in the first place. In this example, we apply this property with a value of `both` to the first paragraph that follows the list of ingredients:

```
                                                            float-clear.html
<!DOCTYPE html PUBLIC "-//W3C//DTD XHTML 1.0 Strict//EN"
    "http://www.w3.org/TR/xhtml1/DTD/xhtml1-strict.dtd">
<html xmlns="http://www.w3.org/1999/xhtml" lang="en-US">
```

```
<head>
<title>float and clear</title>
<meta http-equiv="content-type"
    content="text/html; charset=utf-8" />
<style type="text/css">
.featureimg {
  float: right;
  width: 319px;
  margin-left: 20px;
  margin-bottom: 6px;
  border:1px solid #000;
}

.clear {
  clear: both;
}

</style>
</head>
<body>
<h1>Chinese-style stuffed peppers</h1>
<img src="peppers1.jpg" width="319" height="213" alt="peppers"
    class="featureimg" />
<ul>
  <li>1 tablespoon of oil</li>
  <li>1 crushed garlic clove</li>
  <li>Peeled and finely chopped fresh ginger root</li>
  <li>250g minced pork, beef or Quorn</li>
  <li>1 chopped spring onion</li>
  <li>1 chopped celery stick</li>
  <li>Grated rind of 1 lemon</li>
  <li>Finely chopped red chilli (optional)</li>
  <li>4 large green peppers</li>
</ul>
<p class="clear">These stuffed peppers are lovely as a …</p>
…
</body>
</html>
```

As shown in Figure 9.8, where we've floated the image to the right of the page, this markup causes the paragraph to be pushed down so that it begins below the floated image.

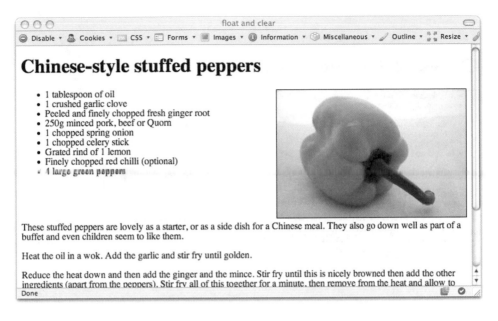

Figure 9.8. The first paragraph displaying clear of the floated image

Discussion

The `float` property takes an element out of the flow of the document: the block-level elements that appear after it will simply ignore the floated element. This effect can be seen more clearly if we apply a border to the elements in our document, as illustrated in Figure 9.9, which adds a two-pixel border to the `ul` and `p` elements in the page.

The floated image basically sits on top of the block elements. The text within those elements wraps around the image, but the elements themselves will ignore the fact that the floated element is there. This means that, in our example, if the height of the ingredients list is less than that of the image, the paragraph after the list of ingredients will wrap around the image, as Figure 9.10 shows.

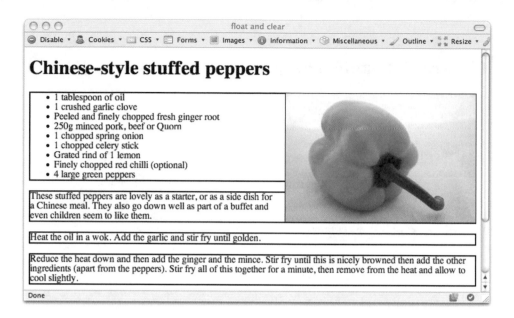

Figure 9.9. Applying a two-pixel border to the ul and p elements

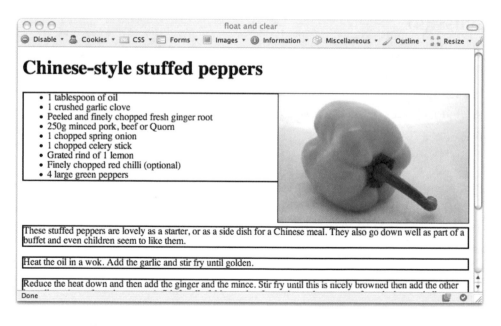

Figure 9.10. Using the clear property to clear the paragraph from the float

To get the paragraph to begin at a point below that at which the image finishes, we can use the `clear` property:

```
.clear {
  clear: both;
}
```

We apply this CSS class to the first `<p>` tag after the ingredients list.

```
<p class="clear">These stuffed peppers are lovely as a starter, or
   as a side dish for a Chinese meal. They also go down well as
   part of a buffet and even children seem to like them.</p>
```

If we leave the borders in place and reload the document as in Figure 9.10, we can see that the paragraph begins below the pepper image; its border does not run behind the image at all.

The `clear` property can also take values of `left` or `right`, which are useful if you want to clear an element only from left or right floats, respectively. The value you are most likely to use, though, is `both`. Be aware that both `float` and `clear` can trigger bugs, particularly in Internet Explorer. We discussed one of these bugs in Chapter 7.

How do I align a site's logo and slogan to the left and right without using a table?

If you've ever used tables for layout, you'll know how easy it is to create the type of effect shown in Figure 9.11 with a two-column table. This method allows you to align the contents of the left-hand table cell to the left, and those of the right-hand cell to the right. Fortunately, the same end result is achievable using CSS.

Figure 9.11. Aligning the logo and slogan left and right, respectively, using CSS

Solution

We can use float to create this type of layout:

```
slogan-align.html
```

```
<!DOCTYPE html PUBLIC "-//W3C//DTD XHTML 1.0 Strict//EN"
    "http://www.w3.org/TR/xhtml1/DTD/xhtml1-strict.dtd">
<html xmlns="http://www.w3.org/1999/xhtml" lang="en-US">
<head>
<title>Stage &amp; Screen - theatre and film reviews</title>
<meta http-equiv="content-type"
    content="text/html; charset=utf-8" />
<link rel="stylesheet" type="text/css" href="slogan-align.css"
    />
</head>
<body>
<div id="header">
  <img src="stage-logo.gif" width="187" height="29"
      alt="Stage &amp; Screen" class="logo" />
  <span class="slogan">theatre and film reviews</span>
</div>
</body>
</html>
```

```
slogan-align.css
```

```
body {
  margin: 0;
  padding: 0;
```

```
    background-color: #FFFFFF;
    color: #000000;
    font-family: Arial, Helvetica, sans-serif;
    border-top: 2px solid #2A4F6F;
}
#header {
    border-top: 1px solid #778899;
    border-bottom: 1px dotted #B2BCC6;
    height: 3em;
}
#header .slogan {
    font: 120% Georgia, "Times New Roman", Times, serif;
    color: #778899;
    background-color: transparent;
    float: right;
    width: 300px;
    text-align:right;
    margin-right: 2em;
    margin-top: 0.5em;
}
#header .logo {
    float: left;
    width: 187px;
    margin-left: 1.5em;
    margin-top: 0.5em;
}
```

Discussion

The float property allows us to align the elements in our header with either side of the viewport. Before adding the float, our elements will display next to each other, as in Figure 9.12.

The elements appear side by side because the HTML that marks them up dictates nothing about their positions on the page. Thus, they appear one after the other. Let's take a look at the markup that controls the slogan's alignment:

Figure 9.12. The elements displaying at their default positions

slogan-align.html *(excerpt)*

```
<div id="header">
  <img src="stage-logo.gif" width="187" height="29"
    alt="Stage &amp; Screen" class="logo" />
  <span class="slogan">theatre and film reviews<span>
</div>
```

By floating the class `logo` to the left and `slogan` to the right, we can move the elements to the left and right of the display. I've also added a rule to align the text in our slogan to the right—without this line, the text that comprises our slogan will still be left-aligned within the `span` element that we floated to the right! Figure 9.13 shows the result.

Figure 9.13. Applying `float` to make the elements display as desired

To provide some space around the elements, let's add a margin to the top and left of the logo, and the top and right of the slogan:

slogan-align.css *(excerpt)*

```
#header .slogan {
  font: 120% Georgia, "Times New Roman", Times, serif;
  color: #778899;
  background-color: transparent;
  float: right;
  width: 300px;
  text-align: right;
  margin-right: 2em;
  margin-top: 0.5em;
}
#header .logo {
  float: left;
  width: 187px;
  margin-left: 1.5em;
  margin-top: 0.5em;
}
```

One thing to be aware of when you're using this technique is that, once you've floated all the elements within a container, that container will no longer be "held open" by anything, so it will collapse to zero height. To demonstrate this point, I've added a large border to my header in Figure 9.14. Here, the elements have not been floated, so the header surrounds the elements.

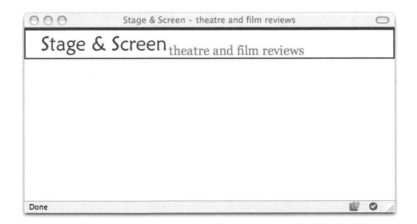

Figure 9.14. Showing the size of the header when elements are not floated

Once I float the elements right and left, the header loses its height, because the elements have been taken out of the document flow. The thick red line at the top of Figure 9.15 is actually the header's border.

Figure 9.15. Floating the elements causing the header to collapse

To avoid this problem, you can set an explicit `height` for the block:

slogan-align.css (excerpt)

```
#header {
  border-top: 1px solid #778899;
  border-bottom: 1px dotted #B2BCC6;
  height: 3em;
}
```

The block now occupies the desired area of the page, as Figure 9.16 shows.

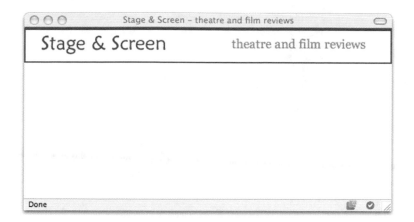

Figure 9.16. The page displaying normally after a `height` is set for the header `<div>`

When you're setting heights in this kind of situation, keep in mind the potential impact that user-altered text sizes may have on your layout. Using ems is a handy way to set heights, as they will expand relative to the text size, so they can accommodate larger text sizes without running the risk of having the floated element burst out of the box.

How do I set an item's position on the page using CSS?

It's possible to use CSS to specify exactly where on the page an element should display.

Solution

With CSS, you can place an element on the page by positioning it from the top, right, bottom, or left using **absolute positioning**. The two blocks shown in Figure 9.17 have been placed with absolute positioning.

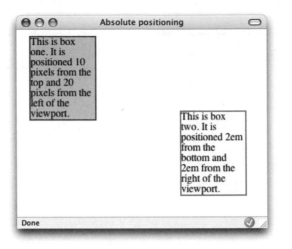

Figure 9.17. Placing boxes using absolute positioning

The code for this page is as follows:

position.html

```
<!DOCTYPE html PUBLIC "-//W3C//DTD XHTML 1.0 Strict//EN"
    "http://www.w3.org/TR/xhtml1/DTD/xhtml1-strict.dtd">
<html xmlns="http://www.w3.org/1999/xhtml" lang="en-US">
<head>
<title>Absolute positioning</title>
<meta http-equiv="content-type"
    content="text/html; charset=utf-8" />
<link rel="stylesheet" type="text/css" href="position.css" />
</head>
<body>
<div id="box1">This is box one. It is positioned 10 pixels from
  the top and 20 pixels from the left of the viewport.</div>
<div id="box2">This is box two. It is positioned 2em from the
  bottom and 2em from the right of the viewport.</div>
</body>
</html>
```

position.css

```
#box1 {
  position: absolute;
  top: 10px;
  left: 20px;
```

```
  width: 100px;
  background-color: #B0C4DE;
  border: 2px solid #34537D
}
#box2 {
  position: absolute;
  bottom: 2em;
  right: 2em;
  width: 100px;
  background-color: #FFFAFA;
  border: 2px solid #CD5C5C;
}
```

Discussion

Setting an element's `position` property to `absolute` removes it completely from the document flow. As an example, if I add several paragraphs of text to the example document shown above, the two boxes will sit on top of the content, as shown in Figure 9.18.

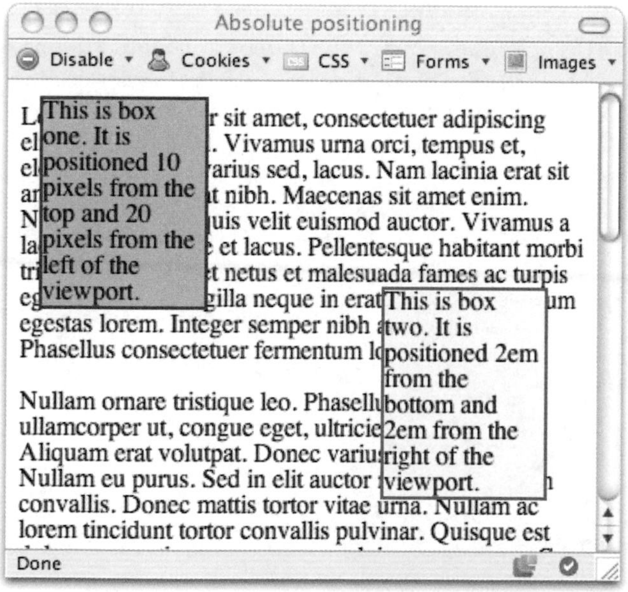

Figure 9.18. The content ignoring the positioned boxes

In the markup that I used to produce this display, the paragraphs follow the absolutely positioned `divs`; however, because the `divs` have been removed from the document flow, the paragraphs begin at the top-left corner just as they would if the boxes did not exist.

As we'll see in "How do I create a liquid, two-column layout with the menu on the left, and the content on the right?", we can create space for absolutely positioned areas by placing them within the margins or padding of other elements. What may not be obvious from this example, though, is that elements need not be positioned relative to the edges of the document (although this approach is quite common). Elements can also be positioned within other elements with the same degree of precision.

Figure 9.19 depicts a layout that contains two boxes. In this example, box two is nested inside box one. Because box one is also positioned absolutely, the absolute positioning of box two sets its position relative to the edges of box one. Here's the markup that produces the display:

position2.html *(excerpt)*

```
<div id="box1">This is box one. It is positioned 100 pixels from
  the top and 100 pixels from the left of the viewport.
  <div id="box2">This is box two. It is positioned 2em from the
    bottom and 2em from the right of the parent element - box one.
  </div>
</div>
```

position2.css

```
#box1 {
  position: absolute;
  top: 100px;
  left: 100px;
  width: 400px;
  background-color: #B0C4DE;
  border: 2px solid #34537D
}
#box2 {
  position: absolute;
  bottom: 2em;
  right: 2em;
```

```
    width: 150px;
    background-color: #FFFAFA;
    border: 2px solid #CD5C5C;
}
```

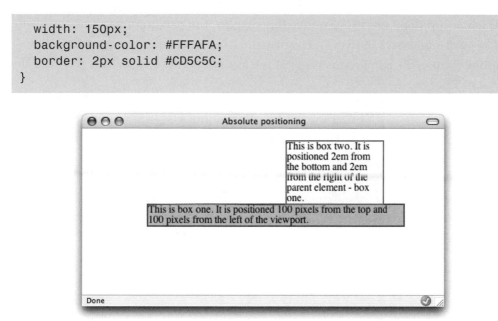

Figure 9.19. Positioning box two within box one

To demonstrate this point further, let's add a `height` of 300 pixels to the CSS for box1:

```
                                                    position3.css (excerpt)
#box1 {
    position: absolute;
    top: 100px;
    left: 100px;
    width: 400px;
    height: 300px;
    background-color: #B0C4DE;
    border: 2px solid #34537D
}
```

You'll now see box two render entirely within box one, as shown in Figure 9.20, rather than appearing to stick out the top of it. This display results because box two is positioned with respect to the bottom and right-hand edges of box one.

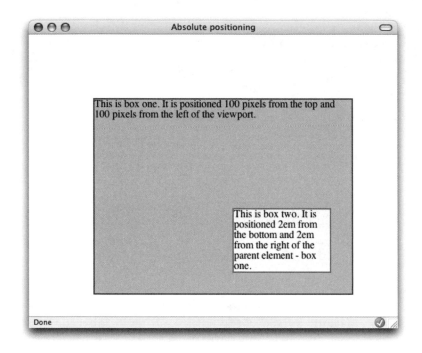

Figure 9.20. Box two rendering within box one

Positioning Starts with the Parent

It's important to note that the parent element (box1) must be positioned using CSS in order for the child element (box2) to base its position on that parent.

If the parent element's position property is not set, then the child's position will be based on the edges of the document—not those of the parent element.

How do I center a block on the page?

One common page layout uses a fixed-width, centered box to contain the page content, as does the one shown in Figure 9.21. How can we center this box on the page using CSS?

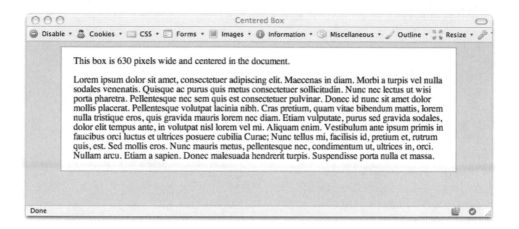

Figure 9.21. Centering a fixed-width box using CSS

Solution

You can use CSS to center a fixed-width box by setting its left and right margins to `auto`:

```
                                                              center.html
<!DOCTYPE html PUBLIC "-//W3C//DTD XHTML 1.0 Strict//EN"
    "http://www.w3.org/TR/xhtml1/DTD/xhtml1-strict.dtd">
<html xmlns="http://www.w3.org/1999/xhtml" lang="en-US">
<head>
<title>Centered Box</title>
<meta http-equiv="content-type"
    content="text/html; charset=utf-8" />
<link rel="stylesheet" type="text/css" href="center.css" />
</head>
<body>
<div id="content">
  <p>This box is 630 pixels wide and centered in the document.</p>
  <p>Lorem ipsum dolor sit amet, consectetuer adipiscing …</p>
</div>
</body>
</html>
```

```
                                                              center.css
body {
  background-color: #CCD3D9;
  color: #000000;
  text-align: center;
}
#content {
  width: 630px;
  margin-left: auto;
  margin-right: auto;
  border: 2px solid #A6B2BC;
  background-color: #FFFFFF;
  color: #000000;
  padding: 0 20px 0 20px;
  text-align: left;
}
```

Discussion

This technique allows you to center boxes easily, and is ideal if you need to center a content block on a page.

When we set both the left and right margins to `auto`, we're asking the browser to calculate equal values for each margin, thereby centering the box. In "How do I create a liquid, two-column layout with the menu on the left, and the content on the right?", we'll see how to create a layout inside a container that has been centered in this way.

The example code provided here contains additional CSS to work around a bug in Internet Explorer 5.x that prevents the margins from centering content. By setting `text-align: center` on the body, then setting it to `text-align: left` on the content `div`, we're able to circumvent the problem, allowing the layout to center in these browsers as well.

How do I create a liquid, two-column layout with the menu on the left, and the content on the right?

Web page layouts like that shown in Figure 9.22, which display a menu on the left and a large content area to the right, are extremely common. Let's discover how to build this layout using CSS.

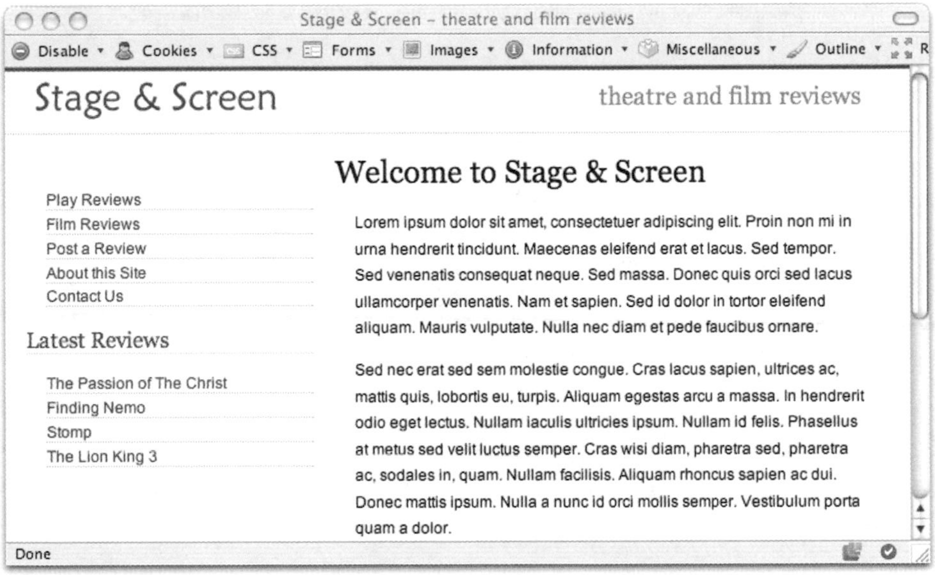

Figure 9.22. Building a liquid two-column layout using CSS

Solution

Here's the markup and CSS that produces the display shown in Figure 9.22:

```
                                                           2col.html

<!DOCTYPE html PUBLIC "-//W3C//DTD XHTML 1.0 Strict//EN"
    "http://www.w3.org/TR/xhtml1/DTD/xhtml1-strict.dtd">
<html xmlns="http://www.w3.org/1999/xhtml" lang="en-US">
<head>
<title>Stage &amp; Screen - theatre and film reviews</title>
<meta http-equiv="content-type"
```

```
      content="text/html; charset=utf-8" />
<link rel="stylesheet" type="text/css" href="2col.css" />
</head>
<body>
<div id="header">
  <img src="stage-logo.gif" width="187" height="29"
      alt="Stage &amp; Screen" class="logo" />
  <span class="slogan">theatre and film reviews</span>
</div>
<div id="content">
  <h1>Welcome to Stage &amp; Screen</h1>
  <p>Lorem ipsum dolor sit amet, consectetuer adipiscing …</p>
</div>
<div id="nav">
  <ul>
    <li><a href="#">Play Reviews</a></li>
    <li><a href="#">Film Reviews</a></li>
    <li><a href="#">Post a Review</a></li>
    <li><a href="#">About this Site</a></li>
    <li><a href="#">Contact Us</a></li>
  </ul>
  <h2>Latest Reviews</h2>
  <ul>
    <li><a href="#">The Passion of The Christ</a></li>
    <li><a href="#">Finding Nemo</a></li>
    <li><a href="#">Stomp</a></li>
    <li><a href="#">The Lion King 3</a></li>
  </ul>
</div>
</body>
</html>
```

2col.css

```
body {
  margin: 0;
  padding: 0;
  background-color: #FFFFFF;
  color: #000000;
  font-family: Arial, Helvetica, sans-serif;
  border-top: 2px solid #2A4F6F;
}
#header {
  border-top: 1px solid #778899;
```

```
    border-bottom: 1px dotted #B2BCC6;
    height:3em;
}
#header .slogan {
    font: 120% Georgia, "Times New Roman", Times, serif;
    color: #778899;
    background-color: transparent;
    float: right;
    width: 300px;
    text align:right;
    margin-right: 2em;
    margin-top: 0.5em;
}
#header .logo {
    float: left;
    width: 187px;
    margin-left: 1.5em;
    margin-top: 0.5em;
}

#nav {
    position: absolute;
    top: 5em;
    left: 1em;
    width: 14em;
}
#nav ul {
    list-style: none;
    margin-left: 1em;
    padding-left: 0;
}
#nav li {
    font-size: 80%;
    border-bottom: 1px dotted #B2BCC6;
    margin-bottom: 0.3em;
}
#nav a:link, #nav a:visited {
    text-decoration: none;
    color: #2A4F6F;
    background-color: transparent;
}
#nav a:hover {
    color: #778899;
}
```

```
#nav h2 {
  font: 110% Georgia, "Times New Roman", Times, serif;
  color: #2A4F6F;
  background-color: transparent;
  border-bottom: 1px dotted #cccccc;
}
#content {
  margin-left: 16em;
  margin-right: 2em;
}
h1 {
  font: 150% Georgia, "Times New Roman", Times, serif;
}
#content p {
  font-size: 80%;
  line-height: 1.6em;
  padding-left: 1.2em;
}
```

Discussion

Our starting point for this layout is the header that we created in "How do I align a site's logo and slogan to the left and right without using a table?". We've added to that layout some content, which resides within a div whose ID is content. The navigation for the page comprises two unordered lists that are contained in a div with the ID nav. As you'd expect, without any positioning applied, these blocks will display below the heading in the order in which they appear in the document (as depicted in Figure 9.23).

Figure 9.23. The content and navigation displaying without positioning information

At this point, the CSS looks like this:

```
2col.css (excerpt)

body {
  margin: 0;
  padding: 0;
  background-color: #FFFFFF;
  color: #000000;
```

```
    font-family: Arial, Helvetica, sans-serif;
    border-top: 2px solid #2A4F6F;
}
#header {
    border-top: 1px solid #778899;
    border-bottom: 1px dotted #B2BCC6;
    height:3em;
}
#header .slogan {
    font: 120% Georgia, "Times New Roman", Times, serif;
    color: #778899;
    background-color: transparent;
    float: right;
    width: 300px;
    text-align:right;
    margin-right: 2em;
    margin-top: 0.5em;
}
#header .logo {
    float: left;
    width: 187px;
    margin-left: 1.5em;
    margin-top: 0.5em;
}
```

Sizing and Positioning the Menu

Let's use absolute positioning to position the menu just under the heading bar, and give it an appropriate width:

2col.css (excerpt)

```
#nav {
    position: absolute;
    top: 5em;
    left: 1em;
    width: 14em;
}
```

As you can see in Figure 9.24, this code causes the menu to appear over the text content, as the absolute positioning we've applied has removed it from the flow of the document.

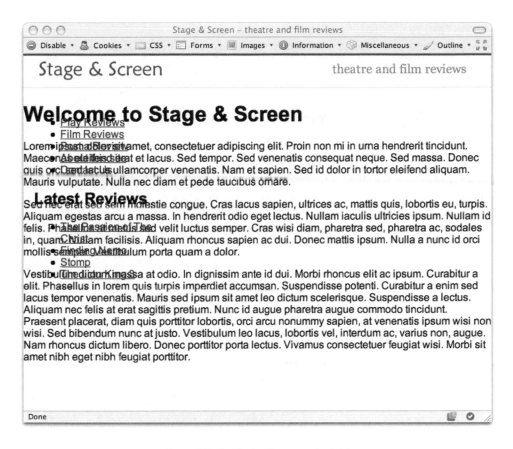

Figure 9.24. Positioning the menu absolutely

Positioning the Content

As we're aiming to maintain a liquid layout, we don't want to assign a fixed width to the content and, in fact, we don't need to. The problem with the content is that it appears in the space required by the menu. To solve this problem, we can simply apply a large left-hand margin to the content area to allow space for the menu. The results are shown in Figure 9.25:

```
#content {
  margin-left: 16em;
  margin-right: 2em;
}
```

Figure 9.25. Adding margins to the content

Now that all the elements are laid out neatly, we can work on the styling of individual elements, using CSS to create the layout we saw back in Figure 9.22. The completed CSS style sheet is given at the start of this solution.

Ems for Positioning Text Layouts

I used ems to position the elements in this layout. The em unit will resize as the text resizes, which should help us avoid any problems with overlapping text if users resize fonts in their browsers. For layouts that are predominantly text-based, the em is an excellent choice for setting the widths of boxes and margins. However, care should be taken if your design involves many images. Images do not resize with text, so you may prefer to use pixels to position elements in cases where you need precise control over the elements' locations on the page.

Can I reverse this layout and put the menu on the right?

Can the technique presented in "How do I create a liquid, two-column layout with the menu on the left, and the content on the right?" be used to create a layout in which the menu is positioned on the right?

Solution

Yes, exactly the same technique can be used! You'll need to position your menu from the top and right, and give the content area a large right margin so that the menu has sufficient space in which to display. The result is shown in Figure 9.26.

Figure 9.26. Building a two-column layout so that the menu appears on the right

Discussion

Positioning the menu on the right doesn't require us to change the markup of the original document at all. All we need to do is change the positioning properties for nav, and the margins on content:

```
                                                    2col-reverse.css
#nav {
  position: absolute;
  top: 5em;
  right: 1em;
  width: 14em;
}
#content {
  margin-left: 2em;
  margin-right: 16em;
}
```

The advantage of using absolute positioning can be seen clearly here. It doesn't matter where our menu appears in the markup: the use of absolute positioning means it will be removed from the document flow and we can place it wherever we like on the page. This can be of great benefit for accessibility purposes, as it allows us to place some of the less-important items (such as lists of links to other sites, advertising, and so on) right at the end of the document code. This way, those who employ screen readers to use the site won't have to hear these unnecessary items read aloud each time they access a page. Yet you, as the designer, are still able to position these items wherever you like for visual effect.

How do I create a fixed-width, centered, two-column layout?

You can use CSS to create a two-column layout that's contained within a centered div on the page.

Solution

Creating a two-column, fixed-width, centered layout is slightly trickier than a fixed-width, left-aligned, or liquid layout, as you don't have an absolute reference point from the left- or right-hand side of the viewport that you can use to position the elements horizontally. However, there are a couple of different ways in which we can deal with this complication in order to achieve the kind of layout shown in Figure 9.27.

Figure 9.27. The fixed-width, centered layout

Whichever layout method you choose, the HTML is the same:

2col-fixedwidth.html

```
<!DOCTYPE html PUBLIC "-//W3C//DTD XHTML 1.0 Strict//EN"
"http://www.w3.org/TR/xhtml1/DTD/xhtml1-strict.dtd">
<html xmlns="http://www.w3.org/1999/xhtml" lang="en-US">
<head>
<title>Recipe for Success</title>
<link href="2col-fixedwidth.css" rel="stylesheet" type="text/css" />
<meta http-equiv="content-type"
```

```
      content="text/html; charset=utf-8" />
</head>
<body>
<div id="wrapper">
  <div id="header">
    <h1>Recipe for Success</h1>
  </div>
  <div id="content">
    <p>The Recipe for Success web site...</p>
  </div>
  <div id="navigation">
    <ul id="mainnav">
      <li><a href="#">Recipes</a></li>
      <li><a href="#">Contact Us</a></li>
      <li><a href="#">Articles</a></li>
      <li><a href="#">Buy Online</a></li>
    </ul>
  </div>
  <div id="footer">Copyright &copy; 1999 - 2007 Recipe for
    success</div>
</div>
</body>
</html>
```

The first and simplest option to achieve this layout is to place the content and navigation elements within the centered block, using absolute and relative positioning, respectively:

2col-fixedwidth.css

```
body {
  margin: 0;
  padding: 0;
  font-family: Verdana, Arial, Helvetica, sans-serif;
  background-color: #FFFFFF;
  text-align: center;
}
#wrapper {
  position: relative;
  text-align: left;
  width: 760px;
  margin-right: auto;
  margin-left: auto;
```

```
  border-bottom: 1px solid #ececec;
}

#header {
  background-image: url(recipe-header.jpg);
  background-repeat: no-repeat;
  height: 150px;
  position: relative;
  border-bottom: 1px solid #ececec;
}

#header h1 {
  margin: 0;
  padding: 0;
  font-weight: normal;
  color: #cb352d;
  font-size: 190%;
  position: absolute;
  bottom: 4px;
  right: 0;
}

#content {
  margin-left: 230px;
  padding: 0 10px 0 0;
}

#content p {
  font-size: 80%;
  line-height: 1.8em;
}

#navigation {
  position: absolute;
  top: 150px;
  left: 0;
  width: 180px;
}

#navigation ul {
  list-style: none;
  margin: 1em 0 0 0;
  padding: 0;
  border: none;
```

```
}

#navigation li {
  font-size: 90%;
}

#navigation a:link, #navigation a:visited {
  color: #cb352d;
  background-color: transparent;
  display: block;
  border-bottom: 1px solid #999;
  padding: 1em 0 0.2em 0;
  text-decoration: none;
}

#navigation a:hover {
  color: #999;
}

#footer {
  font-size: 80%;
  padding-top: 1em;
  text-align: right;
  color: #999;
  background-color: transparent;
}
```

An alternative approach is to simply float the navigation and content against the left and right sides of the centered block, respectively. Floating the elements will give you more flexibility if you need to add other elements to the layout, such as a footer. If you float the left and right columns, you can apply clear: both to the footer to place it beneath the two columns, regardless of their heights. This dynamic placement of the footer within the document flow is not possible if the columns are absolutely positioned:

2col-fixedwidth-float.css

```
body {
  margin: 0;
  padding: 0;
  font-family: Verdana, Arial, Helvetica, sans-serif;
  background-color: #FFFFFF;
```

```
  text-align: center;
}

#wrapper {
  position: relative;
  text-align: left;
  width: 760px;
  margin-right: auto;
  margin-left: auto;
]

#header {
  background-image: url(recipe-header.jpg);
  background-repeat: no-repeat;
  height: 150px;
  position: relative;
  border-bottom: 1px solid #ececec;
}

#header h1 {
  margin: 0;
  padding: 0;
  font-weight: normal;
  color: #cb352d;
  font-size: 190%;
  position:absolute;
  bottom: 4px;
  right: 0;
}

#content {
  float: right;
  width: 520px;
  padding: 0 10px 0 0;
}

#content p {
  font-size: 80%;
  line-height: 1.8em;
}

#navigation {
  float: left;
  width: 180px;
```

```
}

#navigation ul {
  list-style: none;
  margin: 1em 0 0 0;
  padding: 0;
  border: none;
}

#navigation li {
  font-size: 90%;
}

#navigation a:link, #navigation a:visited {
  color: #cb352d;
  background-color: transparent;
  display: block;
  border-bottom: 1px solid #999;
  padding: 1em 0 0.2em 0;
  text-decoration: none;
}

#navigation a:hover {
  color: #999;
}

#footer {
  clear: both;
  font-size: 80%;
  padding-top: 1em;
  text-align: right;
  color: #999;
  background-color: transparent;
}
```

Discussion

For the purposes of this discussion, we'll ignore purely aesthetic style properties such as borders, colors, and fonts, so that we can concentrate on the layout.

Both versions of this layout begin with a centered div, similar to the layouts we worked with in "How do I center a block on the page?". This div is given the ID wrapper:

```
                                   2col-fixedwidth.css or 2col-fixedwidth-float.css (excerpt)
body {
  margin: 0;
  padding: 0;
  text-align: center;
  …
}

#wrapper {
  text-align: left;
  width: 760px;
  margin-right: auto;
  margin-left: auto;
  …
}
```

The results of applying these styles are shown in Figure 9.28.

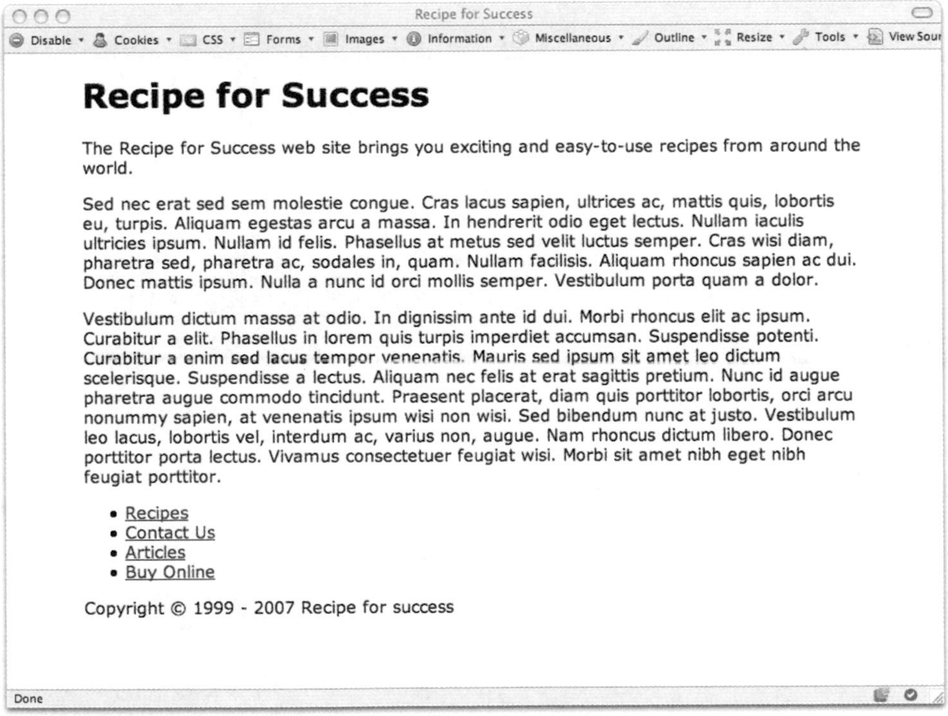

Figure 9.28. Centering the content on the page

Now, in "How do I create a liquid, two-column layout with the menu on the left, and the content on the right?" we saw that we could use absolute positioning to control the navigation's location, and apply enough margin to the content of the page so that the two blocks would not overlap. The only difference in this layout is that we need to position the navigation within the centered `wrapper` block, so we can't give it an absolute position on the page.

Instead of using `absolute`, you can set an element's `position` property to `relative`, which doesn't take the element out of the document flow the way absolute positioning does; instead, it lets you shift the element from the starting point of its default position on the page. If you don't provide coordinates to which you want to shift the element, it will actually stay exactly where the browser would normally position it. Unlike an element that doesn't have a `position` value specified, however, a relatively positioned element will provide a new **positioning context** for any absolutely positioned elements within it.

In plain English, an element with `position: absolute` that's contained within an element with `position: relative` will base its position on the edges of that parent element, not on the edges of the browser window. This is exactly what we need to use to position the navigation within the centered block in this example.

The first step is to set the `position` property of `wrapper` to `relative`:

2col-fixedwidth.css (excerpt)

```
#wrapper {
  position: relative;
  text-align: left;
  width: 760px;
  margin-right: auto;
  margin-left: auto;
  …
}
```

We then use absolute positioning to set the location of the `navigation` block:

2col-fixedwidth.css (excerpt)

```
#navigation {
  position: absolute;
```

```
    top: 150px;
    left: 0;
    width: 180px;
}
```

Finally, we add a margin to the main content of the page to make space for the newly positioned navigation area:

2col-fixedwidth.css *(excerpt)*

```
#content {
    margin-left: 230px;
    padding: 0 10px 0 0;
}
```

As long as the content of the page occupies more vertical space than does the navigation, this layout will work just fine. Unfortunately, since the navigation block is absolutely positioned, it doesn't affect the height of the wrapper block, so if the content is shorter than the navigation, the wrapper block will not be tall enough to contain the navigation. We can see this effect by adding a two-pixel, red border to the wrapper, and adding text to the sidebar so that it becomes longer than the content. In Figure 9.29, you can clearly see that the content in the sidebar extends below the wrapper element.

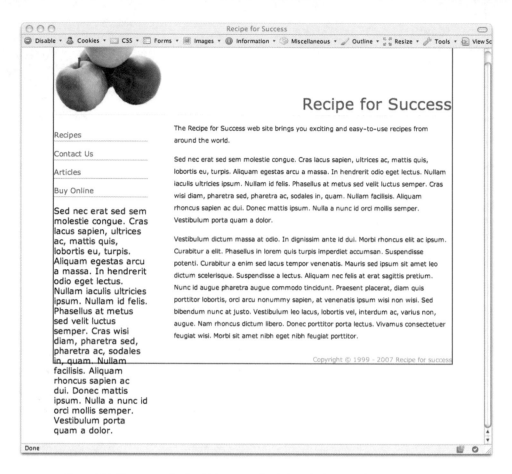

Figure 9.29. The content in the sidebar extending below the bottom of the `wrapper` block

The alternative method of using floated blocks to achieve our design goals is more complex, but it overcomes the limitation I just mentioned, enabling us to position a footer below the columns no matter which column is the longest. First, we float the `navigation` block left and the `content` block right:

2col-fixedwidth-float.css *(excerpt)*

```
#content {
  float: right;
  width: 520px;
  padding: 0 10px 0 0;
}
```

```
#navigation {
  float: left;
  width: 180px;
}
```

As you can see in Figure 9.30, the border of the `wrapper` block now cuts through the page content. This occurs because we floated most of the block's contents, removing them from the document flow. The only element inside `wrapper` that's still within the document flow is the `footer` block, which can be seen in the bottom-left corner of the `wrapper` block, to which it has been pushed by the floated blocks.

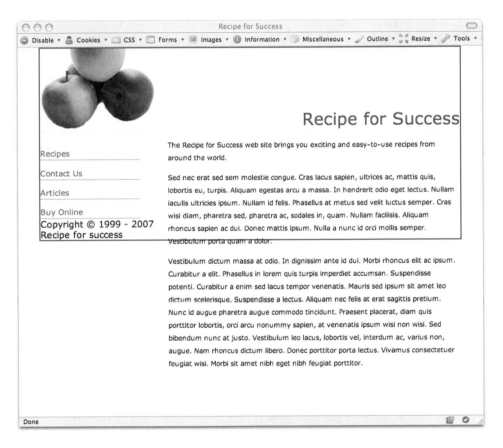

Figure 9.30. Floating the navigation left and the content right

If we set the `clear` property of the `footer` block to `both`, the footer will drop down below both of the floated blocks, thereby forcing `wrapper` to accommodate both the navigation and the content—no matter which is taller. The page now renders as shown in Figure 9.31.

2col-fixedwidth-float.css *(excerpt)*

```
#footer {
  clear: both;
  …
}
```

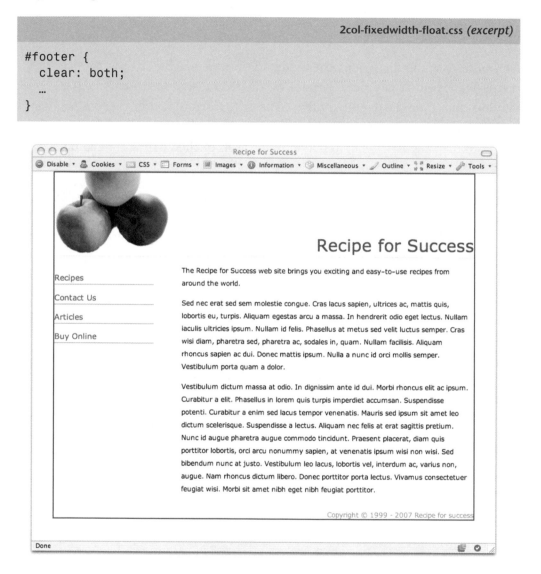

Figure 9.31. The footer set to clear: both

How do I create a full-height column?

If you've tried to add a background to a side column like the one shown in the last example in "How do I create a fixed-width, centered, two-column layout?", you may have discovered that you can't get the column to extend the full height of the taller column next to it, which makes your background look a little strange. For example, applying a background image to the `navigation` element will simply display the background behind the navigation list, rather than stretching it down the column to the end of the content, as shown in Figure 9.32.

Figure 9.32. The grey background displaying only behind the navigation content

Solution

The solution to this problem is to apply the background image to a page element that does extend the full height of the longer column, but to have it display at the same width as our navigation, in order to make it look as though the background is on the navigation column. In this case, we can apply the background image to `wrapper`, as Figure 9.33 illustrates.

```
#wrapper {
  position: relative;
  text-align: left;
  width: 760px;
  margin-right: auto;
  margin-left: auto;
  background-image: url(nav-bg.jpg);
  background-repeat:no-repeat;
  border-bottom: 1px solid #ececec;
}
```

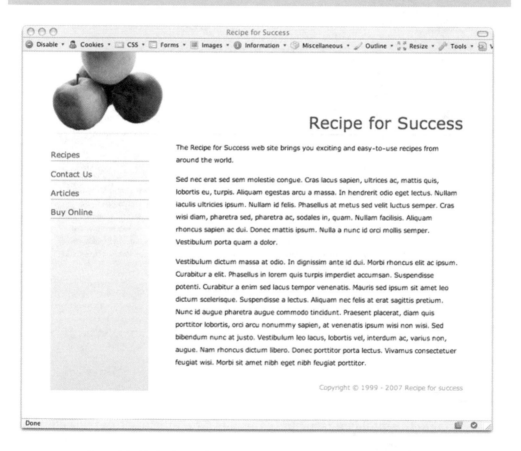

Figure 9.33. The background appearing to be attached to the navigation column

Discussion

This simple technique can be used to great effect in your layouts. In this example, I chose to apply the image to the wrapper block, as I want the background to extend right down to the end of the content, but you could use this technique to have the background stop above the footer, or after a certain section of content: simply apply the background to an element that contains the section of content you want.

Creating Solid Backgrounds

I used a very tall image here, because I was adding a gradient. If you want to display a solid color behind your navigation, use an image that's the same width as the navigation, but only a few pixels tall, and repeat it vertically.

How do I add a drop shadow to my layout?

Drop shadows are commonly used on layouts—particularly on content boxes within a layout. Let's add a drop shadow to a fixed width layout such as the one we worked with in the section called "How do I create a full-height column?".

Solution

We can add a drop shadow to this layout using two images: one for the background, and one to create the shadow effect at the bottom of the layout. Figure 9.34 shows the effect we're working to create.

Figure 9.34. A drop shadow

To create this effect, we need to add some markup that will provide us with hooks to which we can add the two images.

The first image, which I've named **shadow-bg.jpg** and can be seen in Figure 9.35, is a background image that we'll apply to the `div` with an ID of `wrapper`. This image is the left and right drop shadow, and it repeats down the page.

shadow-bg.jpg

shadow-bottom.jpg

Figure 9.35. The files used to create the drop shadow effect

I've increased the width of my `wrapper` block by 20 pixels. I've done this because I want the content area to stay the same width, but I need to allow room for the shadow on either side of the content:

2col-fixedwidth-shadow.css *(excerpt)*

```css
#wrapper {
  position: relative;
  text-align: left;
  width: 780px;
  margin-right: auto;
  margin-left: auto;
  background-image: url(shadow-bg.jpg);
  background-repeat: repeat-y;
}
```

Next, I wrap an additional `div`, which I've named `main`, around the `content`, `navigation`, and `footer` elements, just inside the `wrapper` block:

```html
<!DOCTYPE html PUBLIC "-//W3C//DTD XHTML 1.0 Strict//EN"
    "http://www.w3.org/TR/xhtml1/DTD/xhtml1-strict.dtd">
<html xmlns="http://www.w3.org/1999/xhtml" lang="en-US">
<head>
<title>Recipe for Success</title>
<link href="2col-fixedwidth-shadow.css" rel="stylesheet"
    type="text/css" />
<meta http-equiv="content-type"
    content="text/html; charset=utf-8" />
</head>
<body>
<div id="wrapper">
  <div id="main">
    <div id="header">
      <h1>Recipe for Success</h1>
    </div>
    <div id="content">
      <p>The Recipe for Success web site...</p>
    </div>
    <div id="navigation">
      <ul id="mainnav">
        <li><a href="#">Recipes</a></li>
        <li><a href="#">Contact Us</a></li>
        <li><a href="#">Articles</a></li>
```

```
        <li><a href="#">Buy Online</a></li>
      </ul>
    </div>
    <div id="footer">Copyright &copy; 1999 - 2007 Recipe for
        success</div>
  </div>
</div>
</body>
</html>
```

I add to this div the **shadow-bottom.jpg** image that forms the bottom of our drop shadow. I position it to the bottom-left of the element, and set its background-repeat value to no-repeat. I also add some padding to this div to push the page contents away from the drop shadow:

2col-fixedwidth-shadow.css *(excerpt)*

```
#main {
  padding: 0 20px 20px 20px;
  background-image: url(shadow-bottom.jpg);
  background-repeat:no-repeat;
  background-position: bottom left;
}
```

Voila—our drop shadow is complete!

How do I create a three-column CSS layout?

Many designs fall into a three-column model. As demonstrated in Figure 9.36, you might need a column for navigation, one for content, and one for additional items such as advertising or highlighted content on the site. Let's see how we can accomplish this type of layout using CSS.

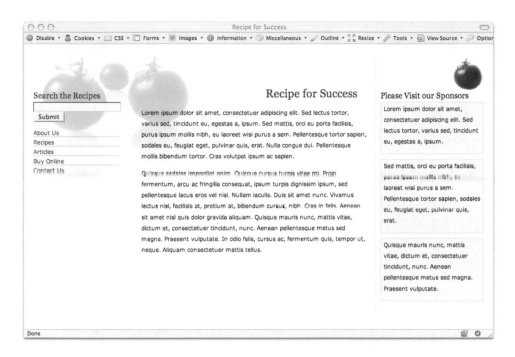

Figure 9.36. A three-column layout developed in CSS

Solution

A three-column, liquid layout is easily created using a simple technique similar to the one we used to build the two-column layout in "How do I create a liquid, two-column layout with the menu on the left, and the content on the right?":

3col.html

```
<!DOCTYPE html PUBLIC "-//W3C//DTD XHTML 1.0 Strict//EN"
    "http://www.w3.org/TR/xhtml1/DTD/xhtml1-strict.dtd">
<html xmlns="http://www.w3.org/1999/xhtml" lang="en-US">
<head>
<title>Recipe for Success</title>
<meta http-equiv="content-type"
    content="text/html; charset=utf-8" />
<link rel="stylesheet" type="text/css" href="3col.css" />
</head>
<body>
<div id="content">
  <h1>Recipe for Success</h1>
  <p>…</p>
```

```
</div>
<div id="side1">
  <form method="post" action="" id="searchform">
    <h3><label for="keys">Search the Recipes</label></h3>
    <div>
      <input type="text" name="keys" id="keys" class="txt" />
      <br />
      <input type="submit" name="Submit" value="Submit" />
    </div>
  </form>
  <ul>
    <li><a href="#">About Us</a></li>
    <li><a href="#">Recipes</a></li>
    <li><a href="#">Articles</a></li>
    <li><a href="#">Buy Online</a></li>
    <li><a href="#">Contact Us</a></li>
  </ul>
</div>
<div id="side2">
  <h3>Please Visit our Sponsors</h3>
  <div class="adbox"><p>Lorem ipsum dolor sit amet, …</p></div>
  <div class="adbox"><p>Sed mattis, orci eu porta …</p></div>
  <div class="adbox"><p>Quisque mauris nunc, mattis …</p></div>
</div>
</body>
</html>
```

3col.css

```
body {
  margin: 0;
  padding: 0;
  background-image: url(tomato_bg.jpg);
  background-repeat: no-repeat;
  background-color: #FFFFFF;
}
p {
  font: 80%/1.8em Verdana, Geneva, Arial, Helvetica, sans-serif;
  padding-top: 0;
  margin-top: 0;
}
form {
  margin: 0;
  padding: 0;
```

```
}
#content {
  margin: 66px 260px 0px 240px;
  padding: 10px;
}
#content h1 {
  text-align: right;
  padding-right: 20px;
  font: 150% Georgia, "Times New Roman", Times, serif;
  color: #901602;
}
#side1 {
  position: absolute;
  width: 200px;
  top: 30px;
  left: 10px;
  padding: 70px 10px 10px 10px;
}
#side2 {
  position: absolute;
  width: 220px;
  top: 30px;
  right: 10px;
  padding: 70px 10px 10px 10px;
  border-left: 1px dotted #cccccc;
  background-image: url(sm-tomato.jpg);
  background-position: top right;
  background-repeat: no-repeat;
}
#side2 h3 {
  font: 110% Georgia, "Times New Roman", Times, serif;
  margin: 0;
  padding-bottom: 4px;
}
.adbox {
  padding: 2px 4px 2px 6px;
  margin: 0 0 10px 0;
  border: 1px dotted #B1B1B1;
  background-color: #F4F4F4;
}
#side1 h3 {
  font: 110% Georgia, "Times New Roman", Times, serif;
  color: #621313;
  background-color: transparent;
```

```
    margin: 0;
    padding-bottom: 4px;
}
#side1 .txt {
  width: 184px;
  background-color: #FCF5F5;
  border: 1px inset #901602;
}
#side1 ul {
  list-style: none;
  margin-left: 0;
  padding-left: 0;
  width: 184px;
}
#side1 li {
  font: 80% Verdana, Geneva, Arial, Helvetica, sans-serif;
  margin-bottom: 0.3em;
  border-bottom: 1px solid #E7AFAF;
}
#side1 a:link, #side1 a:visited {
  text-decoration: none;
  color: #901602;
  background-color: transparent;
}
#side1 a:hover {
  color: #621313;
}
```

Discussion

This layout uses a simple technique. We start with the unstyled XHTML document
shown in Figure 9.37, which has three divs: one with ID content, one with ID
side1, and one with ID side2.

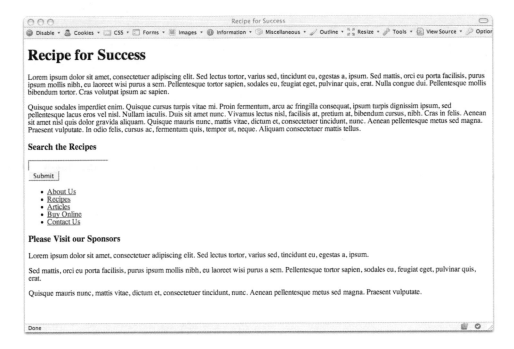

Figure 9.37. The unstyled XHTML document

We create the three columns using the following CSS fragments. We place both the left- and right-hand columns with absolute positioning—side1 is positioned from the left edge of the page, side2 from the right. We also add some significant top padding to these columns to make room for background images that will act as headings:

3col.css *(excerpt)*

```css
#side1 {
  position: absolute;
  width: 200px;
  top: 30px;
  left: 10px;
  padding: 70px 10px 10px 10px;
}
```

3col.css *(excerpt)*

```css
#side2 {
  position: absolute;
```

```
  width: 220px;
  top: 30px;
  right: 10px;
  padding: 70px 10px 10px 10px;
  …
}
```

The `content` block simply sits between the two absolutely positioned columns, with margins applied to the content to give the columns the room they need:

3col.css *(excerpt)*

```
#content {
  margin: 66px 260px 0px 240px;
  padding: 10px;
}
```

Figure 9.38 shows what the page looks like with these initial positioning tasks complete.

Figure 9.38. Three columns appearing with the initial CSS positioning

With our three columns in place, we can simply style the individual elements as required for the design in question. I've used background images of tomatoes on the body and on side2, as you can see in in Figure 9.36.

How do I add a footer to a liquid layout?

If you've experimented at all with absolute positioning, you may have begun to suspect that an absolutely positioned layout will make it impossible to add a footer that will always stay beneath all three columns, no matter which is the longest. Well, you'd be right!

To add a footer to our three-column layout we'll need to use a floated layout. A floated, liquid layout presents an additional problem that we don't have with a floated, fixed-width layout. When we float an element in our layout, we need to give it a width. Now, in a fixed-width layout we know what the actual width of each column is, so we can float each column and give it a width. In a liquid layout such as the one we saw in "How do I create a three-column CSS layout?", we have two columns whose widths we know (the sidebars), and one we don't—the main content area, which expands to fill the space.

Solution

In order to get round the problem of needing to have a flexible column in a floated layout, we need to build a slightly more complex layout, using negative margins to create space for a fixed-width column in a flexible content area. We'll also need to add some markup to our layout in order to give us some elements to float:

3col-alt.html

```
<!DOCTYPE html PUBLIC "-//W3C//DTD XHTML 1.0 Strict//EN"
"http://www.w3.org/TR/xhtml1/DTD/xhtml1-strict.dtd">
<html xmlns="http://www.w3.org/1999/xhtml" lang="en-US">
<head>
<title>Recipe for Success</title>
<meta http-equiv="content-type"
    content="text/html; charset=utf-8" />
<link rel="stylesheet" type="text/css" href="3col-alt.css" />
</head>
<body>
<div id="wrapper">
```

```
<div id="content">
  <div id="side1">
    <form method="post" action="" id="searchform">
    <h3><label for="keys">Search the Recipes</label></h3>
    <div><input type="text" name="keys" id="keys" class="txt" />
      <br />
      <input type="submit" name="Submit" value="Submit" />
    </div>
    </form>
    <ul>
      <li><a href="#">About Us</a></li>
      <li><a href="#">Recipes</a></li>
      <li><a href="#">Articles</a></li>
      <li><a href="#">Buy Online</a></li>
      <li><a href="#">Contact Us</a></li>
    </ul>
  </div>
  <div id="main">
    <h1>Recipe for Success</h1>
    <p>...</p>
  </div>
</div>
</div>
<div id="side2">
  <h3>Please Visit our Sponsors</h3>
  <div class="adbox"><p>Lorem ipsum dolor sit amet...</p></div>
  <div class="adbox"><p>Lorem ipsum dolor sit amet...</p></div>
  <div class="adbox"><p>Lorem ipsum dolor sit amet...</p></div>
</div>
<div id="footer">Copyright &copy; 1999 - 2007 Recipe for
    success</div>
</body>
</html>
```

Within our CSS, we give the new wrapper block a width of 100% and a negative right margin of −230 pixels. This use of negative margins enables us to give the sidebar a variable width that's 230 pixels less than the width of the browser window.

We can then float our sidebars into position, to the left and right of the content:

```
                                                        3col-alt.css (excerpt)
body {
  margin: 0;
  padding: 0;
}

#wrapper {
  width: 100%;
  float: left;
  margin-right: -230px;
  margin-top: 66px;
}

#content {
  margin-right: 220px;
}

#main {
  margin-left: 220px;
}

#side1 {
  width: 200px;
  float: left;
  padding: 0 10px 0 10px;
}
#side2 {
  width: 190px;
  padding: 80px 10px 0 10px;
  float: right;

}

#footer {
  clear: both;
  border-top: 10px solid #cecece;
}
```

As you can see in Figure 9.39, this CSS positions the columns where we need them, and our new footer falls neatly below the three columns. This solution can also be used for a two-column layout; you can change the order of columns by floating elements to the right instead of the left. With a little experimentation, you should be able to get the layout to behave as you need it to, even if it seems a little counter-intuitive at first!

Figure 9.39. The columns floated into place

How do I display a thumbnail gallery without using a table?

If you need to display a collection of images—perhaps for a photo album—a table may seem like the easiest way to go. However, the layout shown in Figure 9.40 was achieved using CSS; it provides some significant benefits that tabled versions lack.

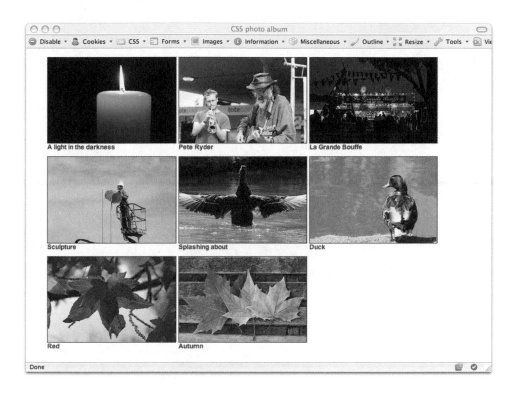

Figure 9.40. Building an image gallery of thumbnails using CSS

Solution

This solution uses a simple list for the album images, and positions them using CSS:

gallery.html

```
<!DOCTYPE html PUBLIC "-//W3C//DTD XHTML 1.0 Strict//EN"
"http://www.w3.org/TR/xhtml1/DTD/xhtml1-strict.dtd">
<html xmlns="http://www.w3.org/1999/xhtml" lang="en-US">
<head>
<title>CSS photo album</title>
<meta http-equiv="content-type"
    content="text/html; charset=utf-8" />
<link href="gallery.css" rel="stylesheet" type="text/css" />
</head>
<body>
<ul id="albumlist">
```

```
    <li><img src="thumb1.jpg" alt="Candle" width="240"
        height="160" />A light in the darkness</li>
    <li><img src="thumb2.jpg" alt="Pete Ryder" width="240"
        height="160" />Pete Ryder</li>
    <li><img src="thumb3.jpg" alt="La Grande Bouffe" width="240"
        height="160" />La Grande Bouffe</li>
    <li><img src="thumb4.jpg" alt="sculpture" width="240"
        height="160" />Sculpture</li>
    <li><img src="thumb5.jpg" alt="Duck stretching wings" width="240"
        height="160" />Splashing about</li>
    <li><img src="thumb6.jpg" alt="Duck" width="240" height="160"
        />Duck</li>
    <li><img src="thumb7.jpg" alt="Red leaves" width="240"
        height="160" />Red</li>
    <li><img src="thumb8.jpg" alt="Autumn leaves" width="240"
        height="160" />Autumn</li>
</ul>
</body>
</html>
```

```
body {
  background-color: #FFFFFF;
  color: #000000;
  margin: 0;
  padding: 0;
}
#albumlist {
  list-style-type: none;
}
#albumlist li {
  float: left;
  width: 240px;
  margin-right: 6px;
  margin-bottom: 10px;
  font: bold 0.8em Arial, Helvetica, sans-serif;
  color: #333333;
}
#albumlist img {
  display: block;
  border: 1px solid #333300;
}
```

Discussion

Our starting point for this layout is the creation of an unordered list—within it, we'll store each image in a `li` element, along with an appropriate image caption. Without the application of CSS, this list will display as shown in Figure 9.41:

gallery.html *(excerpt)*

```
<ul id="albumlist">
  <li><img src="thumb1.jpg" alt="Candle" width="240"
      height="160" />A light in the darkness</li>
  <li><img src="thumb2.jpg" alt="Pete Ryder" width="240"
      height="160" />Pete Ryder</li>
  <li><img src="thumb3.jpg" alt="La Grande Bouffe" width="240"
      height="160" />La Grande Bouffe</li>
  <li><img src="thumb4.jpg" alt="sculpture" width="240"
      height="160" />Sculpture</li>
  <li><img src="thumb5.jpg" alt="Duck stretching wings" width="240"
      height="160" />Splashing about</li>
  <li><img src="thumb6.jpg" alt="Duck" width="240" height="160"
      />Duck</li>
  <li><img src="thumb7.jpg" alt="Red leaves" width="240"
      height="160" />Red</li>
  <li><img src="thumb8.jpg" alt="Autumn leaves" width="240"
      height="160" />Autumn</li>
</ul>
```

Note that I've applied an ID of `albumlist` to the list that contains the photos.

Figure 9.41. The unstyled list of images

To create the grid-style layout of the thumbnails, we're going to position the images by using the `float` property on the `li` elements that contain them. Add these rules to your style sheet:

```css
#albumlist {
  list-style-type: none;
}
#albumlist li {
  float: left;
  width:240px;
}
#albumlist img {
  display: block;
}
```

All we're aiming to achieve with these rules is to remove the bullet points from the list items, and float the images left, as shown in Figure 9.42. Also, by setting the images to display as blocks, we force their captions to display below them.

Your pictures should now have moved into position. If you resize the window, you'll see that they wrap to fill the available width. If the window becomes too narrow to contain a given number of images side by side, the last image simply drops down to start the next line.

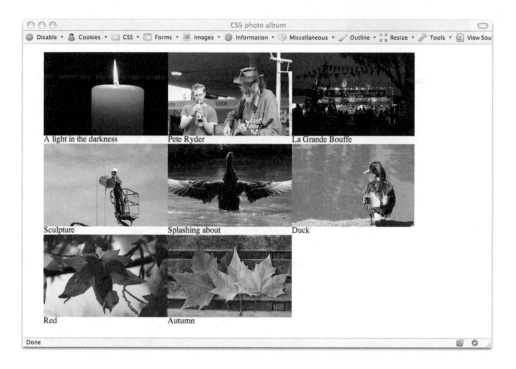

Figure 9.42. The page display after the images are floated left

We now have our basic layout—let's add to it to make it more attractive. For example, we could insert some rules to create space between the images in the list, and specify a nice font for the image captions:

gallery.css *(excerpt)*

```
#albumlist li {
  float: left;
  width:240px;
  margin-right: 6px;
  margin-bottom: 10px;
  font: bold 0.8em Arial, Helvetica, sans-serif;
  color: #333333;
}
```

We could also add borders to the images:

gallery.css *(excerpt)*

```
#albumlist img {
  border: 1px solid #333300;
}
```

The flexibility of this layout method makes it particularly handy when you're pulling your images from a database—you don't have to calculate the number of images, for example, so that you can build table cells on the fly as you create your page.

All the same, you might not always want to permit this wrapping effect to display. You can stop unwanted wrapping by setting the width of the list tag, <ul>:

```
#albumlist {
  list-style-type: none;
  width: 600px;
}
```

This rule forcibly sets the width to which the images may wrap, producing the display shown in Figure 9.43.

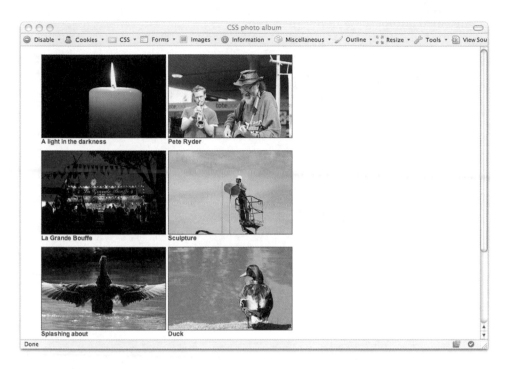

Figure 9.43. The images ceasing to wrap after we set the width of the containing `<ul>` tag

How do I create boxes with rounded corners?

There are a number of approaches you can use to create rounded corners on boxes. Here, we'll look at three different ways of achieving this effect.

Solution 1: The Mozilla `border-radius` Property

If this solution doesn't have you forcibly converting all your friends to Mozilla, nothing will! This solution, illustrated in Figure 9.44, works only in Mozilla-based browsers, and currently uses a Mozilla extension to CSS. Here's the markup and CSS:

corners1.html

```
<!DOCTYPE html PUBLIC "-//W3C//DTD XHTML 1.0 Strict//EN"
    "http://www.w3.org/TR/xhtml1/DTD/xhtml1-strict.dtd">
<html xmlns="http://www.w3.org/1999/xhtml" lang="en-US">
```

```
<head>
<title>Rounded Corners</title>
<meta http-equiv="content-type"
    content="text/html; charset=utf-8" />
<link rel="stylesheet" type="text/css" href="corners1.css" />
</head>
<body>
<div class="curvebox">
  <p>Lorem ipsum dolor sit amet, consectetuer adipiscing …</p>
</div>
</body>
</html>
```

corners1.css

```
.curvebox {
  width: 250px;
  padding: 1em;
  background-color: #B0C4DE;
  color: #33527B;
  -moz-border-radius: 25px;
}
```

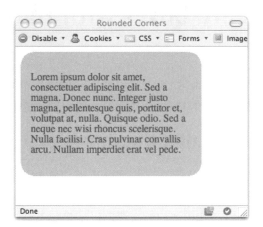

Figure 9.44. Rounded corners, Mozilla–style

This example doesn't use a single image! The CSS property that creates those nicely rounded corners on the box borders is:

```
-moz-border-radius: 25px;
```

Remove this line from the CSS, as I've done in Figure 9.45, and you'll see that the box displays with the usual square corners (as it does in browsers other than those that are Mozilla-based).

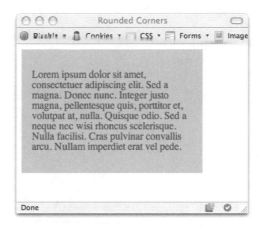

Figure 9.45. Removing `-moz-border-radius: 25px;` to have the box display as normal

The Mozilla-only `-moz-border-radius` property corresponds to the `border-radius` property that will be part of the CSS3 recommendation when it's finalized.[1] Obviously, it's currently only of use to visitors to your site who use Mozilla browsers, so most designers will look to a different solution.

Solution 2: Images and Additional Markup

A solution that works in multiple browsers uses additional images and markup to create the rounded effect. First, create the corner images using a graphics program. You'll need a small image for each corner of the box. The easiest way to create these is to quarter a circle so that you end up with a set, as shown in Figure 9.46.

Figure 9.46. Rounded corner images

[1] http://www.w3.org/TR/css3-border/#the-border-radius

The markup for this example is as follows. The top- and bottom-left images are included in the document itself, within top and bottom `div`s:

corners2.html

```
<!DOCTYPE html PUBLIC "-//W3C//DTD XHTML 1.0 Strict//EN"
    "http://www.w3.org/TR/xhtml1/DTD/xhtml1-strict.dtd">
<html xmlns="http://www.w3.org/1999/xhtml" lang="en-US">
<head>
<title>Rounded corners</title>
<meta http-equiv="Content-Type"
    content="text/html; charset=utf-8" />
<link rel="stylesheet" type="text/css" href="corners2.css" />
</head>
<body>
<div class="rndbox">
  <div class="rndtop"><img src="topleft.gif" alt="" width="30"
      height="30" /></div>
  <p>Lorem ipsum dolor sit amet, consectetuer adipiscing …</p>
  <div class="rndbottom"><img src="bottomleft.gif" alt=""
      width="30" height="30" /></div>
</div>
</body>
</html>
```

The top- and bottom-right images are included as background images in the CSS for the `div`s, with the classes `rndtop` and `rndbottom`:

corners2.css *(excerpt)*

```
.rndbox {
  background: #C6D9EA;
  width: 300px;
  font: 0.8em Verdana, Arial, Helvetica, sans-serif;
  color: #000033;
}
.rndtop {
  background: url(topright.gif) no-repeat right top;
}
.rndbottom {
  background: url(bottomright.gif) no-repeat right top;
}
.rndbottom img {
```

```
    display:block;
}

.rndbox p {
    margin: 0 0.4em 0 0.4em;
}
```

Together, the images, markup, and CSS create a curved box like the one shown in
Figure 9.47.

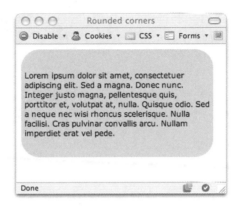

Figure 9.47. A curved box created using images

Solution 3: Using JavaScript

Adding markup and images to your code isn't a particularly attractive option, especially if you have a lot of boxes that you want to have round corners. To get around
the problem, many people have come up with solutions that use JavaScript to add
the rounded corners to otherwise square boxes. The beauty of this solution is that
even if users don't have JavaScript enabled, they see a perfectly usable site—it
merely lacks the additional style of the curved edges.

Various methods have been devised to achieve rounded corners using JavaScript,
but here we'll look at just one—NiftyCube—as it's very easy to drop into your code
and get started. The script is included in the code archive for this book, but if you'd
like the latest version, download NiftyCube from the NiftyCube web site, and unzip
the zip file.[2] You'll find lots of example pages in the zip archive, but all you need

---

[2] http://www.html.it/articoli/niftycube/

to implement this effect in your own pages is the JavaScript file **niftycube.js** and the CSS file **niftyCorners.css**. Copy these files into your site. Our starting point is a square-cornered box created by the following markup:

corners3-start.html

```
<!DOCTYPE html PUBLIC "-//W3C//DTD XHTML 1.0 Strict//EN"
"http://www.w3.org/TR/xhtml1/DTD/xhtml1-strict.dtd">
<html xmlns="http://www.w3.org/1999/xhtml" lang="en-US">
<head>
  <title>Rounded Corners</title>
  <meta http-equiv="content-type"
      content="text/html; charset=utf-8" />
  <link rel="stylesheet" type="text/css" href="corners3.css" />
</head>
<body>
  <div class="curvebox">
  <p>Lorem ipsum dolor...</p>
  </div>
</body>
</html>
```

You have a reasonable amount of freedom in terms of the way you style your box, with one exception—the padding inside your box *must* be specified in pixels. If you use any other unit, such as ems, then your corners won't render properly in Internet Explorer. The result of our work is pictured in Figure 9.48.

corners3.css

```
.curvebox {
  width: 250px;
  padding: 20px;
  background-color: #B0C4DE;
  color: #33527B;
}
```

Figure 9.48. The square box

To add rounded corners to this box using NiftyCube, link the JavaScript file to the head of your document, then write a simple function to tell the script that you wish to round the corners of the class curvebox:

```
corners3.html
<!DOCTYPE html PUBLIC "-//W3C//DTD XHTML 1.0 Strict//EN"
"http://www.w3.org/TR/xhtml1/DTD/xhtml1-strict.dtd">
<html xmlns="http://www.w3.org/1999/xhtml" lang="en-US">
<head>
  <title>Rounded Corners</title>
  <meta http-equiv="content-type"
      content="text/html; charset=utf-8" />
  <link rel="stylesheet" type="text/css" href="corners3.css" />
<script type="text/javascript" src="niftycube.js"></script>
<script type="text/javascript">
window.onload=function(){
Nifty("div.curvebox");
}
</script>
</head>
<body>
  <div class="curvebox">
    <p>Lorem ipsum dolor...</p>
  </div>
</body>
</html>
```

This markup produces the display shown in Figure 9.49.

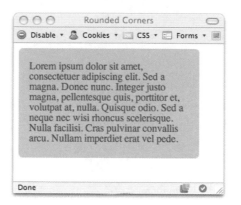

Figure 9.49. Rounded corners without images or extra markup

Discussion

While numerous solutions are available to help you create rounded corners without JavaScript, they all require you to insert additional markup, or ensure that your markup is structured in a certain way.[3] If you only have a few boxes whose corners you want to round—perhaps a main layout container or a couple of larger boxes—the additional images and markup won't be a huge imposition. But if your layout includes many rounded corners, peppering your markup with extra `divs` and images may be an extremely undesirable option. The JavaScript method allows cleaner HTML code, but as with all JavaScript solutions, it doesn't work when the user has JavaScript turned off.

Personally, I feel that using JavaScript in this way—to plug the holes in CSS support—is legitimate. As long as you've checked that your layout remains clear and easy to use without the rounded corners, you're not going to prevent those without JavaScript from using your site. If you do use this JavaScript solution on a project, be sure to check the whole site with JavaScript turned off, to make sure that the users still have a good experience on the site.

---

[3] One attempt at generating rounded corners using semantic markup and no JavaScript is Spanky Corners [http://tools.sitepoint.com/spanky/], created by SitePoint's Alex Walker.

Summary

This chapter should have given you some starting points and ideas for your own layouts. By combining other solutions in this book, such as the innovative use of navigation and images, with your own creativity, you should be able to come up with myriad designs based on the layouts we've explored here. As with tables, most CSS layouts are really just variations on a theme.

Once you have a grasp of the basics, and you've learned the rules, you'll find that you really are limited only by your imagination. For inspiration, and to see what other designers are doing with CSS layouts, have a look at the CSS Zen Garden.[4]

---

[4] http://www.csszengarden.com/

Index

Symbols

ID prefix, 8

* html hack (*see* star html hack)

A

<a> elements (*see* links)

About Debian Linux site, 219

absolute keyword font sizes, 19

absolute positioning, 315, 317

   advantages, 332

   three-column liquid layouts, 351, 355

   two-column fixed-width layouts, 334, 340

   two-column liquid layouts, 328

   within other elements, 318, 340

access keys, 199–202

accessibility

   (*see also* screen readers; text-only devices)

   absolute positioning and, 332

   access keys, 201

   advantages of CSS, 215

   <blockquote> elements and, 45

   designing in, 140

   drop-down menus and, 134

   <fieldset> and <legend> elements, 197

   image text and, 76

   pixel sizing and, 16

   problems with tabular layouts, 135

   reliance on color and, 179

   tabular data, 137

   testing in text-only browsers, 260

accesskey attribute, 201

accounts data spreadsheet, 136

:active pseudo-class, 27, 28, 126

align attribute alternatives, 302

alignment

   of form fields, 189, 193, 194

   of logos and slogan in headers, 309

   of tabular data, 148

   of text, 42, 43, 46

   in two-column liquid layouts, 323, 331

alistapart.com site, 129, 285

alpha transparency and IE6, 237, 242

alt text, 262

alternating column colors, 157

alternating row colors, 150, 153, 205

alternative style sheets, 276–292

   alerting users, 280

   avoiding code duplication, 287–292

   links to, 285

   print style sheets, 265

   style sheet switchers, 282

anchor elements (*see* links)

arrow key navigation, 261

attributes, HTML

   (*see also* class attributes; ID attributes)

   deprecated attributes, 56, 62, 302

   for tabular data, 139

aural media type, 264, 265

author's web site, 222, 251, 260

auto setting, margin properties, 321, 322

B

background colors

   (*see also* highlighting)

I

THE PRINCIPLES OF
BEAUTIFUL
WEB DESIGN

BY **JASON BEAIRD**

THE ART &
SCIENCE
OF CSS

BY **CAMERON ADAMS**
JINA BOLTON
DAVID JOHNSON
STEVE SMITH
JONATHAN SNOOK

INSPIRATIONAL STANDARDS-BASED WEB DESIGN